Slavery, Agriculture, and Malaria in the Arabian Peninsula

Ohio University Press Series in Ecology and History

James L. A. Webb, Jr., Series Editor

Slavery, Agriculture, and Malaria in the Arabian Peninsula

Benjamin Reilly

OHIO UNIVERSITY PRESS

ATHENS

Ohio University Press, Athens, Ohio 45701
www.ohioswallow.com
© 2015 by Ohio University Press

To obtain permission to quote, reprint, or otherwise reproduce or distribute material from
Ohio University Press publications, please contact our rights and permissions department at
(740) 593-1154 or (740) 593-4536 (fax).

Printed in the United States of America
Ohio University Press books are printed on acid-free paper ∞™

25 24 23 22 21 20 19 18 17 16 15   5 4 3 2 1

Library of Congress Cataloging-in-Publication Data
Reilly, Benjamin, 1971–
  Slavery, agriculture, and malaria in the Arabian Peninsula / Benjamin Reilly.
     pages cm. — (Ohio University Press series in ecology and history)
  Includes bibliographical references and index.
  ISBN 978-0-8214-2181-9 (hardcover : acid-free paper) — ISBN 978-0-8214-2182-6 (paperback :
acid-free paper) — ISBN 978-0-8214-4540-2 (PDF)
  1. Slavery—Arabian Peninsula—History. 2. Africans—Arabian Peninsula—History. 3.
Slaves—Arabian Peninsula—History. 4. Agricultural laborers—Arabian Peninsula—History.
5. Malaria—Social aspects—Arabian Peninsula—History. 6. Agriculture—Health aspects—
Arabian Peninsula—History. 7. Agriculture—Social aspects—Arabian Peninsula—History.
8. Agriculture—Environmental aspects—Arabian Peninsula—History. 9. Oases—Arabian
Peninsula—History. 10. Arabian Peninsula—Environmental conditions—History. I. Title.
  HT1316.R45 2015
  306.3'620953—dc23
                                2015026456

Contents

Illustrations

Preface and Acknowledgments

THIS BOOK is intended to be a contribution to two main fields of scholarship. On one hand, it seeks to expand our knowledge of slave practices in the Arabic world, which remain vastly under-studied in comparison to slave systems in the Atlantic world of the seventeenth through the nineteenth centuries, especially that of the American South. In particular, it shines light on agricultural slavery in the Arabian Peninsula, an almost entirely unstudied phenomenon. At the same time, this book seeks to contribute to the field of environmental history, which I would define as the study of human/landscape interactions as mediated by societal, cultural, biological, and genetic processes. While the environmental histories of other parts of the world, such as the American West and the Mediterranean, have been well-charted by multiple scholars, the Arabian Peninsula is still terra incognita from an environmental history standpoint, and this book represents an initial foray into the field.[1]

Since this book is written primarily for scholars of slavery and environmental history, I have adopted a highly simplified Arabic orthography throughout the text. Rather than use special characters for *daad, saad, ta', za',* and *haa',* which are emphasized versions of the English *d, s, t, th,* and *h* sounds respectively, I have transliterated these letters as *d, s, t, th,* and *h.* Similarly, I have transliterated both the *ayn* and *hamzah,* letters which to English-speakers sound like unvocalized breaks in the middle of a word, as apostrophes. I have rendered vowels as the closest English equivalents, without using special English characters; for example, I transliterated ديرة as *deera,* not *dīra.* I did, however, retain the standard special characters in the footnotes and bibliography, and when citing a scholar with their own system of transliteration into English, I generally copied their transliteration and their special characters, though sometimes with clarifying comments. Finally, I have adhered to standard spelling of familiar Arab place names, such as Mecca, even if they are somewhat at variance with this orthography.

WRITING AN academic book, even a relatively short book such as this one, is by necessity a team effort. My loving thanks, first and foremost, to my wife Anita for her support throughout the project as well as her help in editing the text. My sincere thanks as well to my editors, James L. A. Webb, Jr. and Ricky Huard at Ohio University Press. Many thanks as well to the two anonymous readers who reviewed the draft manuscript and whose insightful comments paved the way to numerous improvements in the final draft of the text. Similarly, I would like to thank Peter Stearns at the *Journal of Social History* for his support of my original journal article, "*Mutawalladeen* and Malaria: African Slavery in Arabian Wadis," which served as the nucleus of this book. Thanks also to my mother, Eileen Reilly, for identifying typos on earlier versions of the manuscript. My sincere gratitude as well to Lansiné Kaba, my colleague at CMUQ, for his long-standing support of my work on the Arabian Peninsula, for his mentorship, and for his friendship.

A historian is only as good as his sources, so my sincere thanks to the staff of the CMUQ Library in Qatar and the Hunt Library in Pittsburgh for their assistance. Thanks in particular to Theresa MacGregor at the CMUQ library and to Andrew Marshall at the interlibrary loan desk at Hunt Library—faced with a relentless onslaught of interlibrary loan requests, they never flinched, and delivered me the materials I needed with a smile. Thanks as well to the staff at the library of Georgetown University in Qatar, who have built up the most impressive research library on the Gulf, and whose vast holdings of archival sources greatly enriched this book.

My gratitude as well to my student researchers, including Jonathan Stepp, Mohammed Al-Matwi, Fatima Al-Emadi, Ognjen Popovic, and Raji Kitabe.

A special thanks to the Qatar Foundation for their financial support for the project and for creating the global, interdisciplinary scholarly environment that inspired and enriched this work.

Introduction

THE GOAL of this book is to describe, in as much detail as the sources permit, a system of slave and servile agricultural labor, employing mainly sub-Saharan Africans, which prevailed in the traditional Arabian Peninsula. Previous studies of slavery in the Arabic world have focused almost exclusively on non-agricultural employments of slaves, most notably domestic labor, military servitude, or concubinage. The use of slaves in productive sectors of the economy such as agriculture has rarely been noticed in the literature, much less studied systematically. This book therefore is intended to address a quite considerable lacuna in our understanding of the institution of slavery, particularly African slavery, in the Arab world.

As with most books about slavery, this book will deal heavily with the traditional concerns of social history: hierarchy, social mobility, demographic processes, and the daily lives of subalterns. Nonetheless, this book belongs as much to the field of environmental history as it does to social history. As an academic subfield, the environmental history of the Middle East is only now beginning to be written. Alan Mikhail wrote as recently as 2013 that, despite some good work done in recent decades, the Middle East is "one of the gaping holes in the global story of the environment."[1] This book represents a preliminary attempt to fill in this gaping hole. In addition, I believe this book could serve as an example of the possible benefits that historians studying the Arabian Peninsula could derive from environmental history. I will argue throughout this text that the African contribution to the agriculture of the Arabian Peninsula can be fully understood only within the context of environmental history, in particular the interaction between economics and geography, epidemiology, and human biology.

Overall this study will argue that, as the result of the interaction between economic, cultural, and environmental factors, African agricultural slavery in the Arabian Peninsula had a distinctive, hybrid character. From the cultural and social standpoint, as one might expect, African agricultural slavery in the Arabian Peninsula had obvious affinities to slavery as practiced throughout the Middle East. Nonetheless, from the standpoint of genetics and disease, African agricultural slavery displayed characteristics that were strikingly similar to slave systems in the Atlantic world of the seventeenth through the nineteenth centuries. In both systems of slave agriculture, the malaria threat inherent in the fertile lowland agricultural zones encouraged the dominant population to exploit these dangerous environments by proxy, by means of African slaves with intrinsic or acquired immunity to malaria infection.

The Historiographical Background: African Slaves in Arab Agriculture

Although the slave systems in the Arab world have been the subject of some fine scholarship, on the whole, slavery in the Middle East has been significantly under-studied compared with slavery in the Atlantic world.[2] In 1989, historian Bernard Lewis lamented the "remarkable dearth of scholarly work" on slavery in a Middle Eastern context, and by and large Lewis's observation is still valid today.[3] The literature that does exist about slavery in the Islamic world focuses on nonproductive uses of slaves, such as sexual slavery (concubines), harem guards (eunuchs), slave soldiers, and domestic servants. Indeed, scholars of slavery have long argued that slaves "produced nothing" (Orlando Patterson) or were "not a labor unit" (Philip Curtin) in Islamic societies.[4] More recently, Gwyn Campbell and others have argued that this distinction between productive and unproductive slaves is a "false dichotomy," noting, for example, that even apparently nonproductive slave activities, such as military slavery, are encouraging economic production by providing security for markets and supply routes.[5] Nonetheless, despite this current shift in the literature away from broad assumptions about the "nonproductive" character of Middle Eastern slavery, we still know relatively little about slaves employed in economically vital sectors such as the crafts or agriculture.

Lewis's "remarkable dearth" of Islamic slavery literature has been most pronounced in the study of agricultural slavery within the Islamic Middle East, which is a particularly neglected corner of an underworked field. Our knowledge about the agricultural use of African slaves is limited to a few often-cited examples, all sharply restricted in both space and time. One celebrated use of slave agricultural labor was the employment of the Zanj, an African population used in the ninth century to remove the top layer of the salt-impregnated soils of southern Mesopotamia in order to expand sugar and other agricultural production in "dead lands" in Iraq.[6] The eventual rebellion of the Zanj, inspired by religious sectarianism as well as their miserable living conditions, helped fatally weaken the Islamic Abbasid Caliphate. Nonetheless, another system of African agricultural slavery thrived nearby in the tenth century. According to the Persian traveler Nasir-I Khusraw, "thirty thousand Zanzibari and Abyssinian slaves" worked in the "fields and orchards" of the al-Hasa oasis of eastern Arabia. Their owners were the Qarmatians, a Shi'ite sect that declared independence from the Abbasid Caliphate around the time of the Zanj rebellion.[7] Unfortunately, we have few sources other than Khusraw's account of this curious tenth-century system of African agricultural slavery. One scholar, Salah Trabelsi, has made the case that the employment of slaves in agriculture was fairly widespread throughout the era of the Islamic conquests, during which time captured populations were enslaved and distributed as booty among the victorious Muslims. As Trabelsi himself admits, however, the evidence for this early Islamic agricultural slavery is rather thin, and some of his interpretations are open to question.[8] Moving forward in time, there are some indications that African slave labor was used (perhaps not exclusively) in sugar plantations in early modern Morocco and in Oman, though these slave systems eventually collapsed along with the Islamic sugar industry as a whole owing to a lack of local fuel for sugar refining and competition from cheaper American sugar.[9]

African agricultural slavery again emerged as a theme in various parts of the Arab world in the nineteenth century. According to Gabriel Baer, the use of slaves for agricultural tasks in nineteenth-century Egypt was "not uncommon," and revolved around unpleasant jobs such as sugar production in Upper Egypt and drawing well water throughout the Egyptian rural countryside.[10] Egyptian agricultural slavery probably reached its height in the 1860s, when even Egypt's poor *fellaheen* (peasant farmers) began to acquire enslaved African farmhands to cash in on the short-term cotton price spike that accompanied the American Civil War.[11] Agricultural slavery flourished around the same time in the Ottoman Empire, though for very different reasons: as Ehud Toledano has pointed out, approximately 150,000 Circassian slaves flooded Ottoman domains in the late 1850s and early 1860s, and many of these slaves were employed in agriculture, though most were manumitted by the late nineteenth century.[12] An export-based slave plantation system also arose in Zanzibar and the vicinity on the Omani-dominated East African coast in the mid-nineteenth century, initially to take advantage of high clove prices, and later to produce cereal crops for export to the Arabian Peninsula.[13] Similar plantations were established, though on a much smaller scale, along the Shebelli River of southern Somalia, though in this case these plantation slaves were owned by local pastoralist populations as well as Arab traders.[14] Slave plantations were also established or enlarged in coastal Yemen and Oman in the late nineteenth century to produce dates for export.[15] In addition, a number of sources describe slave-like employment of Africans in agricultural labor in the fertile Saharan oases of North Africa, in particular on the borderline between the Arab-speaking and Tuareg Berber cultural zones, and in the oases controlled by the Sanusi religious order in the nineteenth-century Libyan Desert.[16]

While these nineteenth-century uses of African slaves in agriculture are well attested to in the scholarly literature, the phenomenon of African agricultural slavery in contemporary northern and central Arabia has received virtually no attention. Indeed, I've managed to come up with only a handful of references to it in the current literature. Murray Gordon's *Slavery in the Arab World*, for example, devotes a single enigmatic line to the phenomenon, noting that African slaves "proved adaptable for use on the large estates in the *Hijaz*."[17] Similarly laconic is John Hunwick and Eve Trout Powell's comment in *The African Diaspora in the Mediterranean Lands of Islam* that "in Arabia, agricultural labor was generally considered an inferior type of work, especially by the nomadic peoples. Hence, it was frequently carried out by slaves."[18] In much the same vein, William Ochsenwald notes in his study of the slave trade controversy in the Hijaz that the Arabs there "chiefly wanted servants for work in the home, though some slaves were used for . . . agricultural labor."[19] A few other authors, such as Suzanne Miers, Abdussamad Ahmad, Beatrice Nicolini, and Abd al-'Alim 'Ali Abu Haykal, have also noted the existence of a system of agricultural slavery in Arabia, but give no details.[20] The existing literature, therefore, has nothing concrete to tell us about the origins, scale, or prevalence of African slave agriculture within the Arabian Peninsula interior. This study ventures into almost entirely unexplored ground.

Scope of the Inquiry

Spatial Parameters

In terms of geographic extent, this book will take as its subject the Arabian Peninsula as a whole, so a word or two about the region is in order. Spatially, the Arabian Peninsula occupies more than three million square kilometers, an area nearly ten times as large as Germany and nearly one-third the size of the United States. Desert is overwhelmingly the dominant landform throughout the peninsula, but as might be expected over a territory so large, there are important local variations, which help to divide the territory into a number of useful subregions.

The Hijaz, which means "the barrier" in Arabic, received the name from its rugged, volcanic mountain ranges. These ranges serve as a barrier insofar as they form a wall separating the Arabian interior from the Red Sea, which was in fact created by the same tectonic processes that formed the Hijaz's mountains. The Hijaz is predominantly arid, consisting in large part of gravelly soil or bare rock, including large areas of *harrah*, or basalt lava flows. As a result, pastoralism has historically been the predominant lifeway practiced in the Hijaz, though a few favored drainage channels, such as the Khaybar and the Medina oases, hosted long-established agricultural communities. Despite its overall aridity, the Hijaz has historically boasted of a number of fairly large urban centers, such as Jeddah and Mecca, which accommodated thirty thousand and seventy thousand inhabitants, respectively, in the early twentieth century. The wealth of these cities, however, was derived from religion rather than agriculture. Both Mecca and Medina have historically been almost entirely dependent on Islamic pilgrims for their revenue, and pilgrim income has allowed these cities to subsist on imported foodstuffs, mostly from Egypt. In addition, as we will see later in the book, these cities, and the pilgrims they attracted, played an important role in the history of the African slave trade in the Arabian Peninsula.

West of the Hijaz, and along the entire length of the Red Sea, stretches the Tihamah coastal strip. For the most part, Tihamah is best suited to nomadic pastoralism, as it is very arid even in the south, and hot even by Arabian standards. Nonetheless, Tihamah also supports a number of important port cities, including Jeddah, though as Mecca's main port, Jeddah is usually considered a city of the Hijaz. In addition, agriculture is possible in some areas of Tihamah, especially in the south, where mountain rainfall fuels flash floods, or *sayl*, which penetrate the dry Tihamah and can be harnessed for agricultural production. It should be noted that

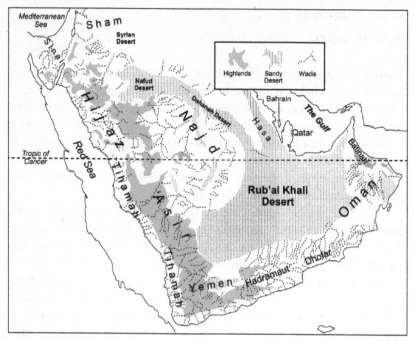

Map I.1. Regions of Arabia

Tihamah is heavily influenced by its close proximity to Africa, not only in terms of flora and fauna, but also in terms of culture. Tihamah's traditional conical grass huts, for example, appear nowhere else in Arabia, but echo building styles on the African side of the Red Sea.[21]

To the east of the Hijaz lies Najd, meaning "highlands" in Arabic. Although far less mountainous compared to the Hijaz, Najd gets its name from a series of local escarpments and (in the north) small mountains which differentiate it from the flatter terrain immediately to the east and west. As with the Hijaz, pastoralism is the predominant lifeway in Najd, but thanks to the widespread availability of groundwater, slightly higher rainfall, and important seasonal watercourses, most notably the Wadi al-Rimah and the Wadi Fatima, agriculture was practiced in Najd to a far greater extent than in the Hijaz, mostly in a series of villages and towns stretching from Jabal Shammar (Mountain of the Shammar) in the north to the inland delta of the Wadi Fatima to the south, and then southwest alongside the Jabal Tuwayq escarpment as far as Ghayl and Sulayyil. Several of the towns of Najd were also important trade hubs, especially 'Unayzah, Buraydah, and Ha'il. The nearby oasis of al-Hasa is often considered to be an extension of

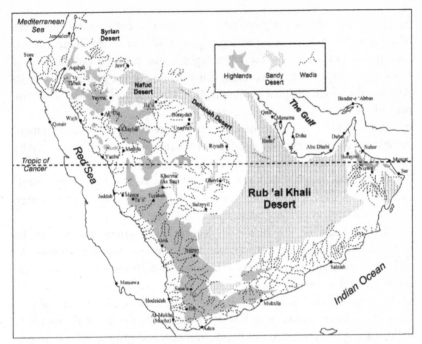

Map I.2. Towns of Arabia

Najd, though as we will see in chapter 1, al-Hasa is almost unique in Arabia for its fertility and population density and could be considered as a region unto itself.

In the southern heel of the Arabian Peninsula lies Yemen, an Arabic term which means "on the right hand." Yemen is the geographical antithesis of al-Sham, meaning "on the left hand," which is the traditional Arabic term for Syria. Both terms presume an eastward-facing hypothetical observer standing in the Hijaz, which in turn tells us something about the centrality of the Hijaz and its holy sites in the traditional Arab worldview. In any case, Yemen shares the mountainous topography of the Hijaz, but differs noticeably from the Hijaz in terms of its abundant summer rainfall. As a result of rain and altitude, the mountain highlands of Yemen enjoy a humid subtropical climate found almost nowhere else in Arabia, and Yemen is unique in the Arabian Peninsula for having far more farmers than nomadic pastoralists. Yemen also played an important historical role in regional and international trade, in part due to its strategic location at the mouth of the Red Sea, a major trading corridor. It also reflects the fact that Yemen was almost unique in Arabia for having a valuable export commodity, namely coffee; indeed, mocha coffee bears the name of the now-derelict coffee exporting city of al-Mukha on the Yemeni coast. Yemen has lost both of these advantages in the modern era because of European competition, however, and is now one of the poorer regions in Arabia, whereas in the past "Arabia Felix," as Yemen was known, was quite possibly Arabia's most prosperous region.

'Asir, in turn, is a transitional zone between the Hijaz and Yemen, notable for its relatively high rainfall, an advantage tempered somewhat by high levels of malaria. Unlike other regions of Arabia, which have names corresponding to geographical features, 'Asir is named for a tribe dominant in the region. Historically, 'Asir has been something of a backwater, the home of fiercely independent mountain tribesmen.

To the west of the historical territory of Yemen, but within its modern-day borders, lies Hadramaut, a collection of massive canyon-like valleys cut through an arid coastal plateau. Hadramaut means "death has come" in Arabic, though the origins of this term are obscure. The Hadrami, as the people of Hadramaut are called, traditionally combined animal pastoralism and agriculture, which is practiced in the depths of Hadramaut's valleys using a combination of flood diversion and groundwater exploitation techniques. Hadramaut is notable for being cut off from the rest of Arabia by mountains and the vast Rub' al Khali desert. As a result, Hadramaut's natural outlet is to the Indian Ocean, and thus it has traditionally been heavily influenced by Swahili, Indian, Malay, and Indonesian culture. This reflects in part the limited resources of Hadramaut, which has encouraged the Hadrami to seek their fortunes abroad. For example, an estimated eighty thousand Hadrami were living in the Dutch East Indies in 1931.[22] It also reflects an influx of non-Arab peoples to the region, such as the wives that Hadrami Arabs had married while overseas. The result was one of the most ethnically and culturally diverse regions in Arabia, to the point that one observer in 1940 was surprised to find that "Malay has become a 'second language' in the Hadhramaut."[23]

Eastward still of Hadramaut lies Dhofar, one of the Arabian Peninsula's more unusual landscapes. In Dhofar, a modest but fairly steep mountain range catches the northernmost fringe of the Indian Ocean monsoon, creating a number of unique microclimates, such as a tropical "mist oasis" environment on the mountain foothills, a zone of incense-producing trees in the mountain rain shadows, and an intermediate "termite savannah" region common in Africa but found nowhere else in Arabia. Dhofar also marks the zone in which the coconut displaces the date palm, which is ubiquitous farther north in Arabia.[24] As might be expected given the variety of microclimates in Dhofar, its peoples practiced a number of overlapping lifeways, such as coastal fishing, incense gathering, and agriculture. They also practiced animal husbandry, including cattle herding, a practice that exists almost nowhere else in Arabia. It should be noted that the area immediately to the north, south, and west of Dhofar's mountains includes some of the most barren and waterless wastelands of the Arabian Peninsula.

Eastward and northward of Dhofar is Oman, a mountainous area near the mouth of the Gulf. The term "Oman" is a rather nebulous one, previously applied to a number of regions that are outside of the modern territory of Oman, including the modern nation of the United Arab Emirates, which was once called "Trucial Oman" by the British. To confuse matters further, even within the core area of Oman, two distinct entities have traditionally coexisted: an outward-looking, cosmopolitan coastal region heavily engaged in the Indian Ocean mercantile world; and an inward-looking, religiously conservative interior, usually ruled by an *imam*, the leader of the Ibadhi sect of Islam. Oman's relatively high rainfall (by Arabian standards), high water table in the mountains, and significant domestic mineral resources (again, by Arabian standards) have combined to ensure that Oman has remained one of the most important and densely inhabited regions of Arabia from as far back as the Bronze Age, four thousand years ago. In addition to these domestic resources, the history of Oman, even more than Hadramaut, is intertwined with the sea. Oman long served as an important trade entrepôt, capitalizing upon its strategic location on the Gulf of Arabia and the Gulf of Oman. What is more, fishing has historically played a major role in Oman's economy; European observer S. B. Miles quipped in 1919 that "the whole coast of Oman is a continuous series of fishing stations."[25] An important subregion within Oman is al-Batinah, an area of intensive palm cultivation on the coast at the foot of the western al-Hajar mountain range. These palms are in decline today, but British traveler J. R. Wellsted observed in the early nineteenth century, with only moderate exaggeration, that the palms of al-Batinah "form a continuous grove" for a "distance of one hundred and fifty miles," and that "a traveler may proceed the whole distance without ever losing their shade."[26]

Moving eastward and up the Gulf from Oman we find ourselves in the Gulf coast of Arabia, a coastal region whose fortunes, to even a greater extent than Oman, are tied to the sea. In the modern day, the Gulf coast is divided into sovereign states: the United Arab Emirates, Qatar, and

Kuwait, with Saudi Arabia claiming a stretch of coastline between the two latter nations. Historically, however, terms such as "Qatar" were mere geographical abstractions, and the coastline of both the Arabian side and the Iranian side of the Gulf was inhabited by highly mobile and shifting populations living in relatively small, mostly autonomous communities.[27] Population movement was constant, triggered by local failures in the water supply, siltation of harbors, shifts in the productivity of the pearl banks, and excessive taxation levied by internal strong men or by states external to the region. Although some pastoralism and agriculture was practiced in this region, both occupations were limited by low rainfall and infertile soils. Rather, the Gulf Arabs depended primarily on the sea for survival, fishing with both boats and weirs, diving for pearls, and participating in both local *cabotage* and long-distance Indian Ocean trade.[28] Gulf populations also earned notoriety by taxing or attacking the trade of others, an occupation that the Gulf Arabs regarded as a legitimate extension of mainland intertribal raiding into the sea, but that British and other European powers interpreted as piracy, thus earning the lower Gulf region the designation of the "Pirate Coast" until the early 1800s.[29]

The only part of eastern Arabia to practice agriculture on a large scale was Bahrain, which, although only a small island archipelago, nonetheless has occupied a disproportional place in eastern Arabian history. Bahrain means "the two seas," which may be a reference to its midpoint location in the Gulf, or may refer to two types of water, fresh and salt. Either meaning would be apt. Bahrain has been an important middleman trading city for nearly five thousand years; the ancient Mesopotamians, who knew it as Dilmun, exported grain and wool there, and received copper, cotton, and other goods in return. In addition, Bahrain's numerous natural springs have long made it a regional center of agriculture and have allowed it to host a much larger population than its small size would suggest. Bahrain's population in the early twentieth century was approximately one hundred thousand souls, nearly four times the population of the nearby peninsula of Qatar, which is fifteen times the area of Bahrain. Bahrain's high population, agricultural productivity, and mercantile wealth, which in the past was bolstered by the presence of nearby pearl banks, has ensured that Bahrain has been the frequent target of expansionist states, including the Ottomans, the Omanis, the Persians, and most recently the British.

The following chapters will attempt to trace the use of African agricultural slaves in all of these regions of Arabia, but the picture that emerges is much clearer in some areas than others. Although it is likely that a certain number of slaves were used in agriculture in 'Asir, where high malaria rates would have made slave agriculturalists an attractive proposition, I have been unable to find any evidence for it. Much the same can be said of Yemen, where I suspect that the presence of a large community of Arab farmers would have precluded the need to employ many slaves in agriculture endeavors in any case. More sources are available for the Hadramaut and Oman, and more still for the Gulf coast countries, al-Hasa, and Bahrain, though the picture that emerges is still somewhat indistinct. It is in the Hijaz and Najd regions that agricultural slavery comes into the sharpest focus. This is not to say that agricultural slavery was disproportionally concentrated in Najd and the Hijaz. The apparent preponderance of slavery in these two provinces could just as easily be an artifact of the evidence itself, given the relatively large number of travelers' accounts available concerning these regions, as compared to the rest of the Arabian Peninsula. Alternatively, the greater visibility of slavery in the Hijaz and Najd may reflect the central role played by the Hijaz in general, and Mecca in particular, in the African slave trade, a subject we will return to in chapters 2 and 4.

Temporal Parameters

In terms of temporality, this study will focus on the nineteenth and early twentieth centuries. This focus, however, reflects the limitations of the sources rather than the reality of the phenomenon under study. The use of African slaves and servile African labor for agriculture in the Arabian Peninsula almost certainly predates this period and may even predate the Islamic era, and I will discuss the evidence for the antiquity of agricultural slavery in Arabia in some detail in chapter 5. Suffice it to say at this point that from the standpoint of environment, economics, and culture, the factors that favored the use of African labor in agriculture in the nineteenth and early twentieth centuries were all present to some degree in earlier centuries as well. Logic, if not hard data, suggests that some African agriculturalists therefore existed throughout the period of traditional Arabian history.

The term I have just used, "traditional Arabian," requires some discussion. Traditional Arabia can only be understood in the context of its counterpart, "modern Arabia." As defined in this text, the period of modern Arabia does not have an exact start date, but is defined instead by a set of fundamental, transformative changes brought to the Arabian Peninsula by a set of new technologies and new political conventions imported from the Western world. The process began at sea in the nineteenth century, where the imposition of British naval power and the advent of the steamship disrupted earlier Arab patterns of naval raiding and tribute collection as well as established techniques of Indian Ocean trade. In the early twentieth century, the arrival of the automotive age crippled the power of Arabia's dominant camel-breeding tribes, in part by destroying the market for Arabia's camel exports, but also by blunting the military advantage of Arabia's camel Bedouins. Bedouin military power was further undermined by the use of the airplane, both by the British and later by newly founded Arab states, for reconnaissance and warfare. The modern era also brought with it fixed national boundaries that struck a death blow to Bedouin camel nomadism, which depended on unfettered scope of movement within their tribal *deera*, or customary pasture grounds. From the standpoint of agriculture, the most transformative technological innovation was the adoption of tube wells and diesel pumps. These new wells drilled into Arabia's deep aquifers and rendered small-scale oasis crop cultivation obsolete. Arabian agriculture is now an industrial venture practiced on a massive (and wasteful) scale, overseen by expatriate technical experts. These technological and political changes were paid for by one further breakthrough: the discovery of oil throughout the northern and eastern portions of the Arabian Peninsula, which transformed some of the world's most impoverished peoples into some of the world's richest.

The glittering lights of Arabia's modern cityscapes, however, should not blind us to the fact that Arabian life in the traditional period took place on a very different scale and followed quite different patterns. In contrast to the modern era, in which the concentration of population into cities has become the norm, Arabia's population was traditionally diffused and scattered. Nomadic pastoralism was the dominant economic activity, both in terms of its territorial expanse within the Arabian Peninsula and the number of people who followed this lifeway. Pastoralists were also the politically dominant group within the peninsula, especially the *sharif* ("noble") camel-breeding tribes, since the mobility they derived from desert-adapted camels gave them a decisive military advantage. These pastoralists lived in symbiosis with Arabia's settled, or *hadr*, population, which was concentrated in small towns and villages throughout the peninsula. The main basis of exchange was desert fats and proteins, desert firewood and charcoal, and hides for the carbohydrates, cloth, finished leather, and metalwork provided by the towns.[30] This exchange was by no means equal; indeed, camel pastoralists were able to expropriate a portion of hadr production for themselves through raids or through tributary payments.[31]

Overall, the economy of the Arabian Peninsula, especially in the interior, was subsistence- rather than market-oriented.

Political structures in the traditional Arabian Peninsula tended to be fairly weak, as the egalitarian traditions of pastoralist tribes curbed the power of desert sheikhs, and the towns commanded few resources and had little sway over the surrounding desert. Significant political entities usually arose only when the sheikh of a pastoral group managed to establish himself as an emir, or local strong man, in one of the towns. This was the case in the nineteenth-century Rashidi dynasty, whose power was defended both by warriors of the camel-breeding Shammar tribe and by a large household of slave soldiers, mostly of Abyssinian origin or descent. Alternatively, political structures could be established when charismatic leaders rallied both hadr and Bedouin populations behind a religious ideology, as was the case in both the rise of Islam in the seventh century and the rise of the nineteenth-century Wahhabi state.[32] Still, other state structures in Arabia resulted from outside patronage, such as the Ghassanid and Lakhmid dynasties in the immediate pre-Islamic period or the emirate of the Arabs established by Egyptian rulers in western Arabia during the Middle Ages.[33] Once established, these political entities tended to prove ephemeral due to the peninsula's precarious resource base, the shifting fortunes and policies of the established states surrounding the Peninsula, or both.

This is not to say that the traditional Arabian Peninsula was unchanging or timeless. Change was, in fact, a constant, especially on the level of politics, where the machinations of internal tribal groups and emirs, combined with interference from external political powers (Egyptians, Byzantines, Persians, Abyssinians, British, etc.), constantly reshaped the political map of Arabia. Other changes occurred intermediately, such as with the rise and fall of specific trade routes along the Red Sea and the Gulf, or through the interior of Arabia.[34] Such temporary changes, however, had a limited impact on the deeper structures of Arabian society and material culture. It is useful, in this respect, to recall the distinction made by the great French historian Fernand Braudel between *histoire événementielle*, the history of specific people and events, and the *longue durée*, the underlying structures and continuously recurring patterns of history that can remain fairly constant over very long periods of time.[35] While Arabian politics and trade route fluctuations occurred at the level of histoire événementielle, the concept of longue durée is more useful when seeking to understand agriculture, pastoralism, and other Arabian Peninsula lifeways. Nasir-i Khusraw's depiction of Arabian Bedouin and hadr populations in the eleventh century, for example, differs very little from those described by Charles Doughty and other European travelers in the late nineteenth century. R. B. Serjeant notes, in a similar vein, that every agricultural practice described in a fourteenth-century Yemeni agricultural manual by al-Malik al-Afdal was still being carried out in Yemen in 1970: a visitor could "actually see, from day to day, these usages enacted before one's eyes in the fields of South Arabia."[36] What is more, Daniel Potts notes that "it is unlikely that there would have been much difference between the [date] gardens of Dilmun during the Bronze Age and those of Bahrain in the early twentieth century." According to Potts, "no significant change, apart from the introduction of *falaj* [qanat] irrigation [in the fourth century CE], seems to have disrupted the essential continuity in agricultural praxis for roughly 4000 years."[37] "Traditional Arabia," therefore, is Arabia of the longue durée.

The process of transition between traditional and modern Arabia occurred at different times in different regions of the Arabian Peninsula. Change occurred earliest in coastal areas such as Oman, where British naval control over the seas surrounding the Peninsula disrupted established trading patterns. One of the more important disruptions, for the purpose of the present study, was an active British attempt to suppress the slave trade in the nineteenth century, though, as we shall see, this trade did survive in a diminished form via smuggling well into the twentieth century. Another early disruption was the collapse of the domestic Arabian handicraft industries in the face of cheaper European and (eventually) Japanese manufactures, and the collapse of the eastern Arabian pearl industry in the face of world wars and competition from Japanese cultured pearls. However, change came much more slowly to the interior and rural regions of Arabia. Traditional Arabia survived longest in the Omani and Yemeni interiors, Najd, and the rural regions of the Hijaz. In Saudi Arabia, the full transition to modernity—in other words, the subjugation of the Bedouin, the centralization of the state, and the shift from a subsistence economy to economic affluence—was still not complete as late as the 1970s.[38]

Source Materials

One of the perennial problems facing scholars of the Arabian Peninsula is the relative paucity of source materials. In contrast to European states, and even in contrast to the established Islamic polities of Egypt and Turkey, the weak and short-lived states of the Arabian Peninsula have produced almost no documentary record. Nor has the Arabian Peninsula produced much in the way of native historians or chroniclers, and those who do exist are far more interested in political and religious matters than in rural affairs. As Salah Trabelsi notes, classical Arab historians were urbanites who "disdain[ed] from evoking the dull and insipid life of the people of the countryside and, *a fortiori*, that of slaves stupefied by this punishing work."[39] A historian of Arabian Peninsula environmental history, therefore, cannot afford to be choosy, and must be willing to consider all information available. This study therefore will draw from diverse academic fields, including archeology, anthropology, medical science, and genetics. Material from these disciplines has its limitations, however. Archeologists have done relatively little work in the Arabian Peninsula, a neglect that some authors have ascribed to the profession's overall disdain for Arabian history, and in any case, slavery or servile labor systems are difficult to distinguish from other forms of labor on the basis of archeological remains.[40] Anthropological sources, in turn, are limited by the fact that most research was done in the Arabian Peninsula during the modern era, or during the period of transition to it, and thus is an imperfect window through which to view traditional Arabian Peninsula lifeways. What is more, anthropologists have worked disproportionally with Arabian Bedouins, such as the Rwala or Al Murrah tribes, and not with the settled populations among whom agricultural slavery was practiced.

As a result, the bulk of the material in this study will be drawn from two distinct, though interrelated, sources: archival materials relating to Britain's "undeclared empire" in the Arabian Peninsula; and published accounts of European, American, and Arab travel in Arabia.[41] Given the central role of these materials as sources for the present study, it is worth our while to discuss each briefly.

During the nineteenth and twentieth centuries, the British played an increasingly important role in the affairs of the Arabian Peninsula, in large part because British hegemony in Arabia was seen by the British as a means to safeguard British India. Indeed, the important southern Arabian port city of Aden, on the Yemeni coast, was ceded by the ruler of Lahaj to British India in 1838, thus becoming an overseas extension of Britain's Indian possessions. Britain was also drawn into Arabian affairs by their concerns regarding the Hajj, the annual pilgrimage that attracted thousands of Muslims from British colonies, which the British feared could serve as a pump for the distribution of disease, sedition, or both back into British territory.[42] The high point of British involvement in Arabia was during World War I, when Arabia became a battleground between the British and the Ottoman Empire. Most importantly for the present study, Britain became involved in Arabian affairs through its policy of suppressing the Indian Ocean slave trade.

Britain's undeclared empire in Arabia was administered by political residents and agents, stationed first in Bushire in southern Persia and later in Muscat, Aden, Jeddah, Doha, Abu Dhabi, and other political centers on the Arabian coast. Officially, these residents oversaw British interests and the welfare of British subjects living in the Arabian Peninsula. Unofficially, these agents served as a shadow government in Arabian coastal areas, most especially in the Gulf and in Oman, where local rulers gave up a great degree of their sovereignty in exchange for British recognition and protection.[43] Fortunately for historians, the bureaucracy of Britain's undeclared Arabian empire generated a trove of documents, mostly in the form of letters between the political residents and agents of Arabia and their supervisors in British India and/or the British Foreign Office. The main limitation of these documents for the study of slavery and agriculture in the Arabian Peninsula is that they privilege maritime affairs and deal primarily with the coastal regions of Arabia rather than the interior. This disadvantage is to some degree counterbalanced by a significant advantage: quite a few of these letters touch on slavery, since both the slave trade into Arabia and the manumission of slaves already within Arabia were ongoing British concerns.

The most valuable single source produced by the British government, however, is the *Gazetteer of Arabia*, a classified reference work produced in 1917 for British diplomatic and military personnel. The *Gazetteer* owes its origins, in part, to a previous British publication, J. G. Lorimer's *Gazetteer of the Persian Gulf, Oman, and Central Arabia*, which, despite its title, included relatively little information on the Arabian interior. This deficiency became a matter of grave concern once Britain entered World War I, and central Arabia became a crucial theater of war between the British (and their Arabian ally, the Sharif of Mecca) and the Ottomans (who were supported by their own Arabian ally, the Rashidi dynasty of Ha'il).

The task of filling in this hole in British intelligence was given to a secretive group of Arabists working in Cairo, who compiled data from many sources, including published travelogues, information collected by Britain's political residents and agents in Arabia, and work performed by the British Government's intelligence service in Cairo, including the archeological-cum-espionage expedition carried out from 1914 to 1915 by T. E. Lawrence in the Ottoman Levant.[44] The *Gazetteer* is not without its limitations, most especially the disproportionate coverage it gives to military affairs, such as the number of tribesmen in arms, the attitude of specific leaders towards Britain, and (in one notable case) the practicability of transporting field guns across the Dhofar coastal plain.[45] Nonetheless, it remains the single best and most comprehensive document concerning demographic patterns in the traditional Arabian Peninsula, and the data it provides on population size, population composition, and well depths will be used as the basis for several systematic investigations in the chapters that follow. It should be noted that edited versions of the first two volumes of the *Gazetteer* were reprinted in 1979. These volumes add some additional material from post-1917 sources, but since the project was apparently discontinued halfway through, the edited 1979 *Gazetteer* does not lend itself as readily to systematic examination.[46]

The other major body of sources upon which this study will rely is the corpus of nineteenth- and early twentieth-century travelogues on the Arabian Peninsula written by European, American, and Arab authors. Some anthropologists, such as Madawi al-Rasheed, have critiqued this body of literature, arguing that European travelers failed to grasp basic concepts that would have been clear to "any social scientist trained in the last fifty years or so."[47] Nonetheless, I am far from the first scholar of the Arabian Peninsula to make heavy use of these documents; a number of influential scholars of the Middle East, including F. E. Peters, Norman Lewis, and Alexei Vassiliev, have all employed these sources in the study of the Arabian Peninsula.[48] Even scholars of the Middle East whose first language is Arabic, such as Jibrail S. Jabbur, Madawi al-Rasheed, Soraya Altorki, and Raouf Sa'd Abujaber, have found these sources indispensable to their investigations.[49] Al-Rasheed herself, for example, relies on thirty traveler's accounts penned by twenty-two different European authors in her study of Ha'il and the Rashidi dynasty.

The authors of these travelogues came to Arabia with various motives. Some, like Charles Doughty, were eccentrics, seeking artistic inspiration and self-affirmation from Arabia's desert landscapes. Others came to Arabia as horse traders, scholars, diplomats, soldiers, or pilgrims. Still others combined one of these erstwhile professions with more clandestine aims, and served as spies for the British or French governments. As Clive Smith has noted, during the nineteenth century "the difference between intelligence work and private travel was never precisely defined."[50] Almost all of them saw themselves not as mere travelers but as explorers, delving into the dark recesses of "unknown Arabia," in the words of R. E. Cheesman.[51] In actuality, of course, these "explorers" were nothing of the sort, and they mostly trod along well-known paths in the company of Arab guides and companions. This study will therefore employ the more neutral term "traveler" to describe such individuals, whatever their stated (or actual) motives for entering Arabia, and despite the pretensions many of them had to original discoveries in the Arabian Peninsula.[52]

It might be expected that, given the various motives and backgrounds of these authors, their work would be highly uneven in quality, a combination of honest reporting and flights of fancy. However, this was not the case, in large part due to the fact that these authors understood themselves to be part of a larger tradition of travel writing on Arabia. Nearly all of these authors were well read on the travels of their predecessors in Arabia, and quite often commented upon or critiqued the findings of other travelers. In his 1884 article "Voyage dans L'Arabie centrale," for example, French traveler Charles Huber commented on the work of nearly all travelers to pass through the same region before, including the Swiss traveler John Lewis Burckhart, the Italian traveler Carlo Guarmani, the Finnish academic G. A. Wallin, and the British travelers Charles Doughty, Lady Anne and Wilfrid Scawen Blunt, and William Palgrave. Huber, for the most part, concurs with the findings of these earlier travelers, with the exception of Palgrave, whom he finds guilty of repeated exaggerations, such as overstating the dangers of the Nafud desert and overestimating the age of a mosque in Buraydah by at least three hundred years.[53] Huber's work, in turn, was weighed and judged (mostly favorably) by later travelers. The result of this constant process of reflection and critique was a corpus of literature that rewarded accurate reporting and aggressively sought out misinformation and hyperbole.

Accurate reporting on Arabian affairs was further fostered by the work of the Royal Geographical Society, founded in 1830. Although this society began as an informal dinner club, by the 1850s it had become a powerful institution under royal patronage with strong connections with British governmental and diplomatic leaders, particularly in the British foreign office. The Royal Geographical Society funded numerous "explorations" of Arabia, and also encouraged travelers to report on their Arabian adventures in public meetings, in which the findings of travelers were commented upon and critiqued by a learned audience. Even travelers who traveled as independent agents without any Geographical Society support, such as the stammering and reclusive Charles Doughty, were encouraged to speak at the Geographical Society. The French maintained an analogous institution, the Société de Géographie, to foster exploration and geographical knowledge, though France sent fewer travelers to Arabia. Both societies were founded and maintained in large part to support European imperialist ventures in Arabia and elsewhere, but they also acted to ensure quality control and accuracy within the corpus of travel literature.

The corpus of European travel writing on Arabia is not without its flaws. Most travelers were creatures of their age, and carried with them a set of Orientalist assumptions about Arabia and its supposedly timeless, primitive inhabitants.[54] The Geographical Society was also highly chauvinistic, banning women from its membership and meetings until 1913. This was not simply an injustice to women, but also to history itself, since it marginalized the work of several important female travelers in Arabia, including Lady Anne Blunt, Mabel Bent, and Gertrude Bell. In addition, the Royal Geographical Society actively worked with the government to ensure that travel into Britain's undeclared Arabian empire remained a British monopoly. In the words of Ameen Rihani, an American traveler of Syrian descent, Arabia was open "only to a few favoured Englishmen who combined . . . the interests of the Royal Geographical Society with those of the Foreign Office."[55] Even Englishmen were not immune to interference by the same institutional establishment, as is the case with G. Wyman Bury, a British political agent and keen student of Yemeni history and demography who was forced out of Yemen entirely after running afoul of his superiors. Our understanding of turn-of-the-century Yemen would undoubtedly be greater had he been allowed to remain. Despite these problems, the work of the Royal Geographical Society probably did more to foster than discourage the collection of accurate knowledge concerning the Arabian Peninsula.

The main limitation of the corpus of Arabian travelogue literature, as it exists today, is its narrow temporal extent. Although European travelers and merchants have long been active in the Middle East, in the period before the nineteenth century, most followed the prevailing trade routes along the Egypt–Red Sea or Mesopotamia–Gulf corridors, and few entered the Arabian Peninsula itself. What is more, pre-nineteenth-century explorers were overwhelmingly interested in antiquities and biblical studies rather than in the contemporary Arab inhabitants of the Middle East.[56] Only in the nineteenth century did travel within the Arabian Peninsula become increasingly common, largely as a side effect of European colonial expansion into Egypt and India.

Once again, however, there are compensating advantages. The most important advantage is the geographical extent of these studies. Since most of our travelers imagined themselves to be explorers, they actively sought to fill in the "blank spaces" in the map of Arabia, and competed to be the first to cross certain desert expanses, such as the Rub' al Khali desert of southern Arabia. As a result of this competition, European travelers observed and recorded notes on nearly the entirety of the Arabian Peninsula during the nineteenth and twentieth centuries, as is clear from map I.3, which shows the approximate paths taken by more than ninety different European travelers during the years 1807–1949. True, some areas are overrepresented (especially in northern Arabia) and others underrepresented (especially in the interior of the country, around Ghayl and Sulayyil). Nonetheless, overall, the competitive pressures exerted by the market for travel books and the Royal Geographical Society were a boon for modern scholars studying the traditional Arabian Peninsula.

Finally, this corpus of travel documents has several advantages that are relevant to the study of the environmental history of Arabia. European and

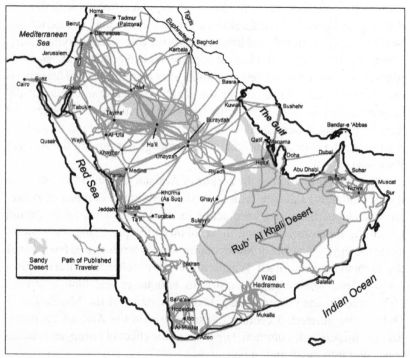

Map I.3. Travelers in Arabia, 1807–1949 CE

American travelers may not have thought like modern social scientists, but they did tend to be fairly observant about Arabian agricultural practices, partially because of their novelty, but also because the small patches of green in the Arabian Peninsula contrasted so starkly with the overall desert bleakness of the landscape. As a long-time inhabitant of the Arabian Peninsula myself, I can understand this sentiment. Even more importantly, nineteenth- and early twentieth-century European travelers were keenly interested in African slavery. In addition to being intrinsically exotic, slavery and the slave trade were then under active assault by European governments and thus were likely to be of interest both to the author and to his or her readers. As a result, these travelogues will serve as the main source of information in the next two chapters, which consider Arabian Peninsula agricultural techniques and the role played by slaves within those agricultural systems.

CHAPTER 1

Traditional Arabian Agriculture

ALTHOUGH SAND and camels dominate most people's impressions of the Arabian Peninsula, agriculture has been practiced in Arabia for over five thousand years, and Arabian farmers have traditionally been quite adept in creating microclimates of luxuriant growth in an unforgiving landscape. These pockets of agricultural fertility, however, have tended to be scattered and infrequent in a landscape characterized by overall sterility. The transition between the barren desert and agricultural fecundity, in fact, could be quite dramatic. For example, when Lieutenant Wellsted of the Indian Navy entered the oasis of Minna in December 1835, he found to his surprise fields green with grain and sugarcane, hedged in by "the lofty almond, citron, and orange-trees, yielding a delicious fragrance on each hand . . . streams of water, flowing in all directions intersected our path." "Is this Arabia," he asked his companions, "this country that we have looked on heretofore as a desert?"[1] As we shall see throughout this book, the abrupt environmental transition between the dry desert on one hand

and the humid fertility of the palm oases and *wadi* drainage channels on the other has played a crucial role in influencing the origins, distribution, and scale of African labor in traditional Arabian agriculture.

Four agricultural techniques dominated traditional Arabian agricultural production, each tied to a different hydrological regime. In a few parts of the Arabian Peninsula, especially in the Yemen and 'Asir highlands, dry (rain-fed) agriculture was possible, mainly with the assistance of agricultural terraces. Farmers also captured rainfall for agricultural production by harnessing occasional floodwaters by means of dikes, dams, and irrigation channels. Groundwater, in turn, was captured in two main ways. High mountain groundwaters could be tapped using *qanat* artificial springs, also called "chains of wells," to divert the water from plentiful mountain aquifers and transport it to agricultural fields, which in some cases lay many kilometers distant. Finally, groundwater could be harnessed almost everywhere using the *jalib*, or draw well, a ubiquitous feature of traditional Arabian agriculture. In the sections below, I will discuss each of these techniques in turn—partially for their own sake, but also because these techniques provide the necessary context by which to understand the roles played by slavery and malaria in traditional Arabian agriculture.

Origins of Arabian Peninsula Agriculture

One of the ironies of the history of the Arabian Peninsula is that, despite its close proximity to the early centers of agriculture in the so-called "Fertile Crescent" of the Levant, Egypt, and Iraq, the Arabian Peninsula was a relatively late adopter of agriculture. This was not due to lack of water resources. Quite the contrary: during the period up until 3000 BCE, the Arabian Peninsula was considerably wetter than it is today, since the ITCZ (Intertropical Convergence Zone), which marks the northern limits of the Indian Ocean monsoon, then penetrated as far north as Sinai and southern Iraq. At that time, most of the Arabian Peninsula's landscape was capable of supporting "comparatively lush vegetation," and would have greatly resembled the modern African savannah, with a mixture of grasslands, scattered medium-sized trees, and shallow, seasonal lakes.[2] From the standpoint of agriculture, however, these ample monsoon rains were a hindrance rather than a help, as the early domesticates of the Fertile Crescent, such as wheat, emmer, and barley, had evolved to live in a Mediterranean weather regime of winter rains and summer drought, and thus had difficulty passing south of the monsoon line. The peoples of the Arabian Peninsula did adopt the domesticated animals of the Fertile Crescent, especially cattle, which became crucial to the economic, social, and religious life of the Peninsula.[3] However, as Arabian archaeologist Joy McCorriston has noted, it would take nearly four thousand years before domesticated plants followed domesticated animals into the Arabian Peninsula.[4] Map 1.1 shows the approximate location of the ITCZ both five thousand years ago and in the modern era.

In addition to serving as an effective rain barrier against Fertile Crescent grains, Arabia's summer rainfall regime also inhibited the cultivation of the date palm, a plant that would become indispensable to Arabian agriculture. Date palms, which probably originated in southern Iraq, prefer wet winters and hot, dry summers. Not surprisingly, then, date palm cultivation in the Arabian Peninsula began only after 3000 BCE, when the

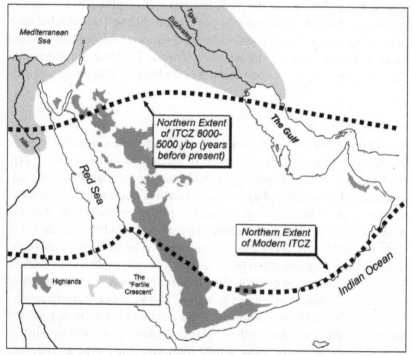

Map 1.1. The ITCZ (Intertropical Convergence Zone), past and present

Source: Juris Zarins, "Environmental Disruption and Human Response: An Archaeological-Historical Example from South Arabia," in *Environmental Disaster and the Archeology of Human Response*, edited by Garth Bawden and Richard Martin Reycraft, 35–49, Maxwell Museum of Anthropology Anthropological Papers 7 (Albuquerque: University of New Mexico Press, 2000).

ITCZ began to shift to its modern position at the southern heel of the Arabian Peninsula, bringing with it summer monsoon rains. The first evidence of date cultivation in the Arabian Peninsula comes from the Hili region in the modern-day United Arab Emirates, where both date stones and date wood were discovered in archaeological sites dating to between 3000 and 2000 BCE.[5] Similar findings in Kuwait, Oman, and Bahrain suggest that the date palm entered Arabia via the Gulf during the third century BCE. From there, the date palm likely jumped from oasis to oasis in central and western Arabia, carried by farmers to the few areas of relatively high groundwater in the increasingly desiccated landscape.

Date palms were crucial to Arabian agriculture not only because they thrived in Arabia's post–3000 BCE climate, but also because the palms themselves created microclimates of shade and humidity that were suitable to agricultural production. The extreme heat and aridity of the Arabian Peninsula was inimical to most of the cultivars of the Fertile Crescent, which could grow poorly if at all in Arabian soils. Palm trees, however, provided necessary protection from the omnipresent sun. The shade of the palms also protected soil moisture, and this moisture, combined with transpiration of water from the palms themselves, meant that the level of humidity within a palm plantation was significantly higher than in the surrounding desert. In the words of Lieutenant Wellsted,

> the instant you step from the Desert within the Grove, a most sensible change of the atmosphere is experienced. The air feels cold and damp; the ground in every direction is saturated with moisture; and, from the density of the shade, the whole appears dark and gloomy.[6]

Wellsted confirmed this impression of a "sensible change" with instrument data. His thermometer indicated that the temperature inside the houses of the Omani oasis he was exploring was 55°F (12.8°C), while the temperature reading in the oasis 6 inches above the moist ground was only 45°F (7.2°C). Wellsted provided no temperature data from outside of the oasis, but the modern average temperature in Oman's interior in December, the time when Wellsted was traveling, ranges between 62.6°F (17°C) and 73.4°F (23°C).

The cooler, moister atmosphere of the oases, as we shall see in greater detail in chapter 4, created near-perfect conditions for the breeding and proliferation of *Anopheles* mosquitoes, the insect vector of malaria.

However, the microclimate under the palms was also highly suitable for agriculture, allowing the cultivation of numerous domesticated plants beneath the canopy of the palms that otherwise could not survive the rigors of the Arabian climate. Arabian traveler Harry St. John Bridger Philby described the fertility and the diversity of one such garden in the Najd oasis town of Hamar as follows:

> The groves of the oasis are of very prosperous appearance containing a rich undergrowth of fruit-trees and vegetables— pomegranates . . . peaches, lemons, cotton-plants, a sort of scarlet-runner trained up the palm-trunks, egg-plants, and chilies.[7]

The same mixture of palms and understory plants was found throughout Arabia, though with a different mix of crops depending on the local climate. In the district of Aflaj in the south of Najd, Philby described the Laila oasis as hosting "lucerne [alfalfa], saffron, cotton-bushes along the borders, pomegranates, figs, and vines, in addition to several different varieties of date trees."[8] In the northern Najd town of Ha'il, crops grown under the palms included grains, pumpkins, millet, "different species of melons," and "gourds of uncommonly large size."[9] In al-Hasa, springwater was so abundant that rice was sometimes cultivated in paddies built within the palm planations.[10] The exact crops grown in any given region depended on the soil and climate, and probably varied seasonally according to rainfall and market prices. Nonetheless, the practice of combining palms with secondary crop cultivation was a constant throughout Arabia.

This form of farming, called *bustan* gardening in the literature (a redundancy, since *bustan* means garden in Arabic), is probably nearly as old as the cultivation of the date palm in the Arabian Peninsula. Such gardens consisted of a number of small fields, averaging about 2 acres in size, and connected to each other and to a water source by a network of irrigation channels. The most commonly used tool for weeding and turning the soil was the hoe, as these fields were, for the most part, too small to be worked efficiently with animal labor, and in any case, the ubiquity of irrigation channels would have left a plow team little room for maneuver. If plows were used, they tended to be ards or scratch-plows. Unlike European moldboard plows, which essentially flip deeper soil back to the surface in order to recover leached-out nutrients, ards kill weeds and aerate the soil without turning it over, thus preventing the loss of precious soil moisture.

Other tools used included sickles and a variety of knives adapted to palm cultivation.[11]

The use of fertilizers was moderate and depended on local availability. Animal manure was usually scarce, since most Arabian oases contained a minimum of livestock due to a scarcity of fodder, but soil and dung was collected from livestock pens, and stubble from previous crops was turned back into the soil.[12] In the al-Hasa area, according to Danish traveler Barclay Raunkiaer, "straw and withered palm leaves [were] burnt and their ashes [were] dug into the earth" to enrich the soil.[13] In nearby Bahrain, farmers fertilized their palms with the fins of the awwal, a "species of ray fish . . . steeped in water till they are putrid."[14] Dutch traveler Daniel van der Meulen reported that bird guano, collected from offshore islands near British Somaliland, was used as fertilizer in tobacco fields in the 1930s in Hadramaut, and in 1934, Freya Stark claimed that dried sardines were employed as fertilizers in the same fields, but it is not clear whether these were recent innovations or long-standing local practices.[15] Some Arabian farms were further fertilized by floodwater sediment, as we will discuss below.

Water

As suggested in the quotation by Wellsted above about the sharp transition from dusty desert to moist fertility, the limiting factor in Arabian agriculture was the availability of water. The Arabian Desert is essentially an extension of the Sahara into Asia, and, as in the Sahara, rainfall tends to be both scant and scattered. Only the southernmost heel of the Arabian Peninsula, which benefits from the Indian Ocean monsoon, receives enough yearly rainfall for dry (that is, nonirrigated) farming. The mountains of Oman receive a significant amount of rainfall as well, from a combination of monsoon rains, winter showers, and the occasional cyclone. As for the rest of the Peninsula, rainfall on average is less than 100 millimeters per year, far below the threshold of dry farming. As a result, pastoralism rather than agriculture is the most prevalent lifeway in the Arabian Peninsula, and the camel rather than the date is the most familiar product of the Arabian Desert.

As a result of the limitations imposed by Arabia's hydrological regime, agriculture in the Arabian Peninsula was traditionally carried out on a very small scale, at least in comparison with Arabia's neighbors. Map 1.2 shows the distribution of the date palm in the Middle East of the 1920s, at

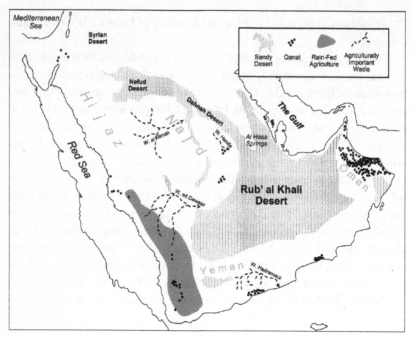

Map 1.2. Palm tree distribution in traditional Arabia and its environs

Source: Paul Popenoe, "The Distribution of the Date Palm," *Geographical Review* 16, no. 1 (1926): 117–21.

a time when modern agricultural techniques such as tube wells had not yet transformed the region's landscape. As is clear from the map, Arabia was a bit player in the field of agriculture, with only a small fraction of the number of palms grown in nearby countries such as Egypt and Iraq. Arabia's agricultural poverty is actually even more profound than this diagram suggests, since palms were the primary mainstay of Arabian agriculture, but played only a secondary role at most in the agricultural production of Arabia's neighbors. Egypt's main crops, for example, were sorghum, millet, and (later) maize, not dates. It should be noted that this diagram is also misleading in that it does not adequately demonstrate the agricultural fertility of Yemen, where high altitudes and summer rainfall were favorable for the cultivation of millet and sorghum but unfavorable for date palms.

While the overall number of palms in the Arabian Peninsula was meager compared to its neighbors, especially the riverine lands of Egypt and Mesopotamia, Arabia's palms, though few in relative numbers, had a profound impact on population patterns within the peninsula. This is clear from a comparison of maps 1.3 and 1.4, which show Arabian Peninsula population distribution and water resources, respectively. The data for map 1.3 were drawn from the British Government's 1917 *Gazetteer of Arabia*, which is an imperfect source: information for this World War II–era government handbook was collected from a combination of European travelers, whose journeys spanned a half century, and Arab informants of various degrees of probity.[16] What is more, while it is probably fairly accurate in terms of coastal regions and areas under strong British influence, like Oman, the Gulf, and parts of Yemen, its information is vague at best for some central regions, most notably the Wadi Dawasir and the borderlands of the Rub' al Khali Desert.[17] Nonetheless, I am confident that map 1.3 probably does represent a fair approximation of the settled population of Arabia c. 1900.

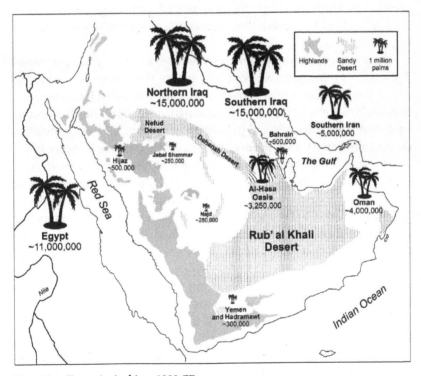

Map 1.3. Towns in Arabia c. 1900 CE

Source: Gazetteer of Arabia (Simla: General Staff of India, 1917).

Errata:

The map on page 28 (currently labeled Map 1.2) should appear as Map 1.4 on page 31.
The map on page 29 (currently labeled Map 1.3) should appear as Map 1.2 on page 28.
The map on page 31 (currently labeled Map 1.4) should appear as Map 1.3 on page 29.

As illustrated by map 1.3, the number and size of towns in the Arabian Peninsula was extremely unevenly distributed, with four main regions of concentrated population predominating:

- Coastal eastern Arabia, with clusters of population on Bahrain Island, in the interior al-Hasa oasis complex, and to a lesser degree, around the port area opposite Bahrain
- Northern Oman, especially (but not exclusively) along the coast
- Najd in the Arabian interior, south of the Nafud and Dahanah deserts
- Yemen, both on the coast and in the mountainous interior, with a secondary arc of population in the eastern Yemen interior in the Hadramaut valley

It is important to note the unique character of population in the province of Hijaz. Although this area hosted some large cities—Mecca, Medina, and Jeddah—these stand almost alone in a landscape dominated by pastoralism.

Why was population so unevenly clustered in the Arabian Peninsula? The answer to this question, or at least part of the answer, is provided by map 1.4, which shows major water sources used by agriculturalists in the Arabian Peninsula. As is clear from a comparison of the two maps, the overlap between water sources and population is striking. The large population cluster in eastern Arabia, for example, is explained by the presence of the al-Hasa artesian spring complex, bolstered by a number of qanat artificial springs, which will be discussed below. Oman's population distribution, on the other hand, correlates almost perfectly with the geographic spread of qanat structures. Najd's ragged string of settlements, in turn, was located largely within or near the base of the Wadi al-Rimah and Wadi Hanifa floodwater channels, and to a lesser degree, near qanat structures, though these are rare in this portion of the Arabian Peninsula. As for Yemen, its somewhat more diffused population can be explained by a combination of rain-fed agricultural land, qanat structures, and the waters of the Wadi Hadramaut floodwater channel. Availability of water, therefore, has profoundly shaped the distribution of Arabia's settled population.

Arabia's farmers employed four main techniques to harness these various water resources: floodwater diversion systems, mountain terraces, qanat artificial springs, and draw wells. The next four sections will discuss each in turn.

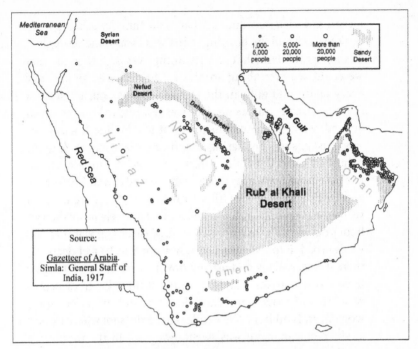

Map 1.4. Water resources in Arabian Peninsula agriculture

Sources: Peter Beaumont, Gerald Blake, and J. Malcolm Wagstaff, *The Middle East: A Geographical Study*, 2nd ed. (New York: Halsted Press, 1988); Fred M. Donner, ed., *The Expansion of the Early Islamic State* (Burlington, VT: Ashgate Publishing, 2008); Dale R. Lightfoot, "The Origin and Diffusion of Qanats in Arabia: New Evidence from the Northern and Southern Peninsula," *Geographical Journal* 166, no. 3 (2000): 215–66; P. G. N. Peppelenbosch, "Nomadism on the Arabian Peninsula: A General Appraisal," *Tijdschrift voor Economische en Sociale Geografie* 59 (1968): 335–46.

Sayl or Floodwater-Diversion Agriculture

One of the oldest agricultural techniques employed in the Arabian Peninsula was the use of diversion dams to contain and redirect water from the sayl, or flash flood. As discussed above, the Arabian Peninsula on average receives very little rain, but when rain does fall it often takes the form of heavy localized cloudbursts. Those downpours that fall on sand are quickly absorbed, but if the rain falls on the gravel, hard-packed soil, or bare rock that characterizes much of the Arabian Peninsula, most of the rain becomes surface runoff that quickly concentrates in low-lying wadis or floodwater channels.[18] Although usually temporary, lasting only a few days or hours, the scale of these floods can be quite considerable. Mid-nineteenth-century British traveler F. W. Holland recorded a memorable firsthand account of a particularly destructive storm and sayl in the Sinai desert:

I never saw such rain, and the roar of the thunder echoing from peak to peak and the howling of the wind was quite deafening. It soon grew dark, but the lightning was so incessant that we could see everything around us. In a quarter of an hour every ravine and gully in the mountains was pouring down a foaming stream, and as my tent was not pitched on very high ground, we kept an anxious look out for the flood, which we saw must ensue. The roaring of a torrent down a narrow gorge behind us showed that the waters were quickly gathering. Soon a white line of foam appeared down the wady [wadi] before us, and quickly grew in size till it formed a mighty stream. . . . It seemed almost impossible to believe that scarcely more than an hour's rain could turn a dry desert wady [wadi], upwards of 300 yards broad, into a foaming torrent from 8 to 10 feet deep. Yet there it was, roaring and tearing down, bearing with it tangled masses of tamarisks, hundreds of beautiful palm-trees, scores of sheep and goats, camels and donkeys, and still worse, men, women, and children. A few miles above the spot where I stood a whole encampment was swept away. . . . In the morning a gently flowing stream, but a few yards broad and a few inches deep were all that remained of the flood.[19]

Despite its dangers, the sayl was harnessed by humans from early times. The earliest evidence for this practice comes from Yemen around 3000 BCE, roughly the same time that monsoon rains began to slacken in the Arabian Peninsula. Archaeological evidence suggests that the cattle farmers of southern Arabia responded to the new weather conditions, which featured a decreasing amount of sustained rainfall and an increase in flash flooding, by building check dams designed to inhibit runoff, capture sediment, and increase infiltration of water into the soil.[20] The dams were probably built initially to increase the available fodder for cattle in a slowly desiccating environment. With increased aridity, these small-scale dams became increasingly sophisticated, and were maintained mainly with the purpose of feeding dense human rather than animal populations.[21] By 2000 BCE, southern Arabian farmers were building check dams on a monumental scale. The most famous dam, in part because its collapse is mentioned in the Qu'ran, was the dam at Ma'rib, built by the Sabaean civilization in what is today north-central Yemen.

The Ma'rib Dam, which probably represents the apex of large-scale sayl diversion in the Arabian Peninsula, was a truly massive structure. A first dam, probably 4 meters high and 580 meters long, was constructed on the site c. 750 BCE.[22] Later, dams of increasing size, height, and sophistication were built or rebuilt continuously by successive southern Arabian governments until 575 CE, when the irrigation system was finally abandoned. Although called a "dam," the purpose of the structure was probably not water impoundment, though this topic is controversial.[23] Rather, the dam was designed to raise the floodwaters of the Wadi Dhana up to the level of Ma'rib's agricultural fields, which were located on either side of the wadi. The dam did so by capturing floodwaters until the water behind the dam rose to the level of two spillways, which then served as primary canals. Excess water was allowed to spill back into the original bed of the Wadi Dhana. The first panel of figure 1.1 shows, in simplified form, the functioning of the Ma'rib Dam sayl diversion system. It is important to note that, while the Ma'rib Dam is the most well-known and famous of these southern Arabian sayl diversion structures, it was merely one of many that functioned between approximately 2000 BCE and 500 CE.

At its height, the Ma'rib Dam serviced an area of about 8,000 hectares, or 80 square kilometers of land. Fields were roughly rectangular, and each was surrounded by a low earthen wall. Water was directed from the primary canals to these individual fields by feeder canals, and each plot of land was flooded to "a considerable depth"—perhaps up to the 80–100 centimeter height of the field walls—when water was available in order to provide enough soil moisture for the coming growing season. Archaeological data suggest that these fields were bustan gardens, in which grains like wheat, barley, and sorghum, as well as various fruit trees, were grown beneath the sheltering canopy of palms. The fields were prepared for planting with the ard, and fertilizer was provided by a mixture of animal manure, ash from burning stubble, and from the rich silt content of the waters of the Wadi Dhana themselves.[24]

Although the silt of the Wadi Dhana contributed to the fertility of Ma'rib's famous gardens, called the *janatayn* or "two paradises" in the Qu'ran, over the long run, the same silt deposits progressively undermined the functioning of the agricultural system. Despite the best efforts of Ma'rib's farmers, who constructed settling tanks at the head of the primary canals to remove excess silt from irrigation water, the silt deposited in Ma'rib's gardens raised the level of those gardens incrementally. Once the soil level of the gardens had reached that of the dam itself, the only solution

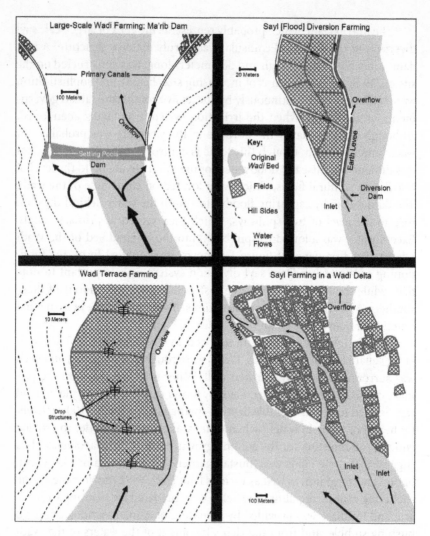

Figure 1.1. Traditional Arabian *wadi* farming techniques

was to increase the height of the dam in order to raise the sayl floodwaters even higher. As a result, the height of the dam, which was originally about 4 meters, rose to 7, to 14, and ultimately to 18 or more meters above the natural bed of the Wadi Dhana.[25] However, each increase in the linear height of the dam meant an exponential increase in the bulk of the dam, and as a result, the dam would have required ever-increasing investments of manpower to maintain. By 542 CE, when the dam underwent major repairs, the manpower of twenty thousand people was required to keep the dam in working order.[26] Investments in such an enormous scale, however, were becoming less and less practical as time went by, in part because of the escalating costs, but also partly due to the decline of the southern Arabian incense trade in particular and the decline of the interior caravan trade of Arabia in general, eliminating the entire *raison d'être* of the southern Arabian states. By the end of the sixth century, the Ma'rib Dam was abandoned permanently; not because of disastrous flood, as the Qu'ran suggests, but because of the increasing costs, increasing logistic problems, decreasing trade profits, and overall decreasing population of the Ma'rib area.[27]

The large-scale dams of southern Arabia, therefore, were designed to make maximum use of the high-volume but infrequent floods of Yemen's interior. In contemporary northern Arabia, a somewhat different system of rainfall capture was used by the Nabataean civilization. The Nabataeans today are best known for the ruins of Petra, their capital city, which features monumental Hellenistic-era tombs and temples carved directly into the sandstone walls of an isolated canyon. Just as impressive, though less well known, is the Nabataean mastery of local water resources for agriculture.

Rainfall in the core area of Nabataean civilization, which overlaps roughly with the northwestern portion of Saudi Arabia plus portions of modern Sinai and Jordan, was somewhat higher than in the rest of the Arabian Peninsula, but still not enough to make dry farming possible. To compensate, Nabataean farmers built a variety of different structures to concentrate, divert, and store rainwater. John Peter Oleason, an expert in Nabataean hydraulics, argued that the Nabataean toolbox included "spring houses, cisterns, reservoirs, dams, wells, enhanced runoff fields, agricultural terraces, wadi barriers, conduits, canals, and water-lifting devices."[28] Perhaps the most important of these techniques was what Oleason refers to above as enhanced runoff fields, but other authors have called "rainfall catchment" or "runoff farming." In such an agricultural system, relatively small plots of land are watered by runoff from much larger catchment basins, upstream from land in which obstructions have been removed and small diversion dams have been constructed in order to facilitate the flow of rainwater into the arable plots. Farmed plots were only about 1–3 hectares in size; in such a case, the catchment basin needed to be 20–60 hectares to provide the necessary runoff rainwater.[29] In addition, on hillsides, in broad basins, or in shallow wadis with more gentle floods, the Nabataeans built containment walls designed to slow down the water and thus increase both water infiltration into the soil and deposition of sediment for agriculture.[30]

What is more, like the Sabaeans, the Nabataeans also practiced sayl diversion agriculture, placing barriers across a wadi bed "to divert excess water flow into channels that carried it to the fields above the wadi bed proper."[31]

After the decline of the Nabatean and Sabaean civilizations, sayl farming continued in suitable locations throughout the Arabian Peninsula, though on a considerably smaller scale. Theodore Bent and his wife described a typical system of sayl diversion agriculture in the Wadi Hadramaut:

> The people were preparing for rain, which may never come; they had none for two years, but if they get it every three years they are satisfied, as they get a sufficient crop. As it comes in torrents and with a rush, each field is provided with a dyke and a dam, which they cut to let the water off. This dyke is made by a big scraper, like a dust-pan, called *mis'hap*, harnessed by chains to a camel or bullocks. . . . When this is done the field is lightly ploughed; there is nothing more to do except sit and wait for rain.[32]

Philby described a similar system of small-scale diversion agriculture near the town of Umm al-Khair, which is located in the Wadi Fatima of the southern region of the Hijaz. Umm al-Khair was

> a hamlet of three or four wretched stone huts with roofs of mud, situated on one side of a considerable tract of alluvial soil, terraced by human industry into cornfields. . . . These terraced fields depend entirely on torrent irrigation, the descending flood being diverted from the storm-channel by flimsy barriers of earth and brushwood into the embanked square plots. With one or more such flushings the soaked soil is ready for the seed, which is scattered upon it broadcast and left to germinate and grow until springtime, when the harvesters descend from the mountains and garner the corn.[33]

When the sayl did come, it utterly transformed life in these arid landscapes. Dutch traveler van der Meulen recorded a delightful narrative of the coming of the sayl in the Yemeni town of al-Jawf:

> With the advent of the sail [sayl] everyone stirs into action: conduits and dykes in the fields must be guarded and kept in

repair; as much as possible of the precious water must be stowed and stored in deeper places in the fields and near the villages. [Children] dive and dash about in the water ... [while] grown-ups come and sit around the little lake while it lasts and enjoy for hours at a stretch the sight and smell of so much water. The water soon disappears but the loam soil retains enough of it to provide sufficient moisture for a quickly-growing crop to ripen.[34]

Figure 1.1 illustrates some of the diverse methods used by traditional Arabian Peninsula farmers to harness the waters of the sayl. The upper right panel illustrates a system of sayl diversion agriculture along a flood channel of modest flow, such as the Wadi Fatima. In such locations, cultivation could not be performed in the wadi itself, since the force of the flood regularly swept the bed of the wadi clean. Agriculture instead was performed along the sides of the wadi. A diversion dam captured some of the water from the wadi flood, but strong embankments prevented the flood from overflowing into the farmed land. The lower left panel, on the other hand, illustrates a possible cultivation scenario in a wadi or depression of less energetic floods. Here, low walls are built within the wadi itself to slow and retain the floods of rainwater, thus trapping both alluvial soil and moisture within the wadi bed for use by farmers. The bottom right panel, in turn, shows a typical sayl harvesting system in the delta of a wadi, where the floodwaters begin to slow and spread outward; in such a scenario, diversion dams are still necessary to direct the water flows, but embankments to protect the fields from the flood are less necessary. Note that in all of these scenarios diversion channels were built into the system to safely release excess water, in order to reduce damage in the case of an extreme flooding event, such as that described by Holland above.

Mountain Terraces

Early nineteenth-century British traveler Charles J. Cruttenden, like many who preceded and followed him, was amazed by the size and scale of Yemen's agricultural terraces:

On leaving El Hudein we ascended gradually for about two hours, when we reached the ridge of the mountains; and from the summit a most magnificent view burst upon us. The hills formed an immense circle, like the crater of a huge volcano, and the sizes of which, from the top to the bottom, were cut regularly into terraces. We counted upwards of 150 in uninterrupted succession; and the *tout-ensemble* was most extraordinary.[35]

Yemen's terraces had hardly changed one hundred years later, when Philby penned an even more appreciative description of Yemen's magnificent terraced landscape:

Here Nature and man have certainly combined to create a scene of astonishing beauty, and it seemed to me that man had actually outdone Nature in their friendly rivalry. Imagine a great table-land thrust up to a height of 9000–9500 feet. . . . The surface of the plateau, plunging steeply down on one side in a series of splendid buttresses, slopes gently on the other in the curves of graceful valleys, forming huge theatres, for which man has provided the seats in terrace after terrace of cornfields. In the middle of June the corn was ripe, and I shall never forget that scene of golden ears soughing and bowing under the gentle breeze, terrace after terrace, down the mighty flanks of those mountains, whose steeper slopes Nature had reserved for her own planting a dense forest of junipers and other trees extending down to the 7500-foot level.[36]

The agricultural terraces of Yemen and elsewhere in the Arabian Peninsula owe their origin to two contradictory characteristics of the Arabian landscape. Rainfall sufficient for dry farming falls, almost without exception, only in the mountainous regions of the Arabian Peninsula. At the same time, the mountains themselves, which have thin soils and steep terrain, are in their natural state almost impossible to farm. Arabian agriculturalists solved this problem through the construction of agricultural terraces, which captured and retained soil, trapped water, and provided a level surface for farming.

Building a terrace is extremely labor intensive. Farmers begin by digging deep into the soil of a hill slope, in part to flatten out the slope of the land but also to excavate enough stone to build the necessary retaining walls. The next step is to build the retaining walls themselves, which follow along the contour of the hill, and which must be set deep enough into the soil to provide sufficient stability to the completed terrace. If the farmers are able to save enough soil from the excavations, the bed of the terraces will be built using that soil; otherwise, soil might have to be brought in by the basketful from elsewhere, usually from alluvial deposits in the valleys below.[37] In most cases, terraces were filled to slightly below the level of the retaining wall, since it was useful to retain a raised lip capable of impounding water and thus allowing it to infiltrate the terrace soil. At the same time, the retaining wall could not be built too high, trapping an excess of water in one terrace, as this would both deny that water to lower terraces and create the danger of a collapse of the overfull terrace under the weight of the impounded water. To avoid both problems, some terraces were fit with overflows, reinforced by earth banks, to release excess water.[38] Broad terraces on gently sloping land were generally planted with grains, and in Yemen, the soil was prepared for planting by the ard. Narrow terraces on steeper land were generally planted with trees instead, which provided greater stability to these more fragile terraces.

Water for these agricultural terraces was provided by various sources. Some water was provided directly through rain falling on the terrace itself. Supplemental water was provided by run-off from uphill slopes, which might have been prepared and cleared for rainfall collection. Runoff water was important because it brought upstream nutrients to the soils of the terrace, reducing or eliminating the need for fertilization of the fields.[39] Ghayl, or springwater, was also used if available, and because of the more reliable nature of this water, terraces fed by ghayl tended to be the most productive.[40] In addition, in more complex terrace systems, water from higher up the hillside might be delivered to lower-lying terraces though subterranean conduits built of masonry. The same conduits also allowed excess water to be drained off safely in extreme rainfall events.[41]

Figures 1.2 and 1.3 illustrate the variety of ways in which terracing was used within the traditional Arabian Peninsula. The first photograph, taken in Yemen, shows mountaintop terraces that clearly depend mainly on direct rainfall, though runoff from the higher slopes to the west might contribute to field moisture as well. In this case, the terraces clearly serve to retain soil from being lost downslope to erosion. In contrast, the second photograph depicts the use of terracing in a mountain village in Oman. Water in this example was provided by a combination of slope run-off and ghayl. The terraces in these cases were created to benefit from upstream erosion, capturing and maintaining moisture and soil washed from higher elevations, and to provide a flat surface for farming in a naturally rugged landscape. Unlike the Yemeni case, some of the terraces in Oman were

Figure 1.2. Terracing in Yemen

Source: Wikimedia Commons, http://commons.wikimedia.org/wiki/File:Yemen_landscape_05.jpg

cultivated as bustan gardens, with a variety of different plants fed by irrigation channels under the canopy of the palms. Bustan farming, it should be noted, is more crucial to agriculture in Oman than in Yemen; in Yemen, the summertime heat is moderated by monsoon cloud cover and moisture, allowing crops to be grown in open fields.

Ghayl and Qanat

In a few favored areas of the Arabian Peninsula, sufficient springwater, or ghayl, was available to make irrigated agriculture possible. By far the most notable area of natural springs in the Arabian Peninsula was al-Hasa oasis of eastern Arabia, where four large and many smaller springs disgorged 150,000 gallons of water per minute into an otherwise very arid desert landscape.[42] Thanks to this abundant water, the al-Hasa region has long been one of the most important agricultural regions of the Arabian Peninsula, with (as of 1955) over 12,000 hectares of land under cultivation, supporting a population of over fifty thousand people.[43] R. E. Cheesman, who visited the oasis in the early 1920s, left a vivid description of his impressions of al-Hasa's natural springs and its resultant fertility:

> We were immediately engulfed in the palm groves. Well-tended gardens surrounded us. Tall date-palms told of the fertility of

Figure 1.3. Terracing in Oman

Photo by Author

the land once it had the necessary water, and here it had plenty. Most of the land below the palms was bright with the fresh green of lucerne [alfalfa]. . . . A greater contrast to the desert outside even than the vegetation is provided by the water flowing on one side, sometimes on both sides, of the paths, and underneath bridges and culverts of rough masonry, with maidenhair ferns growing out of the crevices—not sluggish streamlets, but crystal-clear brooks, with the current and volume of an English mill-race! The arteries of the oasis nearer the source, before the waters are dissipated into side-branches, are swirling rivers.[44]

Outside of al-Hasa and a few mountainous areas of Oman and Yemen, natural springs were a rare anomaly. In many locations in Arabia, however, farmers were able to construct artificial springs, called qanat or *falaj* depending on the region. Qanat technology was first invented in Persia early in the first millennium BCE, but by the sixth century BCE it had spread to Oman, an area under strong Persian influence that was also well suited to qanat construction. Later, waves of cultural diffusion took the qanat to Yemen, eastern Arabia, and finally the Hijaz.[45] It should be noted that although qanat technology is ancient, it is by no means obsolete. Indeed, as late as 1989, more than 4,800 qanats combined to supply 55 percent of all water used for agriculture in Oman, and many are still used today.[46]

Qanat technology depends on a basic principle: that the water table is generally higher in hilly terrain—which, unfortunately, is not well suited for agriculture—than it is in alluvial lowlands where agriculture can be practiced. Qanats could move that water from where it was to where it was needed, but construction of a qanat was difficult, dangerous, and time consuming. First, a "mother well" was dug down to the water table in a hillside. Once water was reached, a chain of wells was dug at regular intervals between the mother well and the intended agricultural land. These wells were then connected laterally by qanat diggers, working in the dark or by the light of oil lamps, who dug out rock and soil which was then lifted to the surface by means of crude winches. Workers on the surface would then dump the soil onto the ground near the well entrance, in part to economize effort, but also in part because creating a donut of soil around each well mouth protected the wells from blowing sand and surface waters. In areas where the qanat main shaft passed through sand or other loose materials, the walls and ceilings would be supported with terra cotta hoops. Once complete, a steady stream of water would flow from the mother well to the other end of the qanat, where it was collected in a basin and then directed to the individual agricultural fields by small surface channels.[47] Figure 1.4 shows a cross-section of a qanat, but keep in mind that most qanat were far longer than the one shown, and might reach a dozen kilometers in length.

Draw Wells

The most ubiquitous method used in the Arabian Peninsula to procure water for agriculture is the draw well. In Arabic, these wells were called jalibs, from the root word *jalaba*, meaning to fetch, to bring, or to get. Jalibs were used in areas where groundwater was available, but could not be extracted horizontally using gravity power by means of a qanat. Rather, as illustrated by figure 1.5, a jalib employed animal power to lift ground-water out of the wells. Once brought to the surface, the water was generally stored in a basin, from which it could be distributed to individual plots of land or individual palms by means of irrigation channels. If the fields of multiple farmers were served by the same jalib, shares of water were divided by units of time, measured during the day by "the hours of prayer, and at night by the stars."[48] Depending on the depth and yield of the well, a given jalib could irrigate about .5–.8 hectares of land.[49]

Unlike qanats, which are still used today, the jalib has been rendered entirely obsolete by tube wells and diesel pumps, and to my knowledge none are still employed in agriculture in modern Arabia. However, several European travelers have left us clear descriptions of their design and use. In the 1910s, for example, Philby described a typical well in Riyadh as follows:

> The mouth of the pit is surmounted by a ponderous triangular superstructure called 'Idda and constructed of palm-logs with *Ithil*-wood for the stays and subsidiary parts; the top cross-beam of the 'Idda is furnished with six pulleys on either side or twelve in all, while the basal beam resting in masonry sockets over the actual mouth of the well is provided with a corresponding number of rollers. Stout hempen ropes, to one end of which are attached the leather buckets generally consisting of whole goatskins, run over the pulleys to be harnessed in this case to . . . donkeys . . . while thinner cords running over the rollers are attached at one end to the donkeys and at the other to the necks of the skin-buckets, which are weighted by stones tied to

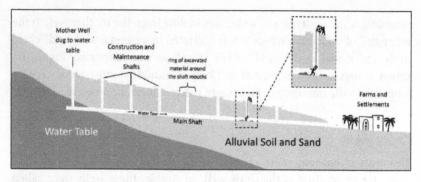

Figure 1.4. Cross-section of a *qanat*, or "chain of wells"

Source: Lightfoot, "Origin and Diffusion."

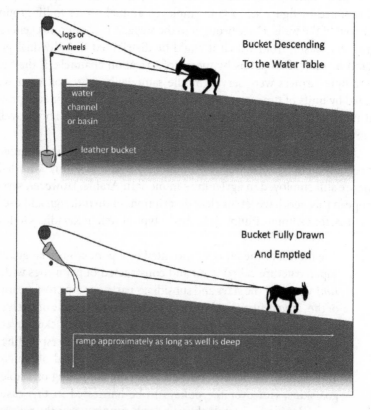

Figure 1.5. Cross-section of a *jalib*, or draw well

Source: Adapted from Henri Charles, *Tribus moutonnières de Moyen-Euphrate*, Documents d'Études orientales, t. VIII (Beirut: l'Institut Français de Damas, 1939).

their thicker extremities. On either side of the well-mouth lies a sharp incline, whose length corresponds to the depth of the pit to water; the donkeys, each harnessed to its bucket by the thick and thin ropes, start in a line, six on each side, down the incline, and as they descend draw up the buckets full of water; when they reach the bottom, the thick ends or bodies of the buckets reach the levels of the pulleys in the upper beam, while their thin ends or necks, being simultaneously drawn over the rollers, discharge their contents into a masonry reservoir immediately below them, whence the water flows out into the channels by which it is distributed over the garden. The animals, having reached the bottom of the incline, pause for a moment and turn round . . . the line then ascends the incline as it descended, and by so doing lowers the weighted [bucket] back into the water, whereupon the process here described is repeated without end.[50]

Although is not entirely clear when the jalib was invented, it dates at least to the pre-Islamic period of Arabian history. The classic Bedouin poet 'Alqama, for example, likened his "weeping eye" to a "water bag, dragged down the well slope by a roan mare, withers bound to the saddle-stay." Another classical-era poet compared the unsteady movement of a sleepless rider to the "swaying of the two ropes of a concave well."[51] Most likely this technique of groundwater extraction is nearly as old as agriculture in the Arabian Peninsula.

Jalibs, when compared to the other forms of irrigation technology described in this chapter, are inherently inefficient. Like qanat agriculture, the construction of a draw well involved considerable costs: Daniel van der Meulen reported that the 100-meter wells sunk into the Hadrami town of Hureidha took more than a year to build, and were the work of well-paid specialized craftsmen.[52] The construction of the collection basin at the base of the well and a network of elevated irrigation channels for the distribution of water throughout the garden would have required further expenses. Building a qanat would cost even more, but once constructed, the operating costs would be lower as the water passes through the system using gravity. This was not the case in jalib irrigation, in which farmers had to work against gravity to draw well water up to the level of their fields. Nonetheless, as we can see from the Philby quote above, Arabian farmers did everything they could to streamline the process. In order to save effort, as well as to extend the life span of the hemp ropes used to draw up the leather bucket, pulleys or rollers were used where the ropes passed over the wooden frame above the well. What is more, the animals used to draw water from the wells walked up and down a built-up ramp (or down-sloping trench), which was highest at the mouth of the well itself. As a result, draft animals walked up the ramp when the leather bucket was empty and down the ramp when it was full, using gravity to compensate for the extra weight of the fully loaded bucket. Nonetheless, this form of irrigation was inherently more demanding in human and animal labor than sayl or qanat irrigation, at least in its day-to-day operation. What is more, gardens irrigated by a jalib, unlike those watered with sayl, had to be provided with fertilizer, though this disadvantage was mitigated to some degree by the manure of the draft animals.

The inherent inefficiency of jalib irrigation was made even worse by the fact that the animals used to draw the water had to be fed, and in the fodder-poor Arabian Peninsula, procuring animal feed was no easy feat. Urban draft animals could not be grazed on pasture land, since there was simply no pasture land to be had; indeed, constant foraging for firewood by urban populations meant that most traditional Arabian towns were surrounded by a dead zone almost devoid of vegetation.[53] As a result, humans competed directly with animals for food in Arabian oasis towns. The "fresh green" crops of alfalfa described above by Cheesman in al-Hasa, for example, were almost certainly grown for consumption by livestock, not humans. One interesting solution employed by Arabian farmers to this local lack of fodder in the oasis towns was to rent camels from Arabia's Bedouin population. These camels would have arrived in the oasis with a full gas tank, as it were, in the form of a hump of fat. The camel would gradually lose that hump while walking up and down the ramps of the jalib, after which the half-starved camel could be returned to its Bedouin owner.[54]

Nonetheless, however inefficient, the jalib was a ubiquitous feature in traditional Arabian agriculture, and was found throughout the Arabian Peninsula. This in part reflects the moderate initial costs of the jalib itself, especially in areas of relatively high groundwater, as compared to the much higher costs of constructing a qanat. It also reflects the fact that, while terraces, sayl irrigation schemes, and qanats could only be built in specific areas with the right geomorphic characteristics, a jalib could be constructed almost anywhere groundwater was available. The exact animals used to provide the motor power for the jalib depended on regional availability:

while donkeys were used in al-Hasa, camels were commonly used in Najd and the Hijaz, while the many draw wells of Omani al-Batinah were worked by bulls "of the humped Brahimee kind," which reflects Oman's close relations with the Indian subcontinent.[55] If animals were not available, a jalib could be operated with human power alone.

So far, this chapter has discussed water sources separately, but in actuality, it was common for any given town to rely on multiple sources of water. In the Najd town of Shaqra, for instance, Philby notes that

> the palm-groves are irrigated in the rainy season by the admission of flood water into the circuit of the oasis through channels for which arched sluices, capable of being closed by boards or brushwood, are provided in the outer wall. Such irrigation gives the palms the annual soaking which their roots require, but perennial irrigation is also carried on for the benefit of the palms and of the important subsidiary crops of fruit, vegetable and corn by means of great wells of the *jalib* type. Donkey and kine and camels are used here to draw up the water. . . . The largest well I actually saw was one of great wheels . . . worked by a team of eight donkeys ascending and descending the inclined plane which, in this case, was only on one side of the well.[56]

In other towns, Philby notes, both sayl and ghayl were used. Arabian farmers probably did not employ multiple water sources in order to maximize production: agriculture in the traditional Arabian Peninsula was, after all, overwhelmingly subsistence rather than commercial in character, and there was little point in producing more food than could be reliably stored. Rather, diversity in water resources provided a level of redundancy and a hedge against famine. What is more, using multiple water sources could help smooth out seasonal and yearly rainfall variations. While the water obtained by sayl was obviously dependent on a given rainy season's rainfall, the water available from qanats and wells depended on average rains for the past few years, and ghayl might be very old indeed. According to carbon dating, for example, the springwater that sustains the al-Hasa oasis first fell as rain between fifteen thousand and twenty-five thousand years ago.[57]

ARABIAN FARMERS, therefore, have used a number of different agricultural techniques over the past five thousand years to create fertile agricultural landscapes within the arid and inhospitable Arabian Peninsula. While some Arabian landscapes were exploited through open agricultural terraces sustained by natural rainfall, the most common overall agricultural system in the Arabian Peninsula was bustan gardening, which employed irrigation to grow date palms as well as secondary crops planted beneath the palms' protective shade. Water for these gardens was derived from multiple sources. Although floodwaters were used in some areas, groundwater was the most typical source of agricultural water, and this was tapped in different places through ghayl, qanat, or jalibs. However, thus far we have not considered the human element: the diggers of wells, the builders of embankments, the harvesters of the dates, and the minders of the camels walking endlessly back and forth up and down the ramps of the jalibs. Who did this work, where did they mainly live, and what was their social status? Perhaps most importantly for the present study, what role did slaves play in the agriculture of the Arabian Peninsula? We will turn to these questions in the next chapter.

CHAPTER 2

Diggers and Delvers

African Servile Agriculture in the Arabian Peninsula

AS DISCUSSED in the last chapter, agriculture in the traditional Arabian Peninsula consisted of a variety of different techniques suited to different hydrological regimes. Not surprisingly, given this regional diversity, slaves served a variety of functions in traditional Arabian Peninsula agriculture. It is important from the outset to make a distinction between slavery as practiced in Arabia and chattel slavery as practiced in the Atlantic world of the seventeenth through nineteenth centuries. Compared to their American counterparts, African slaves in Arabia tended to be more autonomous and more humanely treated, though of course slave treatment could vary depending on local circumstances. At the same time, slave status was more difficult to escape in Arabia—not because manumission was rare, but because a manumitted slave assumed the status of a *mawla*, who continued to be a dependent of his or her former owner, and owed that owner certain obligations. In addition, strong prohibitions against intermarriage with Africans served to keep slaves and mawlas alike apart from the Arab population, to the point that Africans constituted a servile caste in many parts of the traditional Arabian Peninsula.

Of course, not all Africans served as agriculturalists in the traditional Arabian Peninsula, nor were all agriculturalists African. Indeed, the traditional Arabian Peninsula included a number of Arab agriculturalist communities, such as the Baharinah of Bahrain, the Hasawiyah of the al-Hasa oasis, and the Bani Tamim of Najd. Nonetheless, as this chapter will indicate, African slave or servile labor did play an important role in agricultural production throughout the Peninsula. In most parts of the Arabian Peninsula, African slaves and mawlas played a supplementary role in agriculture through the construction of qanats, the digging of wells, the maintenance of palm gardens, and the drawing of water from the jalibs. In a few places, however, thousands of servile Africans were employed in agriculture on a large scale, often as sharecroppers in the service of nearby Bedouin or urban Arab populations. These communities, which I have dubbed "colonies" in the text below, were found throughout the Arabian Peninsula but were particularly common in Najd and the Hijaz.

Slaves and Freedmen

The institution of slavery has been ubiquitous among all human societies from the beginning of history, and the Arabs were no exception. Slaves in early Arabian history were mainly people who had been taken captive in warfare, though some were imported from outside the Peninsula. The *Romance of 'Antar*, which was composed during the pre-Islamic era of Arabian history, mentions not only African slaves, but also slaves from Egypt, Persia, and the Caucasus.[1] 'Antar, the hero of the story as well as the reputed author of the poems, was himself the son of an African slave shepherdess. The institution of slavery was thus already old in Arabia at the time of the Prophet Mohammad, who—as an inhabitant of Mecca—lived in one of the Peninsula's most important slave markets. Indeed, a number of Meccan-born leaders of the early leaders of the Islamic state were, like 'Antar, of partial African ancestry, including the third Caliph 'Omar and possibly Mohammad himself.[2]

Despite the egalitarian ethos of Mohammad's religious vision, Islam did not abolish or even diminish slavery in Arabia, though it did alter the status of slaves in certain ways. The Qu'ran implicitly recognized the rights of slave owners over slaves, who are described euphemistically in the text as "that which your right hand possesses." As Bernard Lewis notes, the Qu'ran "urges, without actually commanding, kindness to the slave . . . and recommends, without requiring, his liberation by purchase or manumission."[3] Muslim slaves were also recognized as being religiously equal to their Muslim masters, and thus superior to pagans and idolaters. In addition, Lewis continues, the "innumerable hadiths" of the Prophet counsel mild treatment of slaves as well, "denouncing cruelty, harshness, or even discourtesy, [and] recommending the liberation of slaves." Lewis therefore argues that "the Islamic dispensation enormously improved the position of the Arabian slave, who was now no longer merely a chattel but also a human being with a certain religious and hence a social status with certain quasi-legal rights."[4] A mistreated urban slave, for example, could appeal to the local *qadi*, or judge, for arbitration and relief. In Bedouin areas, a slave seeking better treatment could benefit from an old customary practice: if a slave injured the horse or camel of an Arab other than his master, custom dictated that the owner of the horse or camel should claim the slave who inflicted the injury as compensation, and this offered slaves a means by which to switch ownership to a master of his or her choice.[5] These laws and customary rights were, of course, not universally respected by all Arab slave owners. T. G. Otte goes so far as to say that the *shari'a* (Islamic religious law) regulations concerning slavery were "honoured as much, if not more so, in [the] breaches as in the observance."[6] In any case, it should be noted that Islam's regulations concerning slavery in effect legitimized and perpetuated the practice. As Murray Gordon has quipped, "in lightening the fetter, he [Mohammad] riveted it ever more firmly in place."[7]

The treatment of slaves in the Islamic world was also moderated somewhat by the tasks they were asked to accomplish, which tended to be consumptive rather than productive in character. The most common use of slaves, both in Arabia and elsewhere in the Islamic world, was as domestic servants, who quite often stayed with a family for many years and were treated as adopted family members, especially if they were involved in raising children. Another common use of slaves was as soldiers or bodyguards, jobs that placed slaves in positions of some power, even if that power was really the reflected glow of the might of their masters. Slaves also served as concubines and eunuchs in the households of wealthy Arabs. Relatively few slaves worked in productive roles, such as water carriers, shepherds, animal drivers, or farmers, though as this chapter will suggest, this last employment of slaves was more prevalent in Arabia than has heretofore been acknowledged. Overall therefore, slavery in the Arabian Peninsula, as with the rest of the Islamic world, was oriented primarily toward status rather than profit, as opposed to the capitalist-driven brutality that characterized slavery in many parts of the Atlantic world of the seventeenth through nineteenth centuries.

Most contemporary observers of traditional Arabian slave systems commented on the relative mildness of Arabian slavery compared to slavery in the Atlantic world, which for these authors was clearly the normative yardstick by which slavery ought to be judged. Typical in this regard is Eldon Rutter, a traveler in Arabia and convert to Islam, who delivered a lecture to a joint session of the Royal Central Asian Society and the Anti-Slavery and Aborigines Protection Society in 1933 to mark the hundredth anniversary of British abolition of slavery in its colonies. Rutter notes that "slavery in Arabia is, in its physical aspect, a slight thing," and that "slavery of the easy-going Muhammadan kind makes contented slaves." Slaves are treated "kindly, and even affectionately," Rutter notes, and he concedes that "the lot of a slave in Arabia is quite as happy as that of thousands of human beings in the most advanced countries of the world." Arabian slavery is so different from its counterpart institution in "the Southern States of North America," Rutter argues, that "we really need a new word to describe the comparatively mild *riqq* or slavery of Arabia."[8] For Rutter, however, the very mildness of Arabian slavery was its worst feature, as slaves in Arabia displayed a dangerous complacency that served to perpetuate the slave system.

Slaves in Arabia, therefore, had more rights and received better overall treatment than their counterparts in the seventeenth- through nineteenth-century Americas. Nonetheless, Arabian Peninsula slaves were at a distinct disadvantage in one respect as compared to their American counterparts. Unlike slaves in the European legal tradition, where the transition between slavery and freedom was clear and well defined, manumission in traditional Arabian slavery did not lead to a dramatic improvement in the legal situation of the former slave. In the Islamic legal tradition, freed slaves generally took on the status of mawlas, a complex term that is best translated as "clients." Although they could no longer be bought or sold, the master retained a set of rights over the mawla. According to Daniel Pipes, a former master could still expect "fealty, aid, and counsel" from his or her freedmen, and in addition "had rights over the *mawla's* inheritance, should the *mawla* die without heir." What is more, since most freed slaves were without property and thus without a means to sustain themselves, most mawlas were obliged to continue performing the same tasks they had performed as slaves, though now as wage earners or sharecroppers. The economic dependency of mawlas was further underscored by that fact that they, unlike slaves, were not entitled to receive food, clothing, and shelter from their owners, but instead had to earn these necessities through their own labor.[9] The continued subordination of the mawlas to their former masters was also dictated by their need for protection, since in traditional Arabian society personal security depended, not on laws and state coercive institutions, but rather on attachment to a tribal entity powerful enough to defend itself. Because of their "disjointed and vulnerable status," Pipes argues, "*mawlas* depended so much on their patrons that they were unfree."[10]

As a result of the continued subjugation of the mawlas to their masters, it is impossible to draw a sharp distinction between slaves and freedmen in the Arabian Peninsula. The Arabs themselves tended to use the term '*abid*, or slave, as a blanket term for people of African ancestry in general, and European travelers were often confused as to the exact social status of any given African individual or community they encountered. Slaves and mawlas alike were often obliged to perform customary duties for free Arab individuals and tribes, and were kept in that position by social restrictions that hindered their ability to marry into "pure" Arab lineages and imprisoned them in what were effectively subordinate hereditary castes.[11] Some of the same traditional obligations and social restrictions also constrained other "free" populations of the Arabian Peninsula, such as the Nakhawila and the Bani Khadhir. As a result, in this study I will often use the term "servile" to describe an African agricultural population in a position of subordination where the exact legal status is unclear.

Two other caveats should be raised about the apparent mildness of the Arabian Peninsula slave regime. First of all, the frequency of manumission in Islamic lands created a constant demand for new slaves, and this demand, in turn, incentivized the wars and slave raids that kept the Middle East's slave markets well stocked. As Ehud Toledano has pointed out in the case of Ottoman slavery, "humanity at home inadvertently perpetuated the brutality from without."[12] Secondly, it is by no means clear that the relatively mild slave regime mentioned in the sources above was necessarily true for the Arabian Peninsula's agricultural slaves. As we will see below, there are some indications that African agricultural slaves were more harshly treated than their non-agricultural counterparts, though the evidence is scanty.

African Slaves as Agricultural Workers

In chapter 1, we examined specific agricultural techniques used in traditional Arabian Peninsula agriculture, including terracing, sayl agriculture,
ghayl agriculture, the qanat, and the jalib. The degree to which African
slave or servile labor was employed in these techniques varied widely. I
have, for instance, found no explicit references to the employment of African servile labor in terracing, which in the Arabian Peninsula is mainly
practiced in Yemen. Indeed, in his survey of Islamic abolitionist thought,
William Gervase Clarence-Smith reports that slavery among the Zaydi
highlanders of Yemen was quite rare, and concentrated in urban Sana'a
rather than the surrounding agricultural countryside.[13] The relative lack of
agricultural slaves in the terraced Yemeni highlands could be explained by
Yemen's somewhat unique social structure. In the rest of Arabia, farmers
tended to be an exploited underclass, subject to the demands of Bedouin
tribes, emirs of the towns, or sometimes both. Not so in the highlands of
Yemen, where tribal groups of farmers living in easily defensible mountain
villages constituted the militarily dominant group, and where agriculture
was a respectable profession for a free man.[14] These military and cultural
factors, combined with Yemen's high population (by Arabian standards),
probably would have made African servile labor unnecessary.

African agricultural slavery might also have been rendered unnecessary by the relative lack of malaria of the Yemeni highlands, since as we will
see repeatedly throughout this chapter and in chapter 4, malaria is strongly
correlated with African agricultural labor in the Arabian Peninsula. Insofar
as agricultural slavery existed, it would have probably been concentrated,
not in the mountain terraces, but in mid-altitude agricultural wadis where
malaria was a chronic problem. Case in point is the Madinat al 'Abid, a
town on a tributary of Yemen's Wadi al-Rimah. The name of the town
means "City of the Slaves," and although British traveler Hugh Scott notes
neither slaves nor Africans when driving through there in 1937, he does
note that the place had an "evil reputation for malaria," to the point that his
guides timed the day's travels to avoid camping overnight in the vicinity.[15]
Nonetheless, while the place name seems to suggest the large-scale use of
slaves in the area at some time in Yemeni history, overall there is no hard
evidence suggesting agricultural slavery was anything more than periph-
eral to highland Yemen's terrace agriculture.

Much the same could be said concerning the contribution of slaves to
Arabia's sayl agriculture. Sayl farming was not particularly time intensive.
The fields and embankments did have to be prepared on a seasonal basis,

which required some short-term effort, but the fields themselves were watered by gravity flow with little human assistance. That is, of course, if the fields were watered at all; if the rains failed, the plot of land would have remained fallow. Thus, given the low and unpredictable labor demands of sayl cultivation, it is unlikely that African servile labor would have been employed, except perhaps on a seasonal basis and in conjunction with other slave employments.

In contrast, African servile labor probably played a significantly greater role in another traditional Arabian agricultural sector, the construction and maintenance of Arabia's qanats and other man-made springs. While the construction of qanats was supervised by well-paid experts, the dangerous grunt work of construction and maintenance was often performed by African slaves or African servile labor. Our best source on slave involvement in qanat construction and maintenance is a remarkable document concerning agricultural slavery, *L'esclave de Timimoun* by F. J. G. Mercadier, which details the life of the African slave Griga in the palm plantations of nineteenth-century French North Africa. Griga recalled to Mercadier the horrors of qanat repairs, a task which to which he was once assigned as part of a general levy of slaves from the village. His party of ten was assigned to clean out ten maintenance shafts, each approximately 36 meters deep, on the plateau overlooking the town. He was sent down one of the shafts without a rope, lowering himself by clinging by hands and feet to the sides of the well: "After a long and painful descent, in which I took stones to the head, I arrived at the water, and crouched in a narrow tunnel which connected two wells." Another slave then joined him, precipitating as he did another "rain of stones" upon Griga, after which they got to work filling baskets with rock and soil by lamplight. Speaking long after the event, Griga was still haunted by this "lonely, superhuman task in a narrow gallery, humid and dim, to open a passage in a cork of sticky clay before which the water mounted inexorably." Griga was terrified all the while, as "it is frequent in the course of such work for supports to collapse, obstructing the channel and burying or crushing the workers."[16] Thankfully, after a period of time, Griga was helped to the surface with the aid of a rope and his place in the qanat channel was taken by another.

As Griga was soon to learn, tunnel collapses were not the only danger that threatened qanat workers. No sooner had he returned to the surface when "suddenly, downstream, we heard cries. We all stopped short, assembled, and discussed. It appeared that someone was calling for aid. We ran to the spot. The slaves [there] explained that when descending into the well, Moumen, a slave of Abdelali had slipped and fallen down a chute 18 meters deep!"[17] Two men descended to retrieve the fallen worker, who was alive but breathing with difficulty, and eventually lifted him to the surface with the help of ropes passed under his armpits. In the end it was to no avail; the injured Moumen later died, leaving his fellow slaves to mourn the loss of life and his Arab owner Abdelali to bemoan the loss of the two hundred francs he had spent on Moumen just a year before.

Although this example hails from North Africa, many such scenes undoubtedly played out, mostly unrecorded, in the Arabian Peninsula. The only explicit account I have come across of African workers laboring in Arabian qanat shafts is given by Harry St. John Bridger Philby, who made note of a team of "a few negroes" working on a qanat shaft near Banna during his travels in Najd in 1918. According to Philby,

> at the time of my visit a few negroes were at work in the last shaft, about three fathoms [5.5 meters] deep, trying to improve the water-supply, which was extremely feeble, by clearing out the channel, but they seemed to be digging in the dark for they confessed they did not know from what direction the water was coming; it looked very much as if the spring, on which the stream depended, was steadily losing its vitality.[18]

African laborers were employed in the construction or maintenance of other large-scale irrigation works as well. For example, in 1907, French archeologists Jaussen and Savignac make note of a team of "five or six negroes" that had been sent out to repair an old reservoir and irrigation channel 6 kilometers south of Taima.[19] Not all such labor was performed by African slaves in Arabia. According to interviews performed by Soriya Altorki and Donald Cole in the 1980s, both free tribesmen and servile Africans were traditionally employed as well-diggers due to the high wages it offered. Nonetheless, the risks that this occupation entailed probably ensured that most well-diggers were servile, as "the men who did it died young," both because of injury and "the smoke [dust] of the clay in the wells."[20]

African servile labor was also frequently used to operate and maintain the jalibs of Arabian farming towns. Altorki and Cole found that these wells were still remembered with nostalgia by the inhabitants of 'Unayzah in the 1980s: "They particularly remember the women singing and speak of the wonderful sound of 'wishshsh' the water made as it emptied into the basin."[21] I doubt that this nostalgia was shared by the workers tasked with the monotonous, mind-numbing task leading the animals up and down the well ramps "throughout the night and into the morning of the next day."[22] This of course assumes animals were available—if not, there was no other alternative than to draw the water by hand. Not surprisingly, workers on the jalib tended to be drawn from the lowest and most impoverished ranks of society, including (where available) African slaves and mawlas.[23]

It is likely that African servile agricultural labor was employed to some degree in Arab agricultural villages through the length and breadth of the Arabian Peninsula. But to *what* degree? Given the limitations of the sources, this is an impossible question to answer. Individual African slaves and freedmen living in predominantly Arab villages are almost invisible to the historian, and families of Africans scarcely less so. In general, African agricultural slaves only become visible to posterity when concentrated into a large community. Luckily for the present-day historian, such communities were not infrequent in the traditional Arabian Peninsula. It is to the phenomenon of African farming colonies that we now turn.

African Agricultural Colonies the Arabian Peninsula

The first difficulty that a historian of African slave communities in the Arabian Peninsula faces is one of terminology.[24] We know from the sources that large concentrations of African servile workers engaged in agriculture existed throughout the traditional Arabian Peninsula, but what term best describes the phenomenon? Neither the Arabs nor the Africans themselves had any special terminology for it. To call these African villages "communities" seems unspecified and vague, and implies a degree of self-containment and independence that does not fit the evidence. The term "estates," which Murray Gordon uses to describe the phenomenon, suggests a small-scale community under a single owner, which was rarely the case.[25] The term "estate" also implies, at least to an American audience, a property that is producing a cash crop (such as tobacco) for an international market, which was rarely true in the traditional Arabian Peninsula, where subsistence rather than commercial agriculture was the norm.

The term that I have decided to use, not without some hesitation, is "colony." This term "colony," like community, is somewhat vague. Nonetheless, the term captures several features common to most of the African agricultural communities that this section will describe. One is their "set apart" status: African agricultural colonies tended to be at some physical distance from Arab communities, which, as we shall see in chapter 4, may reflect the hyperendemicity of malaria in certain areas of the Arabian landscape. These African colonies were also set apart by social conventions, in particular the marriage restrictions that served to establish and maintain African farm laborers as a distinct, servile caste. The term "colony" also suggests the unequal power relationship between the African servile community and a dominant group, usually either Arab urban elites or a sharif camel-breeding tribe. As with most colonies, however, this subordinate position vis-à-vis a dominant outside power did not preclude some degree of autonomy and self-governance within the colony itself.

Although these African colonies can be identified throughout the Arabian Peninsula, they are much better attested (if not more common) in some areas than others. Thus, in the section that follows I will pass from areas of lesser to greater frequency, starting in the Gulf, moving on to southern Arabia, then to Oman, Dhofar and Hadramaut, to Najd and the northern frontier of Arabia, and finally to the Hijaz, where African colonies seem to have been most prevalent. Note that the information given here on the distribution of African colonies in Arabia relates almost entirely to the nineteenth and early twentieth centuries. The degree to which the picture painted by these documents is actually typical of the entire period of traditional Arabian history will be considered in chapter 5.

The Gulf

By and large, the Gulf region of eastern Arabia contained hardly any African agricultural colonies, though I have found two curious exceptions. From the standpoint of agriculture, eastern Arabia is a land of contrasts. Poor soils and low rainfall historically inhibited agricultural development in the region. Nonetheless, abundant springwater in the area between Bahrain Island and the al-Hasa oasis complex has fostered the growth of what is probably the densest concentration of agriculturalists in the entire Arabian Peninsula. However, neither the overall agricultural paucity of the region, nor its islands of agricultural abundance, proved fertile grounds for the development of African agricultural colonies as defined in this chapter.

In Bahrain, al-Hasa, and the Qatif region that lies between, date farming was practiced on a large and productive scale, to the point that al-Hasa was traditionally one of the few food-exporting regions of the Arabian Peninsula. Agricultural labor was provided mainly by two Arab peasant agriculturalist populations, the Baharinah of Bahrain and Qatif, and the Hasawiyah of the al-Hasa area. Neither group was a tribe per se, in the sense of common descent from a shared ancestor. Rather, both groups were defined by their subordinate occupational status—sharecropping farmers—as well as their common Shi'ite identity, which set them apart from a ruling class of Sunni townsmen and Bedouin tribesmen. Although slaves were "fairly numerous" in all three regions, these slaves did not live in distinct African agriculturalist colonies, but rather lived in the communities of their masters, who tended to be members of the Sunni elite.[26] In Bahrain, there were substantial urban populations of "free negroes" and "negro slaves" who did not live with their masters, but it is not clear to what extent such populations were involved in agriculture.[27] Given their urban location, it is more likely that their main employment was pearl diving, which was commonly carried out by slaves in eastern Arabia.

The lack of a large servile African population in the Bahrain–al-Hasa agricultural corridor in the nineteenth and early twentieth centuries is somewhat surprising, given the agricultural fertility of the region, the malarial nature of the local climate, and historical precedent: Nasir-i Khusraw, after all, had counted "thirty thousand Zanzibari and Abyssinian slaves" in the "fields and orchards" of al-Hasa in the tenth century. My sense is that, by the nineteenth and early twentieth centuries, the presence of a large, demographically stable, and politically subordinate Shi'ite farming class in Bahrain, al-Hasa, and Qatif probably rendered the employment of servile Africans in agriculture redundant. This notion is supported by the fact that, while the Africans described by Khusraw have by and large disappeared from view in the Bahrain–al-Hasa corridor, their genes have not. In modern eastern Arabia, a high percentage the population carries the gene for hemoglobin S, a recessive trait of African origin that protects against malaria infection, but which can lead to deadly sickle-cell anemia in homozygous individuals. Eastern Arabians also have high levels of the Duffy-negative antigen, another blood disorder of African origins that protects against the malaria parasite.[28] We will return to this subject in chapters 4 and 5.

Surprisingly, the one area in eastern Arabia where African agricultural colonies are clearly attested to is Qatar, where historically almost no agriculture was practiced. Nonetheless, during a diplomatic trip to the head of ruling al Thani family of Qatar in 1905, the British political agent of Bahrain, Francis Prideaux, came across

> a most refreshing and unexpected sight—a garden enclosed
> by a neat and low mud wall, 100 yards by 200 in area, and
> bordered by a line of tamarisk trees on all sides. Within were

3 masonry Persian wells [jalibs] of the largest size, worked by
donkeys, and irrigating large plots of lucerne grass as well as a
number of pomegranate trees and some 300 hundred [?] date
palms. The garden was only started, I am told, a very few years
ago by Sheikh Jasim but its waters were said by my followers to
be better than they had tasted in Bahrain. The gardeners were
all negroes; in addition to their quarters the garden contained
a small double-storied rest-house and a narrow verandah-like
mosque. The name of this oasis is Sakhama.[29]

Sakhama was only one of two al Thani plantations in Qatar maintained by African servile labor. The other was Wajbah, a "walled garden
with a tower and a mosque" with "three masonry wells, 7 fathoms [about
12.7 meters] deep, containing good water."[30] It should be noted that these
two plantations were the only two permanently occupied sites in the interior of Qatar at the time, since all other inhabitants of Qatar were nomadic
or lived along the coast. Both seem to have served political or social
purposes as well as purely economic ones, as Sakhama was the country
house of the Qatari emir, and Wajbah served as the midway meeting place
between the al Thani family and the Bedouin tribes of the interior. The
locations of these two African agricultural colonies, along with the other
places mentioned in this chapter, are shown in map 2.1.

Southern Arabia: 'Asir and Yemen

African agricultural colonies were apparently uncommon in both Yemen
and in 'Asir, though this could reflect the paucity of the sources as much
as the reality on the ground. What little evidence that does exist concerns
the dry Tihamah coastal plain, which passes along the coastline of both
regions. Although mostly interested in the leadership and fighting strength
of the 'Asir's tribes, for example, the *Gazetteer of Arabia* does make note
of the Ahl Sabya tribe, of whom "the largest element of the population is
of Sudanese blood, partly slaves, but chiefly those who have gained their
freedom. With these are the Mowallads, Sudanese with an Arab strain."
These servile Africans were subordinate to the "pure Arabs" of the district,
including a caste of *ashraf*, or descendants of the Prophet.[31] Much the same
was true of the Bani Shi'ba, a mixed group of nomads and agriculturalists
among whom "the Shaikhs and chief families are Arabs and trace their
descent to Qahtan, but the majority of the tribes are Sudanese, who have
been emancipated for many generations."[32]

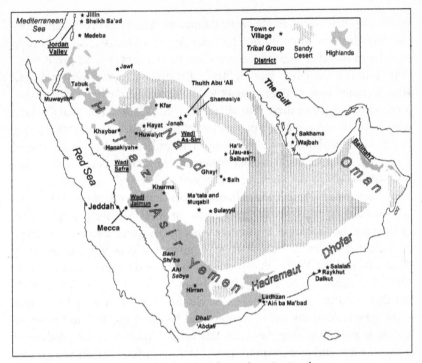

Map 2.1. African agricultural colonies of the Arabian Peninsula

The writings of Wilfred Thesiger, who traveled through 'Asir in 1945, suggest that African agriculturalists were still important to the region a generation later. In his "Journey through the Tihama, the 'Asir, and the Hijaz Mountains," Thesiger includes a long description of the Tihamiyin, the collective name for the settled population clustered along the wadis that conduct mountain rainfall into the dry coastal plain. Physically, Thesiger notes, the agricultural Tihamiyin are "a slightly built race, coffee colored and with black wavy hair," who appeared in Thesiger's eyes to be quite different from nearby Arab Bedouins, who were "light in colour, with hooked noses and light beards."[33] This apparent racial distinction, Thesiger suggests, may be a legacy of slavery. In the past, Thesiger notes, the Tihamiyin included a "considerable slave population, particularly in the Tihamat al 'Asir, but many of them are now free and own land."[34] Thesiger also notes that the Tihamiyin "suffer much from malaria," a theme which will recur frequently in the sections that follow.

Very similar African agricultural colonies existed in the coastal plain of South Yemen, which was part of the British Aden Protectorate. The small emirate of Dhali', for example, was inhabited by "a number of different tribes that have little in common besides their Arab nationality, and few ties to bind them together beyond the need for mutual support and protection." One faction of the Dhali' was the 'Abid, "the descendants of former slaves," who occupied four distinct agricultural villages near the bases of the Jahaf Mountains. Together these four villages included "about 600 souls," which was about 10 percent of the population of the Dhali'.[35] A somewhat larger but more amorphous group of servile Africans lived in the 'Abdali tribe of the Lahaj, an agricultural district immediately inland of Aden. The 'Abdali population, which the *Gazetteer* estimated at fifteen thousand, was comprised mainly of "'Abdali Muwallads, a cross between Arabs and Africans who are only a degree below pure Arabs in social standing, a sprinkling of Somalis, and Khadim, a migratory people of negro descent employed as scavengers." Their main collective occupation was farming in the sandy flood plain of the Wadi Tiban, with its "miles of date-groves and heavily scented gardens of lime, orange, banana, and coconut"; a paradise, providing that one can "stand its malarious climate."[36] Wyman Bury found that these servile Africans were "Swahilis and Nubians mostly," and were for the most part sharecroppers, each having "an interest in the produce of the land they tend as plowmen." These African agriculturalists were under the control of thirty-odd tribal sheikhs, who in turn owed allegiance to the sultan of Lahaj and his bodyguard of "Swahili slaves."[37] Although it is tempting to connect the name of the 'Abdali tribe to 'abid, the name likely derives from the common Arabic surname 'Abdul Ali, meaning "servant of the most high."

Finally, there are some indications that agricultural slavery may have existed in al-Jawf, an interior area of desert lowlands and wadi drainage systems east of the Yemeni highlands. In this "eastern Tihama," as it was called by Joseph Halévy, malaria was a constant threat; Halévy notes that Jews from the highlands would spend only five to ten years at most in the oases of al-Jawf, despite the business opportunities they offered, since "the fevers, the jaundice, and the liver disease occur pitilessly in these low lands."[38] Although most inhabitants of al-Jawf were apparently Arabs, Halévy notes that the town of Hirran on the wadi of the same name was inhabited by "African slaves that the Imam of Sana'a had transported there two or three years ago." Halévy unfortunately does not enter Hirran himself, so it is not clear whether or not these Africans were cultivators (as seems likely) or whether or not they were still enslaved in the second half of the nineteenth century.[39]

Oman, Dhofar, and Hadramaut

In Oman, our information about agricultural slavery goes back somewhat farther than the rest of the Arabian Peninsula, but specific locations and slave numbers are elusive. The earliest reference I have found was from the 1660s, a period of economic prosperity in Oman. During this time the sultan of Oman invested, "as did his admirals, in sugarcane plantations run with slave labor and hired workers to dig new irrigation channels." The Sultan Sayf b. Soltan I himself reportedly owned 1,700 slaves, though some portion of them probably provided military service rather than agricultural labor.[40] Abdul Sheriff infers from this that the overall African slave population at the start of the eighteenth century would have been five thousand, including many agricultural slaves, and assuming a 10 percent death or manumission rate, sustaining this population would have required the importation of five hundred slaves a year.[41] By the early 1800s, sugar was no longer a major crop in Oman, but date palms continued to be a major investment by elite Omanis, and were cultivated in part by African labor.[42] By the end of the nineteenth century, in fact, Arabian and Iraqi dates had become a desirable commodity in the United States, and large-scale American imports probably created a thriving market for agricultural slaves in Omani al-Batinah, which was well suited by geography to participate actively in this trade. Mathew S. Hopper goes so far as to claim that al-Batinah became "the primary destination for slaves in the late nineteenth and early twentieth centuries"—a debatable point, since Mecca has almost always been the peninsula's most important slave market—but nonetheless there can be little doubt that agricultural slavery throve in Oman during this period. African slaves in al-Batinah were employed mainly in jalibs, which "required constant upkeep," and probably maintained the region's many qanats as well.[43]

Nonetheless, it is not clear that these slaves lived in colonies rather than dispersed among the dwellings of their Arab owners. Overall the evidence suggests the latter. In a 1927 summary of the Omani slave trade written to the political resident in Bushire, Bertrand Thomas gave a brief description of African agricultural slavery in Oman. The Omani date gardener, whose slavery "approximates more to that of the European conception derived from 18th century slave methods of American plantations," worked for "perhaps half the year" in "his master's date garden." "He receives no wages," Thomas notes, "but is given food and clothing and in theory it would appear to be in the master's interest to keep him fit." In the other half a year, the slave might join the "great yearly migration north from Oman" into the Gulf, where he would labor as a pearl diver. Indeed, Thomas estimates that at least one thousand slaves from Oman, principally from the al-Batinah coast, migrated to the Gulf during the pearling season. All the wages earned by these slaves, Thomas argues, "go to his master," though it is unclear what mechanism could have compelled these slaves to return and surrender their wages in full to their Omani owners.[44] In his 1931 book, Thomas goes on to say that runaway slaves were common in al-Batinah, due to loose supervision by masters, but most fugitives were quickly found, and often fitted with ankle chains to deter future escapes.[45] Thomas's account suggests that there was a substantial African servile agriculturalist community in Oman, especially al-Batinah, though it is less clear whether these Africans lived in distinct colonies.

Thomas also described widespread African agricultural slavery in the coconut palms that girded the coastline of Dhofar in southern Oman: "Beneath the coco-nut groves wells, served mostly by slaves, bulls or camels, minister to fields of lucerne, sugar cane, plantains, wheat, millet, cotton, and indigo."[46] Thomas does not venture to estimate the number of these slaves, but he does note that Africans (not necessarily slaves) are "the biggest single element in the population of Salalah," the Dhofari capital. As opposed to the African slaves of al-Batinah, who do not seem to have lived in autonomous colonies, Thomas argues that the Salalah African community was "almost self-contained," though one of the slaves of the Omani sultan's court served as their *ab*, or chief magistrate. It is not clear who owned these slaves, or whether they were really slaves at all—here, as elsewhere, slaves and mawlas would have been very difficult for an outsider to distinguish from each other. Still, the fact that the sultan had appointed a supervisor over them from his own slave household suggests that many if not most of them were royal slaves. Thanks no doubt to their numbers and relative autonomy, Dhofar's Africans retained a number of non-Arab cultural traditions, including elaborate funeral rites incorporating elements of the traditional African *zar* spirit possession ceremony.[47] Interestingly, Thomas found that the Bedouins living in northern Dhofar had adopted some aspects of the zar ceremony. In contrast with the frenetic funeral rituals he witnessed in Salalah, however, the Bedouin zar ceremony was a simpler and more toned-down affair, and dominated by men, whereas a woman had been the master of ceremonies in Salalah.[48]

Thomas's observations about the prevalence of African agricultural slavery in coastal Oman are supported by the work of anthropologist Jörg Janzen, who was active in Dhofar in the 1980s. As might be expected,

Dhofar's complex geography and large number of microclimates historically supported a complex mixture of social groups, ranging from high-class
sayyids (descendants of the Prophet) and tribesmen to lower-class freeman
farmers and fishermen. However, the lowest rung of the social structure
was occupied by the 'Abid, the descendants African slaves who had been
imported into Dhofar for centuries, "principally from East Africa and
Zanzibar." According to Janzen, the 'Abid population occupied mainly the
coastal plains and urban areas, where they made up 30–50 percent of the
population, and were historically used for "every sort of heavy physical
labor." While "their chief form of employment was in oasis agriculture,"
they also practiced auxiliary professions like masonry, quarrying, mend-
ing nets, and domestic work. As in Oman, while some of these slaves lived
"on the ground floor of their master's houses," others lived in distinct slave
quarters consisting of "small huts" that were "scattered throughout the
oases" in coastal farming villages like Salkut and Rakhyut.[49]

Much the same social structure prevailed farther down the coast in the
deep valleys and dry coastal towns of Hadramaut. In their book *Southern
Arabia*, the Bents distinguish between four main social classes in Hadramaut: the "wild tribes of Bedouins" who held the top spot by virtue of
their military prowess, the town aristocracy (sadaa and ashraf), the "Arabs
proper," many of whom migrated as far as India or Singapore in search of
employment, and finally "the slave population of the Hadhramout, all of
African origin, and the freed slaves who have married and settled in the
country." Most of the latter, the Bents note, were "tillers of the soil, personal
servants, and the soldiers of the sultans."[50] Another traveler, van der Meulen, also notes the existence of a large number of slave agriculturalists in
the valleys of Hadramaut, especially in the Wadi Do'an.[51]

Although neither van der Meulen nor the Bents identify any distinct
African "colonies" in Hadramaut, a later traveler, Freya Stark, ran into several quite by accident during her own journeys through Hadramaut's valleys. Stark visited Hadramaut a generation after the Bents, in the winter of
1937–38, by which time the British in Aden were exerting more influence
over Hadrami affairs, particularly in regard to the institution of slavery. By
virtue of British declarations, the slaves of Hadramaut were technically free,
but Stark notes that "their freedom only becomes effective when some British official is near."[52] Indeed, African slaves repeatedly accosted her during
her journeys though Hadramaut, perhaps taking her for such an official
rather than for the footloose travel writer that she was. In the village of
Ladhzan on the Wadi Salmun, for example, she found stands of palms and

fields of lucerne and millet "tended almost entirely by slaves." Their owners were local Bedouins, who "scorn to work with their hands and treat their people roughly, with scanty food and beatings, and grudge them even the decent gift of clothes."[53] The same situation reigned at 'Ain ba Ma'bad, an oasis town closer to the coast, where the slave villagers, "tortured and twisted with beatings" administered by their absentee Bedouin owners, "long[ed] for freedom" at the hands of the British.[54] Interestingly, the inhabitants of both African slave colonies imagined that the agent of their liberation would be the British Royal Air Force, which had recently bombed a number of feuding Bedouin tribes to enforce the *Pax Britannica*.[55]

Najd and the North

Although Najd was predominantly agricultural, the employment of African servile labor seems to have been relatively uncommon. This may reflect the region's inland location and resulting isolation from international trade routes, which would have made slaves less available and more expensive. It may also reflect the fact that Najd hosted several large Arab peasant agriculturalist communities, most notably the Bani Khadhir, a low-status tribal group, and the somewhat more respectable Bani Tamim. Of these two groups, the Bani Khadhir appear to have been more numerous in southern Najd, while the Bani Tamim predominated further north.[56] In addition, agricultural labor was also practiced by settled sections of the large local Bedouin tribes, such as the Shammar tribe of the Ha'il region.[57]

Nonetheless, colonies of African servile agricultural labor did exist in Najd, especially in areas that were notable for malaria infection. A number of African agricultural colonies, for example, were situated in the lower reaches of the Wadi al-Rimah where it passed through the major Najd towns of Buraydah and 'Unayzah. The *Gazetteer* notes that this area was "full of palm groves attaining a breadth of as much as a mile; the water here is only 5 to 10 feet below the surface, but it is brackish and fever is prevalent among the negroes who tend the plantations."[58] A generation after these words were written, Arabian traveler Harry St. John Bridger Philby passed through the Wadi al-Rimah and discovered that little had changed. In the wadi town of Janah, Philby found 250 slaves who were property of the free citizens of the town of 'Unayza. Nearby Thulth Abu 'Ali had a population of "300 negroes," though it is less clear whether these Africans were slaves or mawlas. Both communities depended on low-quality wells and springs, which Philby describes as "exceedingly foul and stinking . . . with a scum of yellowish-green slime."[59] Philby later passed through a third settlement of

African agriculturalists in Shamasiya, 15 miles farther downstream from Buraydah, where the Wadi al-Rimah met the sands of the Dahana Desert. Here lived "some five hundred souls scattered about in a number of hamlets over a distance of about a mile."[60] Most of these farmers were African mawlas who worked as sharecroppers for the Bani Tamim, to whom these date plantations belonged.

African colonies were also attested to in the Wadi as-Sirr to the south of 'Unayzah, a "depressed tract" about "forty miles in length from north to south and 20 miles in breadth," containing "wells and springs" but no drainage outlet.[61] British political agent G. Leachman passed through here on the way to Riyadh in 1912 and observed that Arab tribesmen had built "various 'kasrs' or fortified châteaux" in the depression, "dotted about at distances of several miles from each other." Inside each walled compound Leachman discovered "the owner of the land" and his "dependents and slaves, often to the number of sixty and seventy." In sharp contrast to the situation described by Stark in Hadramaut, Leachman notes that "absolute equality seems to obtain between master and servant as regards conversation, and they appear a very happy community."[62] Philby reported only minor changes in the same region which he visited nearly a generation later. Like Leachman, Philby makes note of the local availability of water, though unlike Leachman he found that it was so saline that "it is amazing the palms should be able to derive nourishment from water so salt." These palms, he writes, were tended by a "hundred souls" of a "mixed character, including a number of negroes." Interestingly, Philby notes that local political authority was exercised in part by the Africans themselves, since one of their number served as the village emir.[63] Although neither Philby nor Leachman make note of mosquitoes or malaria in the Wadi as-Sirr, both were undoubtedly common visitors to this lowland drainage basin.

Another African agricultural colony was established farther north in al-Kfar, a satellite town of the Jabal Shammar town Ha'il. The *Gazetteer* describes al-Kfar, which they spell Qafar, as a town of fields and date groves stretching over 4 kilometers in length, worked by three thousand members of the Bani Qasim tribe.[64] According to the Czech Orientalist and traveler Alois Musil, however, the town was also home to "eight hundred families of slaves," who had been settled there by the Rashidi Emir Talal in the mid-nineteenth century. Although Musil does not explicitly mention that this was intended to be an agricultural community, he presents the founding of al-Kfar as part of Talal's goal of "increasing the prosperity of his townships . . . choked-up wells were cleared, the old palm groves were planted and new ones were planted and protected from the sand by high walls."[65] By the time Musil visited al-Kfar in 1915, the community Talal had founded had fallen upon hard times, as it had been "visited by fever (*humma*) which [carried] away the women and children, the men having perished in the wars. Its houses forsaken and its palms felled, al-Kfar grew desolate. Only forty half-ruined houses [were] standing and [those were] inhabited by slaves and aged harlots."[66]

Other servile agriculturalists are attested to in southern Najd. One such colony was Ha'ir, a date plantation town occupying both sides of the Wadi Hanifa. Although Ha'ir was claimed by Bedouins of the Subai' and Suhul tribes, its four hundred inhabitants were all African, including, as in the Wadi as-Sirr, their emir. Although mostly mawlas rather than slaves, these Africans were still known as 'abid by local Arabs. These Africans, Philby notes, were all "*Kaddadid* [agricultural laborers] digging and delving and laboring on the lands of others for a tenant's share of the produce." Philby speculates that the Subai' and Suhul were unwilling to cultivate themselves due to the climate, "which in a narrow valley shut in by lofty cliffs about a strip of water large for Arabia and exposed to all the fierceness of the sun cannot but be unhealthy." The biggest health danger would undoubtedly have been malaria. Indeed, Philby notes that "there was a notable buzz of insect life" in the vicinity of Ha'ir, and "more than once during the night I did hear the ominous song of the mosquito."[67] In addition, the *Gazetteer* notes the existence of "40 houses" of slave cultivators in the poor village of Jau-as-Saibani somewhere in the vicinity of Ha'ir, though in this instance the information given by the *Gazetteer* is rather perplexing.[68]

During his rather extended peregrinations through the Arabian Peninsula, Philby noted the existence of several other African slave colonies in the southern reaches of Najd. Philby found a similar community established in the oasis town of Saih, which stood upon the flood channel of the Batin al Hamar. According to Philby, the "bulk of the settled population of the oasis consists of negro freemen, perhaps some 3,000 souls in all, who have been settled in this locality for many generations, and, to judge by their general appearance, have interbred with their Arab neighbors to a considerable extent."[69] Although some of these Africans were the slaves or mawlas of a clan of immigrant Yemeni ashraf, most were sharecropper cultivators working on behalf of absentee Bedouin owners. A similar African agriculturalist community, though much smaller, subsisted in nearby Ghayl, a town in the rocky hills northwest of Saih. In Ghayl, plentiful springwater nurtured the growth of large date plantations, but the same springs rendered the place "extremely unhealthy for Arabs." Thus the labor in the date palms was carried out by "hired cultivators from the plain villages" (probably including the freedmen of Saih) as well as slaves, who occupied twenty houses in Ghayl.[70]

Colonies of African agricultural labor were also common in the far south of Najd, in a transitional area usually called the Wadi Dawasir. Here, open desert was the predominant landform, and pastoralism was the predominant lifeway, but the Wadi Dawasir drainage system, which originated in the highlands to the west, allowed some agriculture to be conducted in villages scattered throughout the moist wadi bottoms. One such town was the sprawling Sulayyil oasis, which Philby notes contained a sizable mawla population. Interestingly, Philby notes that many of these African freedmen, like the slaves of al-Batinah in Oman, frequently ventured to the Gulf to join pearling expeditions during the summer pearl diving season.[71] Somewhat upstream of Sulayyil, in the area now covered by the modern-day town of al Khamasin, Philby discovered several scattered African settlements, including Ma'tala and Muqabil, which together contained 250 Africans who occupied the plantations "on behalf of *Badawin* owners." Altogether Philby estimated the Wadi Dawasir area to contain as many as two thousand mawlas, mostly sharecroppers for the Mukharim subset of the Dawasir Arabs, which "scorns to live in settled habitations and prefers to roam the deserts with its herds and flocks, coming in only at the date season to reap the benefits of their tenants' industry."[72] According to scholar and diplomat Marcel Kurpershoek, the descendants of the Wadi Dawasir's numerous African agricultural laborers still lived in distinct communities throughout the wadi until the last years of the twentieth century.[73]

African agricultural colonies were also reported in the far northern reaches of the Arabian Peninsula. A number of sources, for example, refer to a large African population in the oasis of al-Jawf, which—like the Wadi as-Sirr—occupied a large drainage basin. Al-Jawf's population, which amounted to perhaps three thousand people, included both Bani Tamim farmers and "negroes and [Mutawalladeen]," the latter being a socially inferior group of mixed racial ancestry.[74] Farther north still, on the poorly defined edges of the Arabian Peninsula, distinct African agricultural colonies existed in several places in the volcanic highlands of the Hauran. The German American archaeologist Gottlieb Shumacher, who surveyed the Hauran in the 1880s, describes the Hauran village of Jillin as "a small, miserable-looking village . . . containing twenty huts, built some of mud and some of stone, with a population of about 100 *negroes*." He found a similar though larger population of African servile agricultural-ists in nearby Sheikh Sa'ad, "a miserable looking place, containing about 60 huts built of stone and mud, many of them now fallen to ruin. It has a population of about 220 souls, all without exception negroes." The inhabit-ants of both towns, Shumacher notes, were mawlas who worked partially in agriculture and partially in the maintenance of a locally revered saint's tomb. Schumacher notes further that both communities "have planted fruit trees and cultivate vegetables and vines" with the aid of local water supplies. Indeed, according to Schumacher, Sheihk Sa'ad suffered from too much water: "There is abundance of water in the neighborhood and this renders the climate rather feverish."[75]

While both Jillin and Sheikh Sa'ad appear to have been satellite colonies of agricultural communities, other African servile colonies in northern Arabia were dependencies of local Bedouin tribes. Archae-ologist H. B. Tristram notes that the agricultural land near the ruins of Medeba was owned by Bani Sakhr camel nomads, but was not farmed by them; rather, the agricultural work was done by a combination of slaves and vassal Arabs of the Abu Endi tribe.[76] In addition, the 'Adwan tribe of what is today Jordan employed slaves, "all black and usually descendants of Africans bought from slave traders," to cultivate tribal land in the Jordan River Valley.[77] It should be noted in passing that Jordan River Valley, due to its heat and high groundwater, had the reputation for being one of the worst malaria hotspots in the Arabian Peninsula. According to William Lancaster, the Rwala section of the 'Anaza tribe also employed slave agriculturalists in both al-Jawf and in the vicinity of Kaf in the Wadi Sirhan.[78]

The Hijaz

The region of Arabia where African servile agricultural colonies appear to be the most common is the Hijaz, the mountainous zone of eastern Arabia running from the Gulf of Aqaba in the north to 'Asir in the south. Several factors probably combined to make African colonies more frequent in this region than elsewhere, including close proximity to the slave markets of Mecca and relatively high levels of malaria infection in the agricultural lands of the Hijaz. However, we cannot discount the possibility that the apparent frequency of African colonies in the Hijaz is to some degree an artifact of the source materials, since this area was frequently visited by European travelers.

As in northern Arabia, most African agricultural colonies in the region were dependencies of powerful local Bedouin tribes. For example, near Muwaylih in the upper Red Sea coastal region, British naval surveyor R. Wellsted observed a number of slave communities growing dates and sorghum on behalf of their owners, the Huwaiyat Bedouins.[79] A similar labor arrangement reigned in the inland oasis town of Tabuk, where, according to Finnish traveler G. A. Wallin, the majority of inhabitants were "emancipated slaves and their progeny, known as [Mutawalladeen]." These African agriculturalists did not own the land itself, but rather were sharecroppers subjected to "heavy exactions by their masters, who despise them."[80]

Several more colonies of African servile farmers lay somewhat south of Tabuk in the Harrat Khaybar, a large tract of volcanic basalt in the north-central Hijaz. One was Hayat (modern Hait), which the *Gazetteer* describes as an "ancient and prosperous oasis village, almost hidden in a cleft of Harrat Khaibar up which its plantations extend for 2 miles." These date palms were worked by "100 houses of negroes, half castes, and Hataim," the latter being an Arab tribe of low social status. About 36 kilometers southwest of Hait lay Huwaiyat, inhabited by "forty houses of negroes."[81] A third town, Hanakiyah, which lay about 160 kilometers southwest of Khaybar, was described by Charles Doughty as a "negro village, of forty houses" scattered through "several palm groves, lying nigh together."[82] However, the largest, most important, and best-known African colony of the region was the town of Khaybar, which boasted a population of 2,500 and is the subject of the next chapter. Although in the past these settlements had owed tribute to local Bedouin tribes, such as the 'Anaza, by the early nineteenth century they had been incorporated into the domains of the Sharif of Mecca, a client king of the Ottomans, to whom they paid taxes. According to the *Gazetteer*, both fever and cholera were prevalent in these Harrat Khaybar oasis towns.[83]

Although the palms of the Harrat Khaybar had spun out of the control of the 'Anaza Bedouin tribe by the 1910s, other Bedouins still retained their traditional rights over African agriculturalists in their territories. Case in point is the Wadi Safra, a valley with "good and abundant" water that bisected the coastal caravan route between Mecca and Medina. Although the *Gazetteer* mentions no African cultivators there, noting only a "fair amount of cultivation of cereals, fruit, and vegetables," British army officer and trained archeologist T. E. Lawrence found that the palms of the wadi were tended by thirteen villages of "blacks originally from Africa, brought over as children by their nominal Takruri [West African] fathers, and sold during pilgrimage, in Mecca."[84] As elsewhere in Arabia, these Africans were serving as tenant farmers of a dominant Bedouin tribe, in this case the Harb, whose tribal deera stretched from Mecca to Najd. According to Lawrence, these African agriculturalists

> formed a society of their own, and lived much at their pleasure. Their work was hard, but the supervision loose, and escape easy. Their legal status was bad, for they had no appeal to tribal justice, or even the Sharif's courts; but public opinion and self-interest depreciated any cruelty towards them, and the tenet of the faith that to enlarge a slave is a good deed, meant in practice that nearly all gained freedom in the end.[85]

In addition, the African agriculturalists of the Wadi Safra seem to have taken advantage of the tradition that the Bedouin land owners could claim shares only of their tenant's dates and grains, and thus any other crops grown belonged wholly to the farmers themselves: "They grew melons, marrows, cucumbers, and grapes, and tobacco for their own account, in addition to the dates, whose surplus was sent across to the Sudan by sailing dhow, and there exchanged for corn, clothing, and the luxuries of Africa or Europe."[86]

Despite the fertility of the wadi—or perhaps because of it—the Harb tribe spent little time in the Wadi Safra, usually less than five months a year. This reflected in part the malarial nature of the area. According to Lawrence, while Africans "flourished" in the Wadi Safra, its "feverish valleys of running water" were too unhealthy for Arab labor. Lawrence found that water was everywhere "three or four feet below the surface," ideal conditions for mosquitoes. The Harb were probably also wary of flash floods in the valley. Lawrence notes that, only a generation before,

> there rolled a huge wall of water down Wadi Safra, the embankments of many palm gardens were breached, and the palm trees swept away. Some of the islands on which houses had stood for centuries were submerged, and the mud houses melted back again into mud, killing or drowning the unfortunate slaves within. The men could have been replaced, and the trees, had the soil remained; but the gardens had been built up of earth carefully won from the normal freshets

by years of labour, and this wave of water—eight feet deep, running in a race for three days—reduced the plots in its track to their primordial banks of stones.

Based on Lawrence's account, it appears that agriculture in the Wadi Safra was primarily conducted using ghayl and sayl irrigation, though the jalibs probably played a supplementary role.

The same seems to have been true of the agriculture in the Wadi Laimun, a drainage basin to the northeast of Mecca. Philby, who visited it in 1918, waxes eloquent about its beauty: "Orange and palm groves, banana plantations, and fields of young corn and lucerne blended their different shades of green in a wild highland setting." These delightful farmsteads were the property of local ashraf, but the actual farm work was done by "cultivating tenants, negro freedmen, tribesmen and others." As in the Wadi Safra, these farmers irrigated their crops using a combination of ghayl and sayl techniques.[87] Although Philby notes that the climate was "unhealthy," especially in the summer, Africans seem to have been in the minority rather than the majority in the Wadi Laimun. This impression is supported by anthropological work carried out by Motoko Katakura in the 1970s. She found that the *muwallad* (a variant of mawla) of the nearby Wadi Fatima were still employed for the most part as agricultural laborers, but comprised only about 5 percent of the overall population.[88] Katakura notes that these muwalid were treated as social equals by the local Arabs, in keeping with the Wahhabi theology of human equality, though marriage between muwalid and Arabs was almost unknown.

Finally we come to Khurma, a wadi agricultural town in the southern Hijaz that may have housed the single largest African agriculturalist colony in the Arabian Peninsula. As is typical of Hijazi farming towns, Khurma lay in a wadi bed, and water was available only inches beneath the sands of the torrent bed and only a few feet beneath the cultivated land below the valley slopes. These waters sustained "several straggling and unwalled groups of mud tenements of the type common to all Najd, but here and there a two-storied house of more pretentious appearance relieves the general dinginess of the place." These "pretentious" houses were likely the homes of Khurma's ashraf elite, who numbered "not more than 200 souls," but who owned much of the land in the village. The rest of the land was the property of the Bedouins of the Subai' tribe, who "wander[ed] the livelong year with their flocks over the Subai' plain," only visiting Khurma at the time of the summer date harvest. Actual agricultural labor was performed by mawlas, who constituted "at least three-quarters of the entire resident population" and upon whom fell "the whole burden of the cultivation of the soil," though one half of their agricultural production went to the ashraf or Subai'. These African sharecroppers were quite numerous, by Arabian standards. Philby estimates that they made up three-fourths of Khurma's population, which he puts at four thousand.[89] Philby's population estimate is roughly comparable with the *Gazetteer's* assertion that Khurma contained "300 houses," plus an equal number of houses and huts in Khurma's "very extensive date plantations."[90]

Given the size of Khurma's African servile farming population, it stands to reason that other towns in the same wadi system would also have hosted some number of African agriculturalists. Although Khurma was the largest town in the region, the upper stretches of the Wadi Sabai' hosted a number of similar settlements, including the substantial upstream village of Turabah and downstream town of Ranyah. All of these towns, like Khurma, contained large date plantations and were swollen by an influx of Sabai' Bedouins during the summer date harvest. What is more, as we have already seen, several towns in the nearby Wadi Dawasir in southern Najd hosted substantial African agriculturalist populations. Unfortunately, Philby's otherwise wide-ranging travels never took him to either of these towns. Indeed, in *Heart of Arabia*, Philby laments that he was unable to visit Turabah, not only for reasons of geographical exploration but also because Turabah was the site of a crucial 1919 battle between the forces of Ibn Saud and the Sharif of Mecca.[91]

The notion that the large African servile population of Khurma was just one of many such colonies in the lower Hijaz receives strong but indirect support from the writings of Maurice Tamisier, a Frenchman who accompanied an Egyptian military expedition into 'Asir in the early 1830s. Tamisier's expedition, like the voyages of Philby nearly a hundred years later, took him through the Wadi Fatima, the Wadi Laimun, and then south through the lower Hijaz and upper 'Asir, before finally taking him to the oasis town of Bishah. During this voyage Tamisier was constantly surprised by the "great number of black slaves among the people who, due to bad luck or curiosity, crossed our paths."[92] Tamisier had the opportunity to interview a group of African laborers in the "unhappy village of Akig [modern Aqiq]," who told him that they were originally from West Africa, but remained in Aqiq after a pilgrimage to Mecca. Aqiq's Takruris claimed to be free men, though they admitted that they sometimes sold their own children into slavery. Tamisier also found another "great number" of

African Takruris farther south Tania (probably modern Theniah), a town between Bishah and the modern town of Tabalah. He further estimates that Bishah itself was inhabited by "about six thousand negroes or *mawla*," though this is probably a gross overestimate.[93] Unfortunately, it is unclear from Tamisier's account whether or not these Africans were primarily agricultural laborers, partly because of his lack of interest, but also because the army he was accompanying disrupted normal social relations in the region through which it passed. Nevertheless, on the basis of Philby and Tamisier's accounts, it is clear that the southern Hijaz/northern 'Asir area hosted a substantial number of African agriculturalists, though where and how many is impossible now to determine.

Scale of the Phenomenon

In the section above, I have endeavored to give an exhaustive list of all locations in the Arabian Peninsula where African servile labor is explicitly attested to in the primary and secondary sources. But does this list represent the entirety of the African presence in Arabian Peninsula agriculture? Almost certainly not. Given the somewhat sporadic nature of the evidence used above, which depends on eyewitness accounts compiled in an unsystematic fashion, it is inevitable that some African agricultural colonies within Arabia did not find their way into the historical record. But how many? And what fraction of all slaves and mawlas in the Arabian Peninsula were employed in agricultural labor, as opposed to domestic service, military servitude, concubinage, or other slave professions?

In most countries, questions like this one would be answered with census data. In Saudi Arabia, however, the first attempt at a census was not made until 1962, when the phenomenon of agricultural slavery was already well into decline, and no complete, reliable census was conducted in the country until 1992.[94] However, the officials of Britain's informal empire in Arabia did keep their own statistics, and one study they conducted has some relevance to the question at hand. The British had a long-standing tradition of emancipating slaves who fled from Ottoman jurisdiction to their embassies, consulates, and ships, and while the Ottomans were no longer in charge of the Hijaz by the 1920s, the British consular officials in Jeddah continued to manumit and document escaped slaves up until the mid-1930s.[95] These manumission documents were compiled and summarized in British political agent A. Ryan's "Memorandum on Slavery in Saudi Arabia," which was published for internal British use in 1934. In it,

Ryan provides data pertaining to the 209 slaves who had fled to the British consulate of Jeddah from 1926 to 33. In addition to recording the gender, nationality, and circumstances of enslavement, Ryan collected evidence concerning the "trade or craft of the slaves," which I used as the basis for figure 2.1.

As can be seen from the diagram, by far the largest number of slaves seeking manumission at the hands of the British were domestic servants, including sixty-two men and forty-four women. The second largest worked in the field of transportation, a grab-bag category that included water carriers (twenty-three slaves), camel drivers (thirteen), seamen (seven), porters (five), and a single chauffeur. Agricultural laborers came in third place with thirty-three slaves. This means they accounted for only 16 percent of the total number of slaves manumitted and recorded by the British, though it should be noted that agricultural slavery was the second largest category in terms of overall numbers.[96]

According to Alaine S. Hutson, a historian who studied British slave manumissions at Jeddah from 1926 to 1936, the agricultural slaves freed in Jeddah were, as a group, quite distinct from other slaves in the data sample. For one thing, agricultural slaves were overwhelmingly male: only five of the freed agricultural slaves were female, compared to forty-four males.

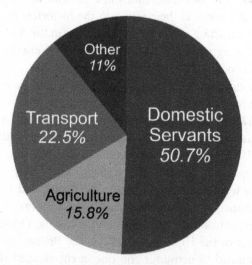

Figure 2.1. Professions of manumitted slaves, Jeddah 1926–33

Source: Sir A. Ryan to the Foreign Office, "Memorandum on Slavery in Saudi Arabia," 15 May 1934, in *The Slave Trade into Arabia: 1820–1973*, ed. A. L. P. Burdett (London: Archive Editions, 2006), 6:683.

Secondly, agricultural slaves were overwhelmingly from sub-Saharan Africa. In all, 62 percent of agricultural slaves claimed to be from the Sudan, while only 19 percent of agricultural slaves claimed to be from the Abyssinian region. One final factor that set agricultural slaves apart from their nonagricultural counterparts was their common complaints of shabby treatment. Hutson notes that 93 percent of the agricultural slaves in the sample cited poor treatment as the reason for running to the Jeddah consulate, while only 54 percent of domestic and a mere 25 percent of commercial slaves complained of the same.[97]

Hutson's precise statistics should be taken with more than the usual grain of salt, since there are all sorts of problems inherent to using these manumission statistics as a data set. In terms of chronological span, the manumission data cover only a small slice of time, and an atypical slice of time at that, since the British had been actively intervening in the slave trade for decades by the time Hutson's data were collected. This study also deals exclusively with Jeddah, and thus may not be representative of slavery elsewhere in Arabia, an issue we will return to below. What is more, men outnumbered women in this data sample by almost three to one, despite the fact that female slaves probably outnumbered male slaves in the Arabian Peninsula as a whole.[98] More importantly, this data set deals specifically with slaves seeking manumission rather than all slaves, meaning that certain professions that were particularly onerous might be overrepresented and more "pleasant" slave professions (if such a thing can be said to have existed) were underrepresented. Furthermore, nearly all of the slaves who sought manumission—171 out of 208—were originally enslaved outside of Arabia, and it is not clear whether the professions held by these slaves were representative of all slaves in general. And of course this data set tells us only about slaves, not mawlas and other African servile agriculturalists. Nonetheless, as is often the case when studying Arabian Peninsula history, we must do the best we can with incomplete and imperfect evidence.

On the basis of the data presented in figure 2.1, and with the caveats listed above, it is probably fair to say that a substantial minority of Arabian Peninsula slaves were engaged in agricultural pursuits. In fact, I suspect that the number of African slaves engaged in agriculture was higher than figure 2.1 suggests. It should be remembered that these statistics were collected in Jeddah, a dry and dusty port where little if any agriculture was practiced. The closest agricultural districts were the Wadi Fatima and Wadi Jaimun, which, as we have seen above, hosted relatively small African agriculturalist populations. Khurma and the Wadi Safra contained more African slaves, but were over 200 kilometers away, and the other colonies listed in this study were still more distant. While agricultural slaves were apparently not well supervised by their owners, 200 kilometers would have been an intimidating journey, especially considering that an escaped slave was under no one's protection and thus could be robbed, killed, or re-enslaved while on the road. In contrast, an urban slave in Jeddah seeking the protection of the consulate had only to walk across town. Thus, we would expect urban occupations like domestic servitude and water carrying to be overrepresented in the study, while rural professions like agriculture would be underrepresented. It stands to reason therefore that the actual proportion of African slaves consigned to agricultural employments was higher than 16 percent, perhaps considerably higher, though as mentioned above, the number of agricultural slaves who sought refuge in Jeddah might also be artificially high due to greater incidence of mistreatment by their masters. Nonetheless, on balance, I would say that 20 percent is a conservative estimate, especially given the evidence for the many African servile colonies that has been given in this chapter.

Armed with this percentage, we can venture an estimate as to the overall number of African servile agriculturalists present in the traditional Arabian Peninsula. Figures on slavery are hard to come by: in 1963, a British official in Jeddah noted that "estimates [on the number of slaves in Saudi Arabia]—it would be more correct to call them guesses—range from between 2000 and 500,000." The same official estimated, based on evidence provided by Aramco as well as other anecdotal evidence, that the true figure was closer to between fifteen thousand and thirty thousand, "scattered all over the country."[99] This figure is exclusive, however, of mawlas, which in the eastern provinces of Saudi Arabia numbered about twelve thousand, or four times the number of slaves.[100] If this proportion is valid for elsewhere in the Arabian Peninsula, that would indicate that there were at least three thousand to six thousand agricultural slaves, and twelve thousand to twenty-four thousand servile mawlas agriculturalists in the Hijaz, Najd, 'Asir, and eastern Arabia as a whole, exclusive of African servile populations in Oman, Yemen, and elsewhere. This is a very rough and speculative estimate, based on data collected at the very end of the traditional era of Arabian history. Nonetheless, it does agree in broad strokes with the survey of African agricultural colonies given earlier in this chapter. In any case, the number of agricultural slaves and mawlas present in the traditional Arabian Peninsula at any given time would have depended largely on price and supply trends in the Indian Ocean slave trade, a theme we will return to in chapter 5.

Common Features of African Servile Agricultural Colonies

Based on the materials provided in this chapter, it is safe to say that a substantial African servile agriculturalist population existed in the traditional Arabian Peninsula, at least in the nineteenth and early twentieth centuries. These African farmers were a mixture of slaves and mawlas who performed similar economic roles and had roughly similar social status in Arabian society. There seems to have been a slight shift from slave to mawla status over time, with the term "slave" used more frequently in the 1831–1918 travelogues, and "freedmen" used thereafter. This shift is probably a result of the gradual diminution of fresh slave imports by the beginning of the twentieth century, a side effect of the European "scramble for Africa" and of Europe's attempts to suppress the slave trade in their newly colonized African territory.[101] Nonetheless, the most common term used by the travelogue authors is "negroes," a purely racial category that tells us nothing about the legal status of the Africans mentioned.

Whether slaves or freedmen, African servile agriculturalists were overwhelmingly associated with date palm cultivation, though there are a few exceptions, such as the slaves of Dhofar, who tended coconut palms, and the slaves of the Bani Sakhr, who plowed wheat fields. Although sayl or ghayl irrigation is attested to in some cases, these water sources generally seem to have been supplemented by ground water, which was probably obtained by means of a jalib. While in many cases there was no clear separation of African servile agriculturalist communities from free Arab communities, in a number of cases Africans seem to have lived in autonomous colonies, which in at least three occasions were led by headmen of African extraction. Most, if not all, of these African agriculturalists were sharecroppers, compelled to surrender a fixed proportion of their dates, and often their grains, to Arab townsmen or Bedouin tribesmen at harvest time. For their own sustenance, they relied on their share of the date harvest as well as crops grown beneath and between the palms. These vegetable foods were apparently supplemented by animal products, such as clarified butter, which they purchased from the Bedouins. The economic basis of this slave system therefore consisted of the symbiotic exchange of oasis carbohydrates for desert proteins and fats, and thus was geared toward the subsistence needs of both parties rather than market forces.

Although both parties benefitted from the exchange of desert for oasis resources, they did not benefit equally. The main beneficiaries of the system were the owners of the land, which in the Hijaz, Hadramaut, the Wadi Dawasir, and the northern frontier area tended to be Bedouin tribes, and in Najd, Oman, and Yemen tended to be ashraf or urban elites, though rights of ownership could fluctuate with changing political circumstances. Both Bedouin and wealthy townsmen received tribute from their slaves and mawla farmers and gave little (if anything) in return, except perhaps protection. It is therefore quite possible that the African servile colonies of Arabia, just like the Sahelian slave oases described by James L. A. Webb, Jr., in West Africa, might have played a role as buffers against Arab famine.[102] In a lean year, the Africans might be squeezed for resources by the dominant Arab tribes, thus transferring the worst of the starvation from the Arab tribes to the African servile agriculturalists of the palms.

The overall treatment of African servile agriculturalists, however, seems have been comparatively mild, and somewhat akin to the treatment of Medieval European serfs. Indeed, it appears from the sources that African agriculturalists enjoyed considerable autonomy, especially those who farmed on behalf of Bedouin tribesmen, who might only visit the palms once a year during the summer date harvest season. Although these African agriculturalists were clearly exploited economically, there are few hints of physical mistreatment of slaves or mawlas, though Freya Stark's "tortured and twisted" slaves of Hadramaut and Thomas's fettered runaways in al-Batinah are notable exceptions to this rule. Two main factors help explain this relatively mild slave regime: (1) agriculture in most of Arabia was geared toward a subsistence economy rather than a market-based economy, and (2) the absence of the Bedouin Arab masters for extended periods, combined with their unwillingness to enter the "feverish" oases themselves for long periods, would have made escape fairly easy and the implementation of a stricter regimentation of labor impossible. I suspect, in fact, that most of the ill treatment that runaway slaves described in the Jeddah manumission surveys was sheer neglect of their basic material needs by their absentee masters, though some agricultural slaves no doubt suffered from physical violence as well. It is also possible that African servile labor may have been overseen more closely in communities headed by ashraf or other non-Bedouin elites who were permanent residents rather than seasonal visitors to oasis agricultural communities.

One final commonality shared by nearly all of the African colonies mentioned above is malaria. With few exceptions, African colonies seem to have been located in areas notable for malaria infections, a subject we will return to in chapter 4.

BASED ON the materials presented in this chapter, it reasonable to conclude that a significant degree of African servile labor was employed in the agricultural landscapes of the traditional Arabian Peninsula. African labor was especially common in the jalib and qanat systems of irrigation, which demanded a large amount of labor for both construction and maintenance. While most African slaves eventually achieved mawla (freedman) status, the social distinction between slaves and mawlas seems to have been minor. Both slaves and mawlas served predominantly as subordinate sharecroppers dependent on Bedouin or Arab townsman masters, though many servile Africans enjoyed some degree of autonomy. The autonomy of servile Africans was probably greatest in the various African agricultural colonies of the Arabian Peninsula. These colonies existed throughout the Arabian Peninsula, but were especially common in Najd and the Hijaz, and tended to be located in areas notable for malaria and/or fevers. We will turn to Khaybar, the location of the best-known of these African colonies, in the following chapter.

CHAPTER 3

Case Study

Khaybar

OF ALL of the African colonies of the Arabian Peninsula, the one that is best documented is Khaybar, a large date plantation community lying on the outer edge of a massive lava field of the same name. In the period between the mid-nineteenth and early twentieth centuries, Khaybar was visited by no fewer than four published European travelers—Carlo Guarmani, Charles Doughty, Charles Huber, and Harry St. John Bridger Philby—and thanks to the rich body of data they provided, the lives of African agriculturalists come into much sharper focus in Khaybar than anywhere else in the Arabian Peninsula. This is not to say that Khaybar is a completely typical example of African agricultural colonies in the Arabian Peninsula; as we shall see, Khaybar was in some ways quite a unique place. Indeed, this uniqueness is probably what attracted the four European travelers to the spot in the first place. Nonetheless, a close analysis of life in Khaybar, as revealed through the work of these four authors, can significantly enrich our understanding of African labor in Arabian agriculture as a whole.

Geography, Geology, and History

Khaybar is located in north-central Arabia, in the eastern portion of the region traditionally known as the Hijaz. The defining feature of the town is the Harrat Khaybar, a huge stretch of volcanic rock that stretches over 150 kilometers northeast, east, and southeast of the town. Khaybar actually lies within the harrah, occupying "gashes in the lava-field" carved out by time and erosion.[1] Although rainfall in the region as a whole is under 100 millimeters per year, the underlying geology of the Harrat Khaybar ensures that Khaybar's clay soil is well supplied with moisture. The basalt rock of the Harrat Khaybar was deposited relatively recently, from 10 million to 730 years before present, and while the surface layer is quite often cracked and porous due to erosive forces, the hard crystalline layers of basalt beneath are generally impervious to water.[2] As a result, what little rain does fall in the Harrat Khaybar is trapped in its shallow aquifers and escapes in the form of natural springs within Khaybar's wadi valleys. The discharge of these springs varies somewhat with rainfall. Philby records being told that "in seasons of good flood . . . the springs of Khaibar send forth streams of river-like proportions, in which fish, as much as two feet long, are found in various pools, and captured for the pot."[3] Philby did not personally see fish anywhere near that large at Khaybar, so it is quite possible that his informants were telling him a bit of a fish story, but even so this tale serves as a vivid illustration for the capacity of Khaybar's springs at full flood.

Even if a convenient spring was not available, it was sometimes possible to create a spring through human ingenuity. European traveler Charles Doughty, who had the opportunity to watch a group of Khaybar farmers at work trying to improve an older spring, describes the process of spring building as follows:

> [Their] iron [crowbars] bit in the flaws of the rock; and stiffly straining and leaning, upon their crowbars, they sprung and rent up the intractable basalt. . . . Three forenoons [mornings] they wrought thus with the zeal of novices: in the second they sacrificed a goat, and sprinkled her blood on the rock. . . . They also fired the rock [lit a bonfire to crack the rock with its heat], and by the third day the laborers had drawn out many huge stones: now the old well-head was become a great bath of tepid water. . . . We had struck a side vein, which increased the old current of water by half as much again,—a benefit forever for the husbandmen of the valley.[4]

It should be noted that the ease with which springs could be built or improved in Khaybar rendered the construction of qanats unnecessary.[5] The easy availability of spring and groundwater also limited the usefulness of the jalib, so for the most part, Khaybar's farmers depended on ghayl irrigation alone. What is more, the water table under Khaybar was rarely more than 2 meters deep, allowing palms to grow with little or no additional irrigation other than natural soil moisture.

As a result of these natural and man-made water sources, Khaybar has probably been inhabited continuously for at least the past five thousand years. Indeed, nineteenth-century traveler Charles Huber asserts that given "the abundant courses of water at Khaybar, it is certain that this oasis ought to be an inhabited center as long as there are inhabitants in Arabia."[6] Nonetheless, Khaybar only appears in the historical record in the sixth century CE, when the town was attacked by the Ghassanids, a Bedouin sheikhdom of northern Arabia that was allied with the Byzantine Empire. At the time, Khaybar was inhabited mainly by Jews, who were reportedly driven out of Khaybar by the Ghassanid attack.[7] The Ghassanid attack seems to have had only a limited impact on Khaybar, however, for by the time of the Prophet Mohammad, Khaybar was not only still controlled by Jews, but was renowned for its wealth and fertility. The Islamic geographer Yaqut notes that at the time of the Prophet, Khaybar was a sprawling oasis consisting of seven distinct settlements, each with its own strong fortress. Yaqut claims that the word *khaybar* itself means "fortress" in Hebrew.[8] In addition to relying on these fortresses for protection, the Jews of Khaybar also paid a portion of their date harvest to the nearby Ghatafan Bedouins, who were supposed to protect them in times of war.[9]

Even so, in 629 CE, when the Prophet launched a military assault on Khaybar, neither Khaybar's walls nor its Bedouin allies prevented it from being conquered piecemeal by the Muslim army. One by one, Khaybar's fortresses were taken, in part because of the inability or unwillingness of the disunited Jewish community to come to one another's defense.[10] Khaybar's land was divided up among the Muslim conquerors, and although the Jewish population was allowed to remain on the land for the time being, they were compelled to pay half the harvest to Khaybar's new Muslim owners. During the Caliphate of 'Umar, the Jews were expelled from Khaybar as well as the rest of the Arabian Peninsula, perhaps because they proved resentful and troublesome sharecroppers on land they had once called their own.[11] The exiled Jews of Khaybar migrated to other parts of the Islamic world, most notably to Egypt, where the Khayabira, or descendants of the

Jews of Khaybar, enjoyed a privileged legal position nearly four hundred years later.[12]

Very little is known about Khaybar's history from the period of the Islamic conquests up to the nineteenth century. According to al-Muqaddasi, a geographer living in the tenth century, Khaybar was "a fortified town" with "a very good mosque," notable mainly for the role it played in the wars of the early Islamic period.[13] Al-Muqaddasi does not explicitly note the existence of a continued Jewish community in Khaybar, though he does note that the nearby town of Qurh (modern al-'Ula) was populated mainly by Jews, 'Umar's expulsion order notwithstanding. Benjamin of Tudela, a Jewish traveler of the twelfth century, declares that Khaybar consisted of "strongly-fortified cities" occupied by a Jewish population of fifty thousand, but his information on Khaybar is based entirely on hearsay and rumor and should not be taken seriously.[14] Nonetheless, Khaybar was still associated with the Jews as late as the sixteenth century, when the intrepid traveler Ludovico di Varthema reports the existence of a mountain town inhabited by "four or five thousands Jews" somewhere north of Mecca. Although Varthema never mentions Khaybar by name, scholars believe that Varthema's "mountain of the Jews" probably reflects the historical memory of the Jewish town of Khaybar.[15]

Khaybar was also associated with agricultural fertility. Indeed, Khaybar's date palms had a legendary reputation throughout Arabia. One traditional Bedouin proverb, for example, likened a generous man to "a palm tree in Khaybar, whose dates fall into the sea"—in other words, Khaybar's palm gardens were so vast and fruitful that they (metaphorically) spilled into the Red Sea 200 miles away.[16] Another traditional proverb likened a pointless and redundant action to "carry[ing] dates to Khaybar," where of course dates were already in abundant supply.[17]

Khaybar in the Nineteenth Century

When Europeans arrived in Khaybar in the nineteenth and twentieth centuries, they found that while some aspects of life in Khaybar had changed little since the age of the Prophet, other aspects had changed dramatically. One thing that stayed the same was Khaybar's sprawling, decentralized nature. Khaybar did have a capital of sorts in the nineteenth century: Qariyat al-Bishr, literally the "Village of Joy." This town probably owed its primacy to its close proximity to Marhab Fort, also known as Qasr al-Yahoudi or "Castle of the Jews," which stood upon an easily defended natural plateau of volcanic rock that overshadowed Qariyat al-Bishr. Marhab Fort, which was named after the defeated Jewish chieftain Marhab Bin Abu Zaynab, served as the seat of Khaybar's governors throughout the nineteenth and twentieth centuries. Surrounding Qariyat al-Bishr were a number of smaller satellite towns, each with its own fort. Our authors exhibit considerable disagreement as to the names of these smaller towns, but I am inclined to believe that Philby's account is the most accurate, since as a long-time resident of Arabia and an intimate of the Saudi family, Philby probably had the best Arabic, the best relations with the local people, and the greatest freedom to investigate the landscape, at least compared to his predecessors. Map 3.1, which is based on a combination of Philby's travel narrative and modern-day satellite photos, shows the general distribution of settlements in the Khaybar oasis area. Figure 3.1 and map 3.2, in turn, show the valleys of Khaybar from the standpoint of Huber, who had a better understanding of nineteenth-century population distribution, but probably a much worse understanding of the area's overall geographic layout than Philby. All told, these scattered towns contained a population of approximately 2,500 or more permanent residents.

While the underlying geography of Khaybar had changed little since the Middle Ages, by the late nineteenth to early twentieth centuries, the

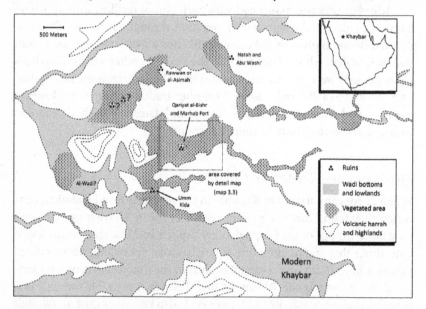

Map 3.1. Khaybar area map

Source: Google Maps; Philby, *The Land of Midian* (London: Ernest Benn Limited, 1957), 32–46.

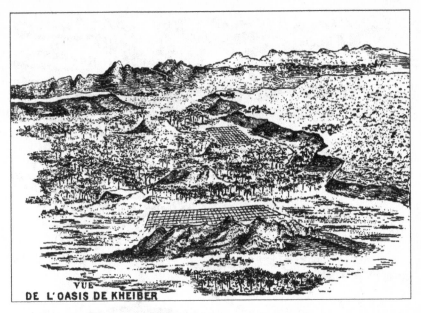

Figure 3.1. Khaybar from above

Source: Inset in Charles Huber's map, "Voyage dans L'Arabie Centrale: Hamâd, Šammar, Qaçîm, Hedjâz," *Bulletin de la Société de Géographie* 1884: 304–63, 468–530.

demographics of Khaybar had changed profoundly. On the strength of Khaybar's history, European travelers in Arabia in the nineteenth and twentieth centuries expected to find Jews in Khaybar, or at least relics thereof. What they found instead, to their evident surprise, was an apparent colony of Africans in the midst of the Arabian Hijaz. In the words of Carlo Guarmani, the first European traveler to reach Khaybar, "the uninitiated stranger, on entering Keibar, would be surprised at the appearance of its inhabitants and think himself miraculously transported into the Soudan [Sudan]."[18] Charles Doughty had a similar reaction, describing Khaybar as "an African village in the Hejaz."[19] As for Charles Huber, he notes that the population of Khaybar "resembles that of El 'Ala," a town where the people were of mixed Jewish-African appearance, "but with a much darker complexion."[20] All three authors note that Khaybar's population was not uniformly of African ancestry; indeed, Doughty observes that the "many nations at Kheybar" included "Kurds, Albanians, Gallas, Arabs, [and] Negroes."[21] Nonetheless, the clear majority of the population, and certainly the majority of the working population, was of African ancestry.

Map 3.2. Map of Khaybar, 1884 CE

Source: Huber, "Voyage dans L'Arabie."

When and how did Khaybar transition from a predominantly Jewish to a predominantly African town? Travelers in nineteenth-century Arabia recorded two stories explaining how this came about. The more fanciful story, provided by Doughty, asserts that following the expulsion of Khaybar's Jews, the remnants of the population united under a certain Okilla, who was a "Slave of Marhab, the Emir of Ancient Khaybar." One day, when a detachment of the Bedouin 'Anaza tribe was encamped within Khaybar's valleys,

> a maiden of the Aarab ['Anaza] entered Kheybar to see the daughters of the town: and there a young man was wounded with her love, who enticed the gazing damsel and forced her:— he was the sheykh Okilla's son! The poor young woman went home weeping:—and she was a sheykh's daughter. This felony

was presently reported in the nomad's menzil [encampment]! And "it was not to be bourne that a virgin should suffer violence!" said all the Beduw. The Annezy ['Anaza] sheykhs sent to require satisfaction from the sheykh of Kheybar:—who answered them shortly that the Annezy should no more water there [Khaybar]. On the morrow the town sheikh, Okilla, rode to the nomad's menzil, with a few horsemen, and defied them. The Beduw set furiously upon them; and Okilla fell, and there were slain many of his people. The Beduw now overran all; they conquered the village, and bound themselves by oath not to give their daughters to the Kheyâbara for ever.[22]

After the battle, Doughty continues, "the Kheyâbara took bondswomen [presumably African slaves] for wives; and at this day they are become a black people," while the "Beduw left the villagers to husband the palm valleys, for half the fruits with them; and thus removed in the wilderness."[23]

Obviously, this story of Khaybar's original conquest contains far more fiction than truth. As we have already seen, the dominant Bedouin tribe in the Khaybar area at the time of the Islamic conquest was the Ghatafan, not the 'Anaza. It is true that the 'Anaza are closely associated with Khaybar, and in fact "Bishr," the name of the main settlement in nineteenth-century Khaybar, was probably derived from Dhana Bishr, one of the two great divisions of the 'Anaza tribe.[24] Whether this connection between the 'Anaza and the town is ancient or more recent is unclear. Virtually all of the historical information concerning the connection between the 'Anaza and Khaybar was drawn from 'Anaza oral tradition, and as Albrecht Noth points out in a seminal 1968 article, such tribal conquest narratives are generally pieced together out of common rhetorical motifs that conceal rather than illuminate actual historical events.[25] Indeed, the 'Anaza tradition of the conquest of Khaybar includes two motifs—the revenge of a rape and taunting exchanges between dueling chiefs—that are common to many such narratives. The point of this story was less to record historical fact than to justify the continued economic exploitation of the African Khaybara, blaming it on a heinous crime committed by a distant ancestor.

The second tale, recorded by Italian traveler Carlo Guarmani, has more of a ring of truth to it:

The population of Keibar [Khaybar] is composed of Moors [sub-Saharan Africans] and Abyssinians, descendants of slaves owned by the Uld-Suleiman and Aleidan [sections of the 'Anaza tribal confederacy]. These slaves stayed on there when their masters, some centuries ago, were killed off in great numbers by smallpox, and believing the water was the cause, the survivors had abandoned the village; without, however, presuming that they had forfeited the right to consider themselves the proprietors, they ceded it to those who remained for a tribute of two bunches of dates from each tree at harvest and permitted them to plant other crops as they pleased. Every year the Uld-Suleiman and Aleidan come to Keibar but do not enter it, believing the water to be fatal to them.[26]

Although divergent in many respects, Doughty and Guarmani's origin stories of Khaybar share two common themes. One is the subordination of the Khaybar farmers to the surrounding Bedouins, either due to conquest, African ancestry, or both. Second, although it is clear from both stories that slavery played a crucial role in both creating and sustaining the population of Khaybar, both stories also suggest that the "Sudan" of nineteenth-century Khaybar were no longer slaves. Rather, their status was more akin to that of peasants or sharecroppers, tied to the soil for a share of that soil's produce.

The Africans of Khaybar belonged to two distinct ethnic groups, the "Sudan" and the "Galla." The Galla were the less numerous group. Although strictly speaking, "Galla" referred to a specific ethnicity within Abyssinia, by the nineteenth century the term had become synonymous with Habash, a general term used for all Abyssinians. Physically, Galla slaves were said to have lighter skin and more Semitic facial features than sub-Saharan Africans. The Galla were considered "more refined and more intelligent than the negroes," according to scholar and traveler C. Snouck Hurgronje, and thus better suited to certain jobs, most notably as body servants, business employees, military service, and concubinage.[27] Correspondingly, such slaves commanded a higher price: in the early 1880s, male Galla slaves were sold for 60–80 MTT (Maria Theresa thaler) in Jeddah's slave markets, and female Galla slaves for 80–150 MTT, while Sudan slaves were worth only 40 MTT, male or female.[28] For the most part, the Galla present in Khaybar in the nineteenth century were in positions of power, either as soldiers or administrators. When Gaurmani visited Khaybar in the 1850s, he was greeted by the governor of the village, an Abyssinian man named Aleidan, who was an appointee of the Rashidi dynasty of Ha'il.[29] By the

1880s, when Doughty and Huber reached Khaybar, the Rashidi governor had been driven out by the Turks, only to be replaced by a permanent garrison of Galla soldiers, led by an officer who was the son of a Galla concubine in Medina.[30]

The second African group present in Khaybar was sub-Saharan Africans, who were generally known as the Sudan, though western travelers often used the term "Negroes" to describe the same group. Like Galla, Sudan was a catch-all term, and it oversimplified a more complex reality; as Charles Doughty perceptively notes, "the blacks are not fewer nations and kindreds than white-skinned men."[31] Nonetheless, a clear distinction was drawn between the Sudan and the Galla slaves, particularly by the Galla slaves themselves, who did not want to be associated with the lower-status Sudan. Doughty writes that the Galla of Khaybar dismissed the Sudan as "not men but oxen, apes, sick of the devil and niggards," unworthy of the title of "children of Adam."[32] The Arabs of Khaybar recognized this distinction between Galla and Sudan Africans as well. While marriages were sometimes contracted between Galla women and Arab men, marriages between the Sudan and Arabs were very rare. Although Doughty does note that "it rarely happens that some welfaring negro villager takes a lone Beduwîa to wife," most marriages among the Sudan of Khaybar were conducted within the Sudan community.[33]

Unlike the Galla, who served primarily as soldiers, and might be only temporary residents of the town, the Sudan of Khaybar were permanent residents employed mainly or entirely in agriculture. The main crop, for which Khaybar was famous, was dates. Huber notes that the date trees of Khaybar were "innumerable," as they proliferated "wherever they are allowed to multiply." Unlike date farmers elsewhere in Arabia, the flowing springs and high groundwater of Khaybar meant that farmers were not burdened with the monotonous toil up and down the ramps of the jalibs. Nonetheless, even with this advantage, date cultivation in Khaybar was not without its difficulties. In order to produce a good crop, date farmers had to perform three seasonal but time-consuming tasks: spring fertilization, late spring thinning of the berries, and summer harvest. Each spring, the farmers of Khaybar would take up climbing gear and a "heavy bill" knife in order to "marry the palm blossoms": a flower bunch was cut from a male tree and then used to fertilize the female flowers, either by shaking pollen from the male tree onto the female flowers or by attaching a small amount of male flowers directly to the female flower clusters.[34] In late spring, the Khaybara (the Sudan of Khaybar) would have to climb the palms again, this time to thin out the number of date berries in each cluster in order to encourage the tree to grow fewer but much larger dates. Each summer, date palm farmers would climb the trees again to collect the fruit before it was lost to the elements or dropped naturally to the ground and spoiled. While performing all three tasks, date farmers were constantly exposed to bodily harm from the date palms themselves, for "at the least instant of inattention, one or more spines, long as a dozen centimeters, very hard and spiny, sharp and wounding, would penetrate deep into a limb or the abdomen and cause wounds difficult to heal."[35]

In addition, the Sudan of Khaybar grew some field crops, including wheat, sorghum, and some barley. Doughty summarizes farming in Khaybar as follows:

> All of their tillage is light. The husbandmen go out after sunrise, when they have eaten, to the plantations. They plough with a pair of their small oxen ... [and] their plough is little more than a heavy sharpened stake [an ard], which may stir the soil to the depth of a handbreadth. Another day [the soil] will be sown down [seeded] with the same hasty hands; there is no dressing, and this is all the care till the harvest, save in their hour in the week of the public water, when they will let the brook upon their field, and it floods at once all the pans of irrigation.[36]

Water rights in Khaybar were overseen by a village elder, who kept records of when and for long each villager might tap into the main irrigation channels. Doughty notes that "amongst these rude Arabian villages are no clocks or watches ... they take their wit [tell time] in the daytime, by the shadowing-round of a little wand set on the channel brink ... [while] at night they make account of time more loosely."[37] According to Doughty, it was common in nearby Medina to measure water rights with a sort of water clock: "a metal cup, pierced with a very fine eye," which was designed to fill with water and sink in a set amount of time.[38] This custom was apparently not known in Khaybar, however. Irrigating fields required little effort: farmers merely used "foot and spade" to cut the embankment separating an enclosed field from an irrigation channel, and then rebuilt the embankment at the end of their allotted time.[39]

Although none of our European eyewitnesses in Khaybar make the point explicitly, it seems likely that irrigated agriculture in Khaybar was limited to some degree by soil salinization. While the springs that fed Khaybar were not particularly salty themselves, the excess of water in the valleys of Khaybar combined with high rates of evaporation in the subtropical sun ensured that salt levels built up over time in Khaybar's soils. Philby gives a memorable description of a "low-lying saline mud-flat" south of Qariyat al-Bishr "whose surface shone with pools of liquid or solid salt against a dark-green background of palms."[40] Similarly, Doughty writes that "a glaze of salt is seen upon the small clay bottoms in the Harra."[41] The same salt flats are still clearly evident today in satellite imagery as large patches of white, in sharp contrast to the predominantly dark, volcanic landscape of Khaybar. To deal with the salt, Khaybar's farmers carefully removed the "infected salt-crust" and then flooded the "brackish land" that remained with water. Once this is done, Doughty notes, "every year [the soil] will become sweeter."[42] The salinity of Khaybar's soils may help to explain why Khaybar's farmers planted relatively few secondary fruit trees under the shade of the palms. In contrast with other oases, Huber notes, Khaybar's farms contained "neither vines, nor peaches, nor figs, nor pomegranates," possibly because these plants, in comparison to the palm tree, are all fairly intolerant of salinity.[43]

Although the farmers of Khaybar were apparently overwhelmingly of sub-Saharan African descent, it is far less clear whether they were free or slave. Certainly, some of Khaybar's farmers in the nineteenth century had the formal status of slaves. According to Doughty, it was common for Khaybar's wealthier hadr (settled) Arabs to purchase a "stout negro slave" as a sort of wedding present for their sons. These slaves were often freed after three years, married to another freed slave, and then set up with "certain palms for their living." Although these mawlas would be nominally independent of their master, they were bound by custom to "be his servants, and partisans of his children forever."[44]

Unfortunately, while Doughty gives us a fairly clear picture of how slavery looked from the elevated standpoint of the Arab owners, neither he nor any other author in the Arabian Peninsula records the voices of the slaves and mawlas themselves. One exceptional slave narrative does exist: L'esclave de Timimoun, which recounts the story of Griga, a sub-Saharan African enslaved at the age of fourteen and ultimately sold to a date plantation owner in the oasis town of Timimoun. Griga's story provides only an imperfect parallel to that of the slaves and freedmen of Khaybar: not only is Timimoun a North African rather than Arabian town, but Timimoun was also under French control and subject to some French interference in domestic matters during Griga's own lifetime. Nonetheless, since his narrative recounts the life of an agricultural slave in a late nineteenth- to early twentieth-century Arab date plantation, Griga's experiences are analogous enough to those experienced by Khaybar's slaves and mawlas to give us some insight into social conditions in Khaybar.

According to F. J. G. Mercadier, the French colonial official who recorded Griga's story, Griga spent years as an agricultural slave in Timimoun, employed primarily in date cultivation, though as we saw in chapter 2, he was also at one point involved in repairing a damaged qanat. Once freed by his master, he found himself with few options. Returning home to sub-Saharan Africa was not possible, as a freedman who left the towns risked robbery, re-enslavement, or death, since he could not count on anyone to protect him. Instead, Griga accepted his former master's offer of a piece of land within his plantations. With the help of his master's slaves, he constructed an irrigation basin at the highest point of the garden, so that it would receive a share of water from the qanat, and using that water, he cultivated a crop of wheat beneath the palms. However, at harvest time, he was obliged to give up four-fifths of his crop to his former master, leaving him without sufficient production to feed and clothe himself and his wife for the coming year. As a consequence, Griga told Mercadier that he "was less happy than the slaves, who are nourished, clothed, and lodged by their masters." Thus, despite being freed, Griga concluded that his status had "not changed at all except on paper." Indeed, Griga lamented that his freedom soon gave way to a new variety of slavery: debt to merchants, from whom he had to borrow during bad years in order to survive.[45] In all likelihood, the freedmen of Khaybar found freedom to be just as much of a mixed blessing as did Griga and the other mawlas of Timimoun.

While some of Khaybar's Sudan were slaves or recently freed, the majority of the Khaybara were Africans born within Arabia. In social terms, the Khaybara were analogous to European peasants: while they did not themselves own the land which they farmed, which technically belonged to the Bedouins by right of conquest, they did have freedom of person and certain inalienable rights to Khaybar's soils. According to Doughty,

> every Possession is reckoned in Khaybar upon the Bedouin Partnership; even the villagers' houses are held betwixt them and the absent nomads. At midsummer the Annezy ['Anaza] tribes (which remain in the south) descend to gather their part of the date harvest. Every béled [land holding] is thus a double inheritance; there is a Bedouin landlord and a black village

partner, and each may say, "it is mine." The villagers are free husbandmen: they may sell their half-rights to others, they may even neglect their holdings, without contradiction of the Beduwy; and the tribesman cannot put another in his room. If the villager sow the soil, the harvest is all his own; the absent Beduwy had no part therein.[46]

Doughty continues:

The absent tribesmen's land-right is over no more than the palms. As they decay the villager should set new plants, and the Beduwy is holden to pay him for every one a real [riyal, a unit of currency] but if his land-partner be poor and cannot requite him, he may leave the ground unplanted, or he may sow the soil himself. Nevertheless the Bedouin lordship remains in the land, and his nomad partner may, at any time, require the village partner to set palms there, for the half fruit, only requiting his labour . . . besides the villagers possess in their singular right certain open lands, which (from antiquity) were never planted with palms.

Although the Bedouin tribesmen who theoretically owned the palms lived most of the year with their animals in desert pastures, they did descend upon Khaybar during the summer date harvest in order to secure their half-share of the crop, temporarily swelling Khaybar's population to as much as fifty thousand or sixty thousand souls.[47] Rather than enter the valleys of Khaybar, which had a bad reputation for mosquitoes and fever, the Bedouins encamped upon the Harrat Khaybar surrounding the oasis, penning their animals in *marabit* (stables) built of "basalt blocks roughly thrown together" to form "roofless compounds."[48] These extensive livestock pens are still clearly visible today in the harrahs surrounding Khaybar, as can be seen in map 3.3.

Although the Khaybara had some recognized rights over the waters and soil of Khaybar, as well as control over their own labor, they still occupied a distinctly subordinate position. While in a good year the Sudan would produce enough to feed themselves as well as purchase household sundries, in a bad year they might be forced to borrow from a "nomad marketer," leading to a downward-spiraling trajectory of debt and poverty. What is more, if there was famine in the desert, it was customary for

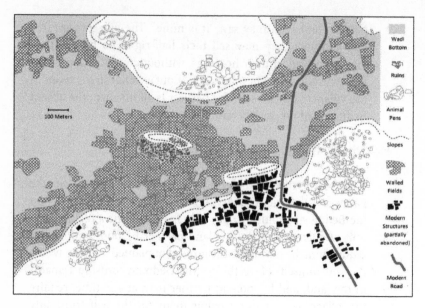

Map 3.3. Detailed map of modern Khaybar

Bedouins to seek hospitality in Khaybar, essentially forcing the Khaybara to provide free suppers. As Doughty notes, despite the natural bounty of the land, the Khaybara's obligations to the Bedouin ensured that "the negroes are poor in the abundance of their palm valleys."[49]

Although the Khaybara can be understood as a class of peasant farmers, it would be just as accurate to define them as a caste. As with many other subpopulations of the Arabian peninsula, the Khaybara were walled off from the remainder of the Arabian Peninsula population by strictly defended marriage taboos, to the point that a number of authors have commented on the "caste-like" nature of Arabian Peninsula society, in which marriages almost always occurred between families at the same social level and where exogamy was strongly discouraged.[50] These marriage restrictions were defended with particular zeal by the sharif Bedouin camel-breeding tribes, such as the 'Anaza and the Shammar. Among the Rwala tribe, a section of the 'Anaza, intermarriage was allowed only between other sharif tribes, but no Rwala "dares marry a member of the Sleyb, Hawazem, Fheyjat, Shararat, or Azem tribes," Bedouin tribes of the second rank. What is more, "a Rweyli [member of the Rwala] may not marry the daughter of a blacksmith or other mechanic," since these people "have no recognized genealogy" and "they marry newcomers from various towns, settlements, and tribes regardless of whether they are free, autonomous, dependent, or slaves." The strongest prohibition, however, was against intermarriage with people of African descent: "Marriages of slaves or rather negroes are also forbidden. A man marrying a slave would be killed by his kin. No one dares defile the blood of his kin."[51]

As we have already seen in this chapter, and will see in greater detail in chapter 5, the prohibition against intermarriage between Sudan Africans and Arabs was not absolute. Khaybar included some relatively poor Arabs, "bankrupts of the desert," who presumably settled in Khaybar after losing their livestock to famine, raids, or disease. Apparently around fifteen lived in Khaybar in Doughty's day, and lived and worked alongside the Khaybara, who would even lend them "ploughs and plough-oxen, and the husbandmen's tools."[52] Such refugees from the desert often had few other options than to marry Sudan Africans. This apparently did not happen during Doughty's stay, but Doughty did notice many "Arab-looking, and even copper-coloured village faces, and that some young men [there] wore their negro locks braided as the Nomads [Bedouins]." Indeed, a group of Khaybara of such intermediate appearance claimed to Doughty that they were not African at all, but rather kinsmen of the Jeheyna Bedouin tribe, despite having the "lips and noses [of] the Kheyâbara from the Sudan." This earned them the derision of Doughty's Arab companions, who invited these would-be Arabs to "let this wise stranger [Doughty] feel each of your noses, and declare to you what ancestry you be of."[53] Nonetheless, although the lines dividing Arab and African were occasionally tested, they functioned well enough to maintain a distinct Khaybara class well into the twentieth century.

The Khaybara were also distinct from other communities within the Arabian Peninsula from the standpoint of culture. In most respects, the Khaybara assimilated into Arab culture despite their African ancestry, but nonetheless a few traditional African cultural practices remained. We have already seen how Khaybara well builders attempted to reactivate a spring with an animal sacrifice, an act that falls well outside of mainstream Islamic traditions. Another example of African cultural influence was the prevalence of witchcraft accusations among the Khaybara. Indeed, according to local traditions, Khaybar's nights belonged to the witches, who "assemble in the dead hours of the night, and sitting in a place of ordures [filth], they strip off their smocks, and anoint their bodies with cow milk," which according to Doughty was widely considered to have medicinal properties. If an innocent passerby encountered a witch, and refused her sexual advances, he would be changed "into the form of some beast—an ox, a horse, or an ass" and afterward lose his mind, in the end perishing miserably.[54]

Doughty also notes that the Khaybara preserved the African tradition of zar, or spirit possession, though the "spirits" of Khaybar were Islamized into *jinn*, supernatural creatures mentioned frequently in the Qu'ran. In one case, an informant of Doughty told him that he had cured his wife of possession by firing a pistol beside her head, which had banished the jinn, as they "cannot abide . . . the smell of sulphur."[55] Such traditions survived elsewhere in Arabia as well, particularly in areas with large subpopulations of African descent, though most likely not to the degree that they persisted in Khaybar.[56] The zar rituals of the Khaybara probably served several functions: in addition to allowing them to foster a sense of collective African identity, the zar rituals may represent an attempt by Khaybara slaves and freedmen to assert some control over their destinies in an Arab-dominated society. As Ehud R. Toledano has argued, zar rituals were used by enslaved Africans as a way to cope with the isolation and alienation imposed by the dislocation of slavery, and thus were "indicative of agency and defiance" on the part of the slaves.[57]

Toledano makes the interesting argument that the spread of the zar cult into Arab territories was of relatively recent provenance, dating only to the 1820s, when it and similar Bori cult practices from the Sudan were first noted in Ottoman Egypt.[58] However, circumstantial evidence suggests that Khaybar's zar cult may have been of considerable antiquity. In his *Sirat Rasul Allah*, a biography of the Prophet written in the eighth century, Ibn Ishaq notes that Khaybar was the home of a "sorceress who had a familiar spirit" and who often served as an intermediary in disputes between local Bedouin tribesmen.[59] Of course, this does not prove that zar rituals existed continuously in Khaybar from pre-Islamic times to the nineteenth century. The rituals may very well have gone into abeyance and then been reintroduced, perhaps repeatedly, over the centuries with the ebb and flow of the slave trade. We will return to this point in chapter 5, which considers African servile agricultural labor in the Arabian Peninsula over the longue durée.

In addition to being set apart from other groups in the Arabian Peninsula by zar rituals and by caste distinctions, the Khaybara were also set apart from the Bedouins by their malarial environment, which more than anything else helped to secure Khaybar's autonomy and special identity within the wider Arabian Peninsula community. For the Arabs, Khaybar was synonymous with malaria, and Khaybar's "valley fever," carried by its large population of mosquitoes, was recognized and feared throughout the Hijaz. In the twentieth century, Philby found that the insects were still ubiquitous in the "mosquito-infested swamps of the oasis," especially in the lowland basins where agriculture was conducted.[60] Philby speculates that the seat of government was located in the elevated fort of Marhab because of its relative freedom from nocturnal mosquito invasions as compared to the valley below, rather than its defensive advantages.

The Khaybara did what they could to cope with mosquitoes, constructing two-story dwellings so that the second floor sleeping areas were to some degree protected from the marauding insects.[61] For the most part, however, mosquitoes and the malaria they carried were a fact of life in Khaybar, to be endured rather than avoided. According to Doughty, the worst season for malaria was March and April, when the air was "still and sultry" and "when the new date berries [were] first formed on the trees." Due to previous exposure, most adult Khaybara had some degree of acquired immunity to the disease: "If the valley fever come upon the grown negro people," Doughty notes, "they do but languish a day or two." However, the children of the Khaybara, who might have had some genetic protections against malaria but lacked the acquired immunity, suffered from a much higher rate of mortality. Doughty "daily wondered to see almost no young children," and was told that children die in Khaybar's pestilent air.[62] Thanks to Khaybar's omnipresent burden of malaria, Khaybar had a reputation of being inhabitable only by Africans. "Only blacks can live at Kheybar," one of Doughty's informants told him, "or else, we had taken it from them long ago."[63] We will return to this relationship between Arabian agriculture, slavery, and malaria in greater depth in the next chapter.

Khaybar from the Twentieth Century to the Present

The last of our four travelers to visit Khaybar was Harry St. John Bridger Philby, who visited Khaybar and its environs in 1950. Philby was moved to visit Khaybar in part by his deep admiration for Charles Doughty. "In Khaybar I had a feeling of being on holy ground," Philby writes, "trodden by Charles Doughty more than seventy years before, and described by him with a charm and distinction." Overall, Philby felt that relatively little had changed in Khaybar since Doughty had visited there, in part because no motor-road had been built into Khaybar proper. One notable change was the construction of a number of new settlements on the ridges of the harrah south of Khaybar, in highlands that were believed to be "more healthy" and "freer of mosquitoes" than Khaybar's valley basins. However, Doughty found that even on the harrah, his home "was full of the horrid insects." These "new" buildings constructed south of Khaybar, which are shown in black in map 3.3, are now themselves falling into disrepair as the town of Khaybar has shifted even further south, as indicated in map 3.1.

The overall impression that Philby received of twentieth-century Khaybar was one of stagnation. By the 1950s, the Bedouins were apparently no longer exerting any right of ownership of Khaybar, presumably due to the Saudi government's policy of subjugating and settling the Bedouin tribes. However, the void of ownership was not filled by the Khaybara, who are described by Philby as a "long-suffering and rather miserable popula-tion."[64] Rather, Khaybar's soils were falling under the ownership of foreign investors, such as 'Abdulla al Hindi, an Indian citizen of Medina who had settled in Arabia after a 1908 pilgrimage.[65] Despite this influx of outside funds, it is clear from Philby's account that Khaybar was fast becoming a backwater. By the 1950s, some oil money was beginning to invigorate the Saudi economy, but as Philby notes, "Khaibar has seen none of the vast wealth which the flood of oil has swept into the coffers of the realm."[66]

Khaybar's stagnation extended to the cultural sphere as well. Accord-ing to Philby, under the rule of the religiously conservative Saudis, a num-ber of local "superstitions" were suppressed. Philby's guides pointed out to him an old well, the Bir al Wuthairi, where "the people of Khaibar used to foregather before the days of Ibn Sa'ud's rule, to celebrate their pagan games and superstitious sacrifices in the meadows sloping down to the channel." Philby was unable to get any further information about these "pagan games" from his guides, who were too young to have participated in them, and were in any case probably unwilling to "talk about such evil things under the shadow of a new dispensation."[67]

After a lightning tour of four days, Philby left Khaybar, never to return. Old Khaybar itself soon followed in his footsteps. While some agriculture is still carried out in Khaybar's valleys, most of Khaybar's remnant popula-tion has since relocated to the harrah bluff south of the old town, and then (in a second wave of migration) to a new and presumably healthier city site near a sandstone ridge about 3 kilometers south of Qariyat al-Bishr. The area of Khaybar called the "new town" by Philby is now, ironically, called al-Qadeema, or "the old town." Today, Khaybar is a fairly unimport-ant stop on the new King Abdullah Road, which connects Medina in the south to Tayma and Tabuk to the north. Modern Khaybar is strikingly forward-looking, as epitomized by the modernistic sculptures that adorn its town center. However, little or no attempt is made by the modern town to revere its rich history. No major archeological projects have been carried out, and to my knowledge none are planned. Indeed, Marhab Fort itself has been fenced off, perhaps because the current Saudi government would just as soon forget that it was once known as the "Castle of the Jews". This is regrettable, both for the city's own sake as a landmark with a rich cultural history, and for that fact that any archaeological excavations in Khaybar could only further our knowledge of what was once one of the largest and most distinctive African agricultural colonies within the Arabian Peninsula.

AS WE have seen in this case study, Khaybar was different from other African servile colonies in the Arabian Peninsula in several important ways. It depended on ghayl irrigation, along with high levels of groundwater, rather than the jalib and qanat technologies that are associated with servile African labor elsewhere in the Arabian Peninsula. What is more, Khaybar's gardens were only partially bustan gardens, since high soil salinity seems to have limited the number of secondary crops that could be grown under Khaybar's palms.

In most aspects, however, Khaybar was quite typical of African servile colonies in the Arabian Peninsula. As elsewhere, the African servile population of Khaybar included some slaves, but most Khaybara were mawlas or their progeny, as might be expected of an established agricultural settlement of considerable antiquity. The Khaybara, like other servile African populations in the Arabian Peninsula, were predominantly sharecroppers, surrendering a portion of their harvest to Bedouin tribesmen who shared ownership of Khaybar's palms. The Khaybara seem to have enjoyed considerable autonomy from their absentee Bedouin landlords, and perhaps as a result retained some distinctly African cultural practices, though these decayed in the face of the Wahhabi cultural onslaught in the mid-twentieth century. Socially, the Khaybara represented a distinct, subordinate caste, which rarely intermarried with Arab populations, though unions between wealthier Khaybara and "desert bankrupts" were not unknown. Finally, Khaybar was notorious for malaria, a distinction it shared with many of the other African colonies discussed in chapter 2. We will explore this association between malaria, agriculture, and African slavery in some depth in the next chapter.

CHAPTER 4

Oasis Fever

Malaria as a Factor in Arabian Agricultural Slavery

AS IS clear from our survey of Khaybar's history in the previous chapter, malaria was a force to be reckoned with in the traditional Arabian Peninsula. While most people (including some scholars) associate the Arabian Peninsula only with sandy desert, in reality, Arabia consists of a patchwork of arid desert and moister lowland environments that were well suited for both irrigated agriculture and the proliferation of *Anopheles* mosquitoes, the vector of malaria plasmodia. Malaria, in turn, strongly influenced the demographics of the Arabian Peninsula. Native Arabs tended to avoid these wetter landscapes, associating them with fevers, hostile spirits, or both. Consequently, Arabs often exploited these moist lowlands through African servile agriculturalists who enjoyed intrinsic defenses—most notably Duffy negativity and hemoglobin S—against malarial infections. In this way, agricultural slavery in the Arabian Peninsula was surprisingly similar to agricultural slavery in the Atlantic world of the seventeenth through nineteenth centuries, where Africans were similarly used as proxy farmers by a malaria-vulnerable population to unlock the economic potential of unhealthy lowlands.

Fevers and Jinn

The pernicious, debilitating impact of malaria in Arabia is one of the most constant themes in nineteenth- and twentieth-century European travel literature, and indeed, a large number of European travelers themselves ran afoul of malaria in the Arabian Peninsula. Case in point is the sad story of British archeologists Theodore Bent and Mabel Bent, who, in early 1897, set out on a scouting expedition into the Yafei and Fadhli regions of Yemen. On their way inland, they were detained in the town of Khanfar, where the mosquitoes were "awful," though this did not stop them from "taking long walks through the cultivated fields" along the Wadi Banna while negotiating with the local sultan for passage into the interior. About fifteen days later, during their tour of the highlands behind the town of Shukra, both Bents were laid low by a severe fever. "My malarial fever was constant," Mabel Bent later recounts, "and I had no tertian intervals, I lost my strength completely. We both, and several others, were very ill, and we were not strong enough to get at our medicine-chest." Unable to walk or even ride a camel, Mrs. Bent reports, "I had to be carried to the sea, 17 miles, on my bed, which was strengthened with tent-pegs and slung on tent-poles."[1] Although they subsequently returned to Britain to convalesce, Theodore Bent's health had been ruined by his bout with malaria, and he died on May 5, 1897, only a few days after their return.

The Bents were certainly not the only European travelers to suffer from malaria in the Arabian Peninsula. A number of the authors upon whom I have relied for ethnographic materials, including Freya Stark, Charles Huber, William Palgrave, Harry St. John Bridger Philby, Ameen Rihani, and J. R. Wellsted, contracted malaria at some point during their journeys. Ameen Rihani suffered from it repeatedly throughout his trip though Najd, and later notes, with black humor, that many of his journal entries were "written when I was in the lap of Dame Malaria, who enveloped me, saturated me, with the heat of her love."[2] While Rihani survived to tell the tale, other European travelers did not, including Louis Burckhardt, a talented young Swiss traveler and scholar who died of malaria or similar malady in 1817 at the age of thirty-three.[3]

Despite these testimonials from travel literature, the prevalence of malaria in the traditional Arabian Peninsula has often been overlooked or underappreciated in the scholarly literature. A study of the historical prevalence of malaria in the Arabian Peninsula conducted in 1968 claims that malaria was present in only a small fraction of the Arabian Peninsula, most especially in Tihamah, the southern Yemeni coast, the al-Hasa region, and some portions of the Hijaz.[4] In the Arabian regions that were malarial, the report suggests, malaria infections were relatively infrequent, with only 10–50 percent of adults exposed to the disease. Other scholars have gone so far as to argue that the *lack* of malaria in Arabia has left a mark on human genetics. Medical researchers Anderson and Vullo, for example, speculated in 1994 that "the absence of malaria in the African and Arabian Deserts could explain why . . . high lactase activity predominates" among Arab and Berber pastoralist populations.[5] As we shall see below, there may be some truth to these scholars' claims about a negative correlation between malaria and the LP (lactase persistence) gene, but I imagine that the bereaved Mrs. Bent would have taken exception to their claim concerning the "absence of malaria" in desert Arabia.

Indeed, an overwhelming body of evidence suggests that malaria has been a constant danger to both visitors and indigenous inhabitants of the Arabian Peninsula over at least the past two thousand years. As early as the first century CE, the *Periplus*, a survey of the Arabian coastline written by an anonymous Greek mariner, notes that the incense-producing province of Dhofar was "very unhealthy, and pestilential even for those sailing along the coast."[6] Although the *Periplus* only suggests malaria infection, other early sources are more explicit. According to eighth-century historian Ibn Ishaq, when the Prophet and his companions fled from Mecca to the agricultural oasis of Yathrib (Medina), they found it to be the "most fever-infested land on earth." Many of the Companions became "delirious and out of their minds with a high temperature," including Abu Bakr and the freed slave Bilal.[7] Mohammad himself died of fever in Medina, and the apparently recurrent nature of his illness is suggestive of malaria.[8]

While it may seem that their nomadic ways and tendency to occupy more arid landscapes would offer them some protection, Bedouin populations were actually disproportionately vulnerable to malaria. In a pre-Islamic Bedouin ode, the poet Shanfara likens his cares and worries to "quatran fever"—in other words, fever that recurs at seventy-two-hour intervals, which is typical of a *Plasmodium malariae* infection.[9] Bedouin concern about such fevers is well attested to in early Islamic historiography, which describes the Bedouins' persistent fear of "damp, low-lying, febrile and insect-ridden places."[10] As one Bedouin supposedly complained to his Caliph, "O Commander of the Faithful, we are not a people who can endure watering places where mosquitoes devour us and fevers grip us."[11] Arabian Bedouins were, in fact, even more vulnerable to malaria than Arab townsmen. Unlike hadr Arabs, Bedouins had little prior exposure to malaria infection, and thus lacked even the modicum of resistance that prior exposure affords. What is more, owing to their milk-rich diet, camel Bedouins had high levels of blood riboflavin, which may facilitate malaria parasite propagation in red blood cells. This is in sharp contrast to village and town-dwelling Arabs, whose milk-poor diet rendered them mildly riboflavin deficient and thus potentially less susceptible than the Bedouins.[12]

Bedouin fears of malaria are manifested clearly in their folk traditions, which tend to associate watery and fertile landscapes with fevers, jinn, or both. While following the trace of the Wadi Jirdan in southern Yemen, for example, Dutch traveler Daniel van der Meulen was astonished to find that, although portions were covered with "fresh, green grass and 'ilb trees," the wadi was completely without "any traces of inhabitants." He soon discovered why: the wadi was "full of mosquitoes . . . so ravenous that we could kill ten of them at a time on our arms." Pondering the matter, van der Meulen speculates further: "Might not malaria have driven settlers away from this fertile, dank piece of land? The siyāras [guides] said that it was a country full of evil spirits which is perhaps a different way of saying the same thing."[13]

A number of other travelers recorded similar stories of Arabs associating moist lowland depressions with dangerous fevers and spirits. We have already seen how the Bedouins surrounding Khaybar associated its abundant waters with fevers that were especially dangerous to people of non-African ancestry. Bertrand Thomas was told similar horror stories about the waters of the Wadi Andhaur in the Oman interior, which tasted sweet, but caused "a fever that kills." Thomas discovered the cause of this folk belief "when a mosquito, the first [he] had seen since Ja'alan, buzzed in [his] ear, and the only inhabitant of the place, a Bait ash Shaikh tribesman, came to [him] with a large spleen and malaria symptoms."[14] Other Bedouins ascribed fever not to water but to specific times of the year. When traveling in the interior valleys of Yemen, for example, Freya Stark was warned by her "camel-men" to avoid the "cloud-steaming lowlands" of the Wadi Hajir in the hot months, as "all who go there when the dates are in flower, fall ill with a fever and die."[15] In still other cases, Bedouins contended that certain ill-favored locations were the haunt of dangerous fever-causing jinn. The Al Murrah tribe of eastern Arabia, for example, exploited the palms of the Jabrin oasis, but never camped within its confines out of a "dread of the spirits that are said to haunt the ruined forts."[16]

As a general rule, Bedouins "shun[ned] the confinement of even an hour" within a desert oasis, and if they did venture into the verdure of a palm plantation, they were careful to leave it by nightfall, an eminently sensible precaution in areas frequented by malaria-carrying mosquitoes.[17] When Bedouins did choose to interact with oasis towns in a large-scale or sustained way, they often did so through intermediaries or proxies in order to protect themselves from the inevitable oasis fevers. For example, after the powerful Rwala camel Bedouin tribe of northern Arabia conquered the town of al-Jawf in the early twentieth century, they garrisoned it with "thirty-five soldiers, most of them young negroes, who never set aside their loaded rifles."[18] In a parallel case, though slightly outside our area of study, the Shammar Bedouin of the northern Iraqi plain employed their African slaves as overseers and tax-collectors in the fertile villages they controlled along the Euphrates River. In their study of the legacy of slavery in Iraq, Juwaidah and Cox ascribe this to social factors—free men were hesitant to collect taxes from their peers—but an equally compelling explanation would be the typical Bedouin hesitation to venture into the notoriously malarial date plantations.[19] Perhaps because of these pragmatic practices and folk beliefs, which led them to avoid oasis environments, Bedouins had the reputation of being somewhat healthier than their town-dwelling counterparts. J. R. Wellsted, for example, noted in the early nineteenth century that the inhabitants of Oman's interior oases "constantly suffer[ed] from sickness," including "violent fevers," and "have not the vigorous and healthy look of the Bedowins." Wellsted ascribed these fevers to the oases' "swamps and pools of water, bordered by rank and luxuriant vegetation," and as we will see below, he was not far off the mark.[20]

While malaria was undoubtedly a scourge of both Arabian farmers and pastoralists, it did provide some measure of protection against outside attack. Diseases, including no doubt malaria, contributed to the failure of the first century BCE Roman expedition into southern Arabia under the generalship of Aelius Gallus.[21] The Egyptian and Ottoman armies that repeatedly invaded Arabia in the nineteenth and early twentieth centuries were also weakened by malarial infection. Italian mercenary soldier Giovanni Finati, for example, describes how, in 1815, 90 Egyptian soldiers died of illness in just three months while garrisoned in the lower Hijaz oasis town of Turaba. Finati blames this on the use of local ammonium salts, though commentators on his work believe that "intermittent fevers" and other diseases were the likely cause of this mortality.[22] The Ottomans lost far more men to disease during their ill-fated 1904–05 occupation of the highly malarial Najd district of Qasim: of the 4,500 troops sent out, only 1,000 returned, largely because the occupying troops were "decimated by disease."[23] Ottoman troops suffered similar problems from malaria during World War I, during which north Arabia became a battlefield between Ottoman and British forces. Czech scholar and wartime diplomat Alois Musil recalls how one Ottoman military expedition against the British was completely undone by malaria. Of the 176 soldiers on the expedition, fully 130 were rendered *hors de combat* by "fever and malaria," and many cases were so serious they had to be evacuated to Damascus for medical treatment.[24]

Malaria and Mosquitoes

The disease agent responsible for most of the havoc described in the anecdotes above is *Plasmodium*, the genus that includes several deadly malaria parasites and is probably almost as old as the human species itself. *Plasmodium* has three important species, known as plasmodia: *P. falciparum*, *P. vivax*, and *P. malariae*. All three of these plasmodia are carried by mosquitoes and cause debilitating fevers, though they differ somewhat in their clinical manifestations. The two most common malaria plasmodia, *falciparum* and *vivax*, cause "tertian" fevers, thus named because the fever episodes strike at forty-eight-hour intervals, and thus the original fever recurs on the third (tertian) day. The less common *malariae* strikes its victim at seventy-two-hour intervals, thus recurring on the fourth day and earning it the name "quartan fever." These characteristic fevers are the result of the plasmodia attacking the red blood cells. After an intermediate stage in which the plasmodia multiply in the liver, the plasmodia infiltrate red blood cells, where they are safe from the human immune system, reproduce, and then issue forth, rupturing and destroying the red blood cells in the process. The amount of time needed for the malaria parasites to reproduce in the red blood cells—about forty-eight hours for most plasmodia, seventy-two hours for *malariae*—accounts for malaria's recurring tertian or quartan character.

The severity of any given malaria epidemic depends on a number of different factors, including the strain of malaria, the general state of health of the infected individuals, the acquired or genetic defenses present in the affected population, and the local mosquito vector of the plasmodia. By far the most deadly strain is *falciparum*, also known as "tropical malaria" since it can only survive in warmer climates with year-round mosquito activity.[25] In a *falciparum* infection, the plasmodia invade blood cells much more aggressively and indiscriminately than the other strains, and can thus infect or destroy up to 80 percent of the blood cells of its host.[26] The *falciparum* strain also has the nasty habit of forcing its host red blood cells to grow surface proteins that make the cells sticky and likely to adhere to the walls of blood vessels. This behavior prevents the infected blood cells from being detected and destroyed by the spleen, but unfortunately these sticky blood cells can also block blood from flowing into the brain or other vital organs, triggering cerebral malaria and death. As a result, untreated *falciparum* infection has a 20–50 percent death rate.[27] In contrast, the death rates of *vivax* and the other less common plasmodia strains are much lower, usually only 1–2 percent, though they can reach 5 percent in cases where victims have compromised immune systems.[28] This fact would be small comfort to a *vivax* victim, however, who would still suffer the splitting headaches, chills, fevers, and lethargy characteristic of all malaria plasmodia strains. What *vivax* lacks in virulence it makes up in effective range: since it has the ability to survive winters in hypnozoites hidden in the liver, *vivax* epidemics have been described as far north as southern Canada and the Russian port of Archangel on the Arctic Sea.[29]

The outcome of any given malaria infection is also dependent to some degree on the health, resistances, and immunities of the host. Young children, who often have little previous exposure to malaria by virtue of their age, are generally killed by malaria at a disproportional rate, as are pregnant women, whose immune systems are weak as a side effect of the pregnancy. People who are living in chronic malarial zones, and thus have been subjected to continuous infection and reinfection, tend to reach a kind of equilibrium with the parasite. In the words of Margaret Humphreys, in such people "active bouts of fever no longer occur," but they "may never be entirely well."[30] People living in such conditions are often characterized by anemia and malaise, and can be identified by swelling on the left side of the abdomen caused by an enlarged spleen, though sometimes these symptoms are absent. In addition, a number of different genetic abnormalities, most notably thalassemia, sickle-cell trait, and the Duffy-negative antigen, can provide some degree of protection. These traits function by changing the normal properties of red blood cells, often in ways that are detrimental to the carrier of the gene, but they also protect against malarial infection. We will discuss these malaria-protective blood abnormalities in some detail later in this chapter.

As with all diseases, the negative effects of the malaria plasmodia on the human body are incidental side effects of the real objective of the organism, which is to jump to new hosts and ensure the survival of the species. Malaria plasmodia do this with the help of mosquitoes, specifically the *Anopheles* mosquito, which is the only mosquito genus capable of hosting the organism. When an *Anopheles* feeds on the blood of a malaria victim, it ingests thousands upon thousands of copies of malaria parasite gametocytes, which are the sexually active form of the organism. These gametocytes mate in the stomach of the mosquito, producing the "seed" form of the parasite called sporozoites, which then infect the mosquito salivary glands. When the mosquito bites a new human victim, the sporozoites are injected along with saliva, and then pass on to the liver, where they reproduce asexually, creating millions of merozoites. Most of these colonize the red blood cells of the new host, but others differentiate into male and female ookinetes, which join sexually to produce new gametocytes, allowing the process to begin again when the host of the plasmodia is bitten anew by an *Anopheles* mosquito. When explained in this way, the malaria plasmodia life cycle seems to have a Rube Goldberg complexity to it, and indeed scientists are now looking for a weak spot in the cycle, since if any one step can somehow be short-circuited, the plasmodia could be eradicated or neutralized as a threat. In the meantime, malaria remains one of the world's greatest killers, reaping an annual death toll of between 1.1 and 2.7 million.[31]

One final factor that can decrease or increase the severity of a malaria infection is the specific species of *Anopheles* mosquitoes found the area. *Anopheles* means "good for nothing" in Greek, and while one might think this is true of all mosquitoes, several other genera of mosquitoes exist, including *Culex, Aedes,* and *Mansonia.* Even within the genus *Anopheles,* considerable diversity exists, and different *Anopheles* mosquitoes exhibit various feeding habits, with marked preference for human or animal hosts, indoor or outdoor feeding, and daytime or nighttime activity. The diversity of the *Anopheles* genes is on full display in the Arabian Peninsula, which occupies an intermediate position "in the world zoogeographic regions, the Palaearctic region from the north, the Ethiopian (Afrotropical) region from the southwest and the Oriental region from the east." As a result, the Arabian Peninsula is "the border of many mosquito species gradient zones and geographical adaptations."[32] Indeed, a 1956 survey of Arabian mosquitoes identified forty-six different species, including seven varieties of *Anopheles* mosquitoes, and subsequent research has detected even more local diversity, with one 2012 study showing more than thirteen different *Anopheles* mosquito varieties in Saudi Arabia's eastern province alone.[33]

Even within the *Anopheles* genus, not all species are created equal. By far the most common *Anopheles* mosquito collected in central Arabia is the *An. dthali*, but this mosquito is not known to be a significant transmitter of malaria to humans in the Arabian Peninsula. Rather, this dubious distinction belongs to a few important vector species. In eastern Arabia and Najd, the most common vector species has traditionally been *An. stephensi*, though as many as thirteen other *Anopheles* species have colonized this region, and of them, *An. multicolor*, *An. gambiae*, and *An. sergenti* probably played a role in malaria transmission as well.[34] On the other side of the Arabian Peninsula, in the highly malarial province of 'Asir, *An. arabiensis* and *An. sergenti* are the known vector species, though *An. stephensi* and *An. multicolor* are found in this region as well.[35] *An. arabiensis* and *An. sergenti* are also the primary vectors of malaria in Mecca and the southern Hijaz as well as in Yemen, though in the latter area *An. culicifacies* have also been implicated in malaria transmission.[36] It is important to note, however, that the exact mosquito species composition in any given part of the Arabia is usually in flux, as yearly variations in rainfall and temperature favor some species at the expense of others, and the invasion of new mosquito species into a region—especially those that prey on the larvae of other mosquitos—can lead to dramatic changes in mosquito numbers over time.

Anopheles Mosquitoes and Arabian Agriculture

Unfortunately for Arabian farmers, the relatively few areas of the Peninsula that were suitable for agriculture were also good habitats for the *Anopheles* mosquito. The link between agriculture and *Anopheles* is, of course, the presence of water.

With the exception of inland Yemen, coastal Oman, and the Jabal Shammar region of Najd, the Arabian Peninsula receives less than 100 millimeters of rain a year, and what little precipitation the peninsula does receive occurs sporadically with "long, dry spells broken by sudden, brief downpours that are sharply restricted in area."[37] When this rain falls upon the mountain slopes, rock pavement, gravel plains, or sand dunes that comprise the bulk of the Arabian Peninsula, much of it is quickly lost, as it is either sloughed off in the form of sheet flooding or, in the case of dunes, quickly absorbed into the sand itself. These landscapes can be exploited by pastoralists, but there is little water available either for farmers or mosquitoes.

As a result, the areas best suited for both *Anopheles* and agriculture are Arabia's numerous wadis and other drainage basins, where water concentrates after the infrequent rainfall events. As we saw in chapter 1, Arabian agriculturalists have centuries of experience with exploiting this water, either during the flood via sayl irrigation practices, or long after the floodwaters have percolated into the groundwater by means of qanats, harnessing ghayl water flows, or the jalib. What is more, Arabian farmers knew the importance of growing a canopy of palms to trap soil moisture and to create a temperate microclimate of humid air suitable for agricultural production, a technique called bustan gardening. These combined techniques made agriculture possible in an otherwise forbidding climate. However, they rendered the intrinsically moist wadi bottoms even more suitable for the breeding of *Anopheles* mosquitoes, which, like all mosquitoes, spend their egg and larval stage in pools of stagnant water, and as adults prefer humid environments without temperature extremes. Arabian farmers rendered the wadi environments even more *Anopheles* friendly by constructing houses, animal enclosures, and other rude structures that could provide shelter for mosquitoes as well as human and animal inhabitants.

Bustan gardening, therefore, vastly increased the risk of malaria plasmodia infection by ensuring that *Anopheles* mosquitoes and human beings lived in close proximity. The transmission of malaria to humans was also facilitated by the relative paucity of livestock in traditional Arabian agricultural oases. This was due in large part to the lack of good grazing in the vicinity of oases, which were generally surrounded by a dead zone containing little to no vegetation because of constant foraging for cooking fuel by oasis inhabitants. Traveler Julius Euting found that "the area around [the Jabal Shammar town of] Ha'il for a radius of several hour's travel [had] long since been stripped of every out-door plant."[38] Under such circumstances, the only way to maintain livestock in the oasis would be through fodder crops like sorghum or barley, and as a result livestock and man would be competing for finite soil, manpower, and water resources. Consequently, many Arabian oasis towns resembled al-Jawf, where, as Wilfrid Blunt notes, "there [were] no horses, asses, or other beasts of burden in the oasis, a few camels only being kept to draw water from the wells."[39] With so few animal meals to choose from, even predominantly zoophilic mosquitoes like *An. stephensi* would be forced to focus on human blood meals.[40]

Although the deadly impact of *Anopheles* mosquitoes and malaria plasmodia on Arabian Peninsula farming populations is clear from innumerable anecdotes in the literature, I have found only two systematic studies describing the phenomenon. The first is Norman Lewis's excellent 1949 depiction of malaria problems in the Selemiya oasis of Syria, which lies somewhat outside the Arabian Peninsula and the 100 millimeter rain line but nonetheless provides clear parallels to the situation in the Arabian Peninsula. For its water, Selemiya depended primarily on thirty-nine qanats, which were known as *foggara* in local parlance. Lewis found that these qanats were poorly maintained, "blocked by vegetation" and full of silt and mud swept in by floods and rain, causing overflow into depressions surrounding the qanat channels and into swamps along the irrigation canals. The problem was made worse by an excess of water, since the qanats provided more water than Selemiya could use, especially during the winter and spring seasons where water availability was at its height but the water needs of the crops were minimal. During those seasons, Lewis found, the canals fed by qanats carried "slow-moving, half-stagnant water," excellent conditions for the proliferation of *An. sacharovi* mosquitoes, the local malaria vector.[41] As a result, 20 percent of the patients admitted to a mobile clinic that visited the region in 1942–43 were suffering from malaria, and in late summer this percentage rose to 80 percent; indeed, Lewis notes, "sometimes practically the whole population of a village was found to be infected." Not surprisingly, malaria epidemics on this scale led to significant mortality in the Selemiya region, with the town of Tell et Tout suffering fifty deaths (nearly a tenth of the entire population of the village) in 1941 alone.[42]

Interestingly, Lewis found that survivors of malaria in Selemiya suffered from chronic weakness, which is what led to the neglect of basic qanat maintenance and, as a consequence, the proliferation of *Anopheles* mosquitoes and the persistence of endemic malaria. Most of the malaria infection suffered at Selemiya was preventable, or at least reducible, given proper maintenance measures on the qanat: cleaning detritus and vegetation from the lower end of the qanat, repairing the banks and irrigation channels, reducing water wastage, and repairing damage done by occasional floods. However, since "malaria causes debility and apathy amongst the villages," these necessary maintenance and repair tasks were often neglected, thus perpetuating the cycle of malaria infection.[43] Lewis's linkage of malaria and neglect is supported by observations of nineteenth- and twentieth-century travelers in the Arabian Peninsula. Charles Huber recalls that the verdant oasis town of Qusaibah near 'Unayzah in Qasim "appeared to be a paradise," but upon closer inspection contained "numerous abandoned properties" and a "tired, emaciated, weak-bodied, thin, and stunted population." The main reason for this, Huber speculates, were the "two very disagreeable scourges" that plagued Qusaibah: "mosquitoes and fevers," both of which arose from its foul air, "saturated with miasmas, owing to the numerous [bodies of] stagnant water."[44]

The second study of the impact of malaria in an oasis environment is Richard Daggy's 1940s–50s study of malaria in Qatif and the al-Hasa oasis complex. Daggy, who worked for the medical department of ARAMCO (the Arab-American Oil Company), found malaria infections to be simultaneously highly prevalent and narrowly circumscribed in the al-Hasa oasis:

> Oasis malaria is characterized by its sharp delimitation to island-like cultivated areas in a sea of sand. The oasis population is concentrated in one or two main centers and the remainder in scattered small villages surrounded by irrigated date palm groves. Within this area are also concentrated the breeding places of the anopheline vectors; primarily *Anopheles Stephensi*. Hence, man, mosquito, and parasite are closely confined to the cultivated areas; and here malaria is hyperendemic. A few miles from the well defined borders of these oases, Bedouins or other travelers are relatively safe from the disease.[45]

Even within the settled parts of the al-Hasa oasis, Daggy found some areas to be far more malarial than others. In 1947–48, Daggy conducted a survey of children two to fourteen years old in which he measured plasmodia levels in the blood as well as the degree of spleen enlargement, a trademark symptom of chronic malaria infection. In urban areas, he found malaria rates to be relatively low: 14 percent in Hofuf, and 16 percent in Hofuf's sister city al-Mubarraz. In rural palm plantations, where humans lived and worked beneath the shade of the date palms, the malaria parasite rate ranged from 71.4 percent to 98.1 percent, and spleen enlargement rates ranged from 91.7 percent to 98.2 percent.[46] In such communities malaria was holoendemic, meaning that nearly all individuals had the plasmodia in their body almost all the time. The most common type of malaria infection overall—or at least the most commonly reported infection—was *falciparum*, which accounted for 33.7 percent of known malaria cases. Another

28.4 percent of cases reported *vivax*, while *malariae* accounted for only 1.3 percent of the cases. In 35.9 percent of the cases, the exact plasmodia was undetermined, while in .8 percent of cases, patients were infected by two or more types of plasmodia, though Daggy suspects that such mixed infection cases were grossly underreported in the data.[47]

Not surprisingly, Daggy found that malaria exacted a heavy annual death toll in the al-Hasa oasis. In the years 1941–47 alone, malaria killed forty-three people in ARAMCO hospitals, and in two of those years (1942 and 1943), malaria was the single highest cause of death. Most of these deaths seem to have been the result of *falciparum* malaria, though *vivax* occasionally turned deadly as well. Daggy argues that in al-Hasa both *falciparum* and *vivax* occurred year-round, though *vivax* infection tended to be more common in the winter (January through March) and late summer (August through October), while heat-loving *falciparum* was prevalent especially in the spring and early summer (April through July) and, surprisingly, in the fall (November through December). Although he does not make the point explicitly, Daggy suggests that al-Hasa's hot water springs may have had a moderating effect on the local environment, allowing both malaria and mosquito to thrive in cold weather seasons when both the vector species and the parasite normally exhibited lower levels of activity.[48] In any case, the high death toll exacted by malaria plasmodia in the al-Hasa oasis is all the more remarkable given the presence of ARAMCO's hospitals in the region, though it may be that wartime scarcity reduced or depleted ARAMCO's stocks of quinine. In traditional Arabia, the mortality rate would presumably have been substantially higher.

In Daggy's opinion, these malaria deaths were tragic, and also to some degree preventable, since by and large, "malaria in the Qatif and al-Hasa oases is largely *man-made malaria*," the direct result of "inefficient irrigation and drainage systems which have been constructed in the past." Like Lewis, Daggy found that drainage channels were quite often "clogged with vegetation," slowing or stopping the current and thus creating ideal mosquito breeding grounds. What is more, seepage from poorly constructed irrigation channels created "grassy pools ideal for anophelines," since these temporary bodies of water were devoid of the fish populations that normally keep mosquito larvae in check. *Anopheles* mosquitoes also colonized the shallow wells of the al-Hasa and Qatif areas, as well as small, shallow puddles created by the "accumulations of waste water, spillage from buckets used to bring water from deep wells, or other sources." In addition, Daggy notes that increases in the water table were also responsible for mosquito breeding, especially when the water table rose to the point where "shallow surface-water accumulations [became] common in low-lying, water-logged areas." While some of the rise in the water table was natural— there was an overall tendency for it to rise in the winter due to higher rain-fall and lower evaporation rates—certain human activities could lead to soil waterlogging as well, most especially "excess irrigation, water wastage, [and] poor drainage." [49] Overall, Daggy found *Anopheles* and agriculture to be inextricably linked in the traditional Arabian Peninsula.

Malaria, Genetics, and Slavery

As might be expected of a human society living in subtropical and tropical regions where both *falciparum* and *vivax* infections are a chronic threat, Arabian Peninsula populations do exhibit some genetic traits that provide protection against malarial infection. Medical researcher Laila Zahed found twenty-five different strains of β-thalassemia, a debilitating blood disorder that nonetheless confers upon its carriers some measure of resistance to malaria, in Saudi Arabia, the UAE, and Kuwait.[50] Saudi Arabia also has one of the world's highest rates of α-thalassemia, another blood disorder that is presumed to be protective against malaria. This mutation is widespread throughout the Arabian Peninsula, but is particularly high in Eastern Saudi Arabia, where 45 percent of the population are heterozygous carriers of the trait.[51] Interestingly, genetic mapping suggests that, while Arabia probably received β-thalassemia via gene flows from outside the peninsula, Arabia's α-thalassemia mutation most likely originated in the Arabian Peninsula itself. While other areas with high α-thalassemia rates do exist worldwide (such as Thailand and Nepal), they are geographically scattered and unconnected by territories exhibiting the trait, which suggests independent mutations in areas that shared a high rate of endemic malaria.[52]

Nonetheless, while thalassemias α and β are protective against malaria, Arab populations historically lacked two important malaria-protective genetic traits that are widespread in sub-Saharan African populations, namely the Duffy-negative antigen and hemoglobin S, better known as the sickle-cell trait. Duffy negativity is an inherited condition in which the Fy^a and Fy^b receptor proteins normally found on the surface of red blood cells are absent. While Duffy negativity is associated with higher levels of asthma and some other minor medical problems, it also endows its carrier with near immunity to *vivax* malaria. Not surprisingly, then, the rate of Duffy negativity is between 85 and 100 percent in sub-Saharan Africa, which was likely the place of origin for *vivax* malaria.[53]

While Duffy negativity is associated with only mild health disadvantages, the same cannot be said for the sickle-cell trait. Individuals who are homozygous for hemoglobin S are afflicted by acute and frequent episodes of pain and weakness, and may suffer organ damage and early death. Even with the benefits of modern medicine, the average life span of homozygous sickle-cell patients in America as of the 1990s was forty-two years for men and forty-eight years for women, decades below the national average.[54] The hemoglobin S trait survives mainly because those who are heterozygous for the trait show few symptoms of sickle-cell anemia, and in addition suffer only one-tenth the normal mortality rate from *falciparum* malaria.[55] As a result of this malaria resistance, the trait persists (despite its deadly drawbacks) at the 10–15 percent level in areas where *falciparum* is common, such as the Congo and Niger River valleys in Africa.[56] Farther north, in the sub-Saharan region that was the source for the bulk of the Sudan slaves sent to Arabia, the hemoglobin S rate ranged between roughly 4 percent and 12 percent.[57]

As Kenneth Kiple points out in his 1984 text, *The Caribbean Slave*, the intrinsic genetic resistance to malaria enjoyed by sub-Saharan Africans helps to explain the cruel logic driving the Atlantic slave trade of the sixteenth through the nineteenth centuries. Almost as soon as the Americas were discovered, they were colonized by Eurasian and African pathogens, including *vivax* and *falciparum* malaria. These diseases rendered the Caribbean and mainland lowlands of América extremely unhealthy to Europeans, especially Northern Europeans native to areas where *falciparum* is absent; as the Spanish cleric Abbé Raynal argued in the eighteenth century, "of ten men that go into the Islands, [by nationality] four English die; three French; three Dutch; three Danes; and one Spaniard."[58] While European and Amerindian laborers withered in the face of tropical fevers, Africans were observed to be resilient—as Bartolomé de Las Casas observed (rather unkindly) in the sixteenth century, "the only way a black would die [in the Caribbean] would be if they hanged him." The observed superiority of Africans in terms of malaria resistance was, paradoxically, used to support the belief in African racial inferiority. African resistance to fevers, many Europeans believed, was a sign of their descent from "lower animals," and thus the same antimalarial advantages that made sub-Saharan Africans desirable slaves in the tropical lowlands was spun into a justification for their enslavement.[59]

I would argue that the same factors that explained the predominance of sub-Saharan African agricultural labor in Kenneth Kiple's Caribbean can also explain the prevalence of sub-Saharan African agricultural labor in the oasis environments of the Arabian Peninsula. The wadi and other lowland agricultural environments of the Arabian Peninsula, like the tropical lowlands of the Americas, were potentially fertile but highly malarial, discouraging indigenous Arabs from exploiting them directly. At the same time, there was some awareness on the part of the Arabs that sub-Saharan Africans possessed a degree of intrinsic resistance to oasis fevers. Slave traders in Upper Egypt in 1810, for example, told Swiss traveler John Lewis Burckhardt that "Nubian" slaves of sub-Saharan Africa had a reputation for both hard work and a "healthier constitution," suffering "less from disease" compared to slaves of Abyssinian origins.[60] What is more, as mentioned in the last chapter, Arabs of the Hijaz understood that Africans were better able to withstand the rigors of certain fever-prone climates, such as Khaybar. Interestingly, even foreign governments who invaded Arabia recognized that Africans from certain areas were better able to withstand Arabia's climate than others. A Sudanese regiment sent by the Egyptians in 1835 to fight Wahhabi rebels in the Hijaz, for example, suffered an extremely high death toll from disease, which Egyptian ruler Mohammed 'Ali ascribed to the fact that these African soldiers were recruited from mountainous areas. In the future, he told his subordinates, only Africans from "the plain parts of the Sudan" should be sent, presumably because these lowlander Africans were understood to be more resistant to malaria.[61]

Arab popular knowledge about the disease resistance of different African populations may have influenced decisions about the employment of slaves in agriculture in the Arabian Peninsula. In almost all cases, the African agriculturalists described in chapter 2 were identified as of either Sudan or Takruri (West African) origins. More commonly, the servile African agriculturalists were identified simply as "Negroes," a blanket term for sub-Saharan Africans. Slaves of Abyssinian (Galla) origin, however, were rarely if ever employed as agriculturalists according to the literature. To a certain degree, this apparent preference for sub-Saharan African slaves as farmers was a function of their price: male Abyssinian slaves were approximately 30–50 percent more expensive than male sub-Saharan African slaves during the nineteenth century.[62] Not surprisingly, ownership of such expensive slaves brought higher status to their owner, and Arabian Peninsula Arabs usually showed off these slaves by assigning them to be domestic servants, bodyguards, or soldiers. Nonetheless, it is also possible that the preferential use of sub-Saharan slaves in agriculture reflects the marked genetic differences between such slaves and their Abyssinian counterparts. Sudan slaves were captured from a region where the level of Duffy negativity is fairly high, usually between 80 and 100 percent. Takruri slaves hailed from a region of even higher Duffy negativity: in West Africa, rates of Duffy negativity are generally 90 percent or higher. In contrast, in the Horn of Africa region from which Abyssinian slaves were captured, the gene frequency for the Duffy-negative antigen is generally 50–70 percent, which is still high by world standards but is much lower than that of sub-Saharan Africa. Much the same holds true for hemoglobin S. While Takruri and Sudan slaves were native to regions where hemoglobin S levels averaged between 4 and 12 percent, Abyssinian slaves were captured from a region with much lower hemoglobin S frequencies, usually from 0 to 3 percent.[63] This is not to say that Arabian Peninsula slave-buyers were conscious of the genetic differences between Africans of different regional origins. Even without such awareness, however, it is reasonable to assume that the disease resilience of sub-Saharan Africans as compared to their Abyssinian counterparts in Arabian agricultural landscapes would have ensured that those Abyssinians employed in agriculture had a higher mortality rate than slaves from sub-Saharan Africa, no doubt reinforcing an existing Arab tendency to purchase cheaper Sudan and Takruri slaves for agricultural employments.

The small amount of numerical data that is available on slave employments in Arabia reinforces my contention that lower prices and higher disease resistance combined to make sub-Saharan Africans the preferred type of slave for Arabian agriculture. As mentioned in chapter 2, Alaine Hutson found that only 19 percent of all agricultural slaves manumitted in Jeddah were Abyssinian, as compared to 62 percent who were Sudanese.[64] However, I suspect that even these lopsided numbers overestimate the Abyssinian contribution to Arabian servile agriculture. In my own survey of the primary source data, I have not found a single reference to Abyssinian (or Galla) slaves serving as agriculturalists anywhere in the Peninsula. In the few instances where Abyssinians are noted in an oasis town, such as the Galla of Khaybar, they are present in the capacity of soldiers, not farmers. As we saw in chapter 2, when the origins of an African agricultural population are mentioned, they were universally Sudan or Takruri. This apparent contradiction between Hutson's findings and the primary source data may be a reflection of the weakness of Hutson's data set: as Suzanne Miers has pointed out, many of the slaves freed by the British Consulate did not know their own national origins, forcing the Consuls to "guess this from their appearance."[65] There may have also been a conscious or subconscious tendency for sub-Saharan Africans to pass themselves off as Abyssinian at the consulate, since the latter ethnicity had a higher social status in the traditional Arabian Peninsula.

Quantitative Study: African Labors, Distance to Mecca, and Well Depths

As suggested by the evidence above, a link undoubtedly exists between sub-Saharan Africans, agriculture, and malaria in the Arabian Peninsula. So far, however, the evidence provided has been primarily anecdotal. As is clear from chapters 2 and 3, Arabian travelers tended to associate malaria infections with African servile labor, but since no authors entered Arabia with the intention of describing African servile agriculture in any sort of systematic way, their observations were by necessity piecemeal and incomplete.

In order to conduct a more quantitative survey of the linkages between African servile labor and agriculture, I turned to the one data source that provides an encyclopedic approach to the demography of the Arabian Peninsula in the traditional era: the indispensable *Gazetteer of Arabia*. In its pages are recorded two crucial pieces of data: the general location of farming towns, and the sources of water available in those towns, including the depths of any wells present. The latter piece of information is vital in establishing the relative malarial character of these towns, since, as we have seen in the work of Lewis and Daggy, malaria is correlated strongly with open water, shallow wells, and high overall water tables. The *Gazetteer* also mentions, occasionally, the presence of Africans in farming towns, though on this latter point I had to supplement the information from the *Gazetteer* with the travelers' accounts described in chapter 2.

My methodology in conducting this survey was as follows. I chose to examine only the Hijaz and Najd, where our information about African servile labor is particularly rich. For each town listed in these regions in the *Gazetteer*, I plotted that town on a map (map 4.1) as accurately as I could using the 1917 *Arabia: Districts and Towns* map that accompanied the *Gazetteer*, Hunter's 1908 *Map of Arabia*, and if necessary, data from modern atlases and Google Earth. I then recorded the well depth for each village and town in the data sample, a task complicated by the fact that some towns were listed as having wells of various depths and others were

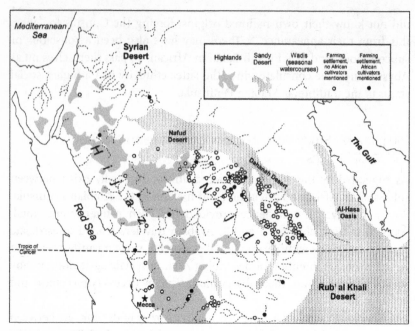

Map 4.1. Well depth survey locations
Source: Gazetteer of Arabia.

watered by both wells and other sources, including springs and qanats. In such cases, I took the average of the highest and lowest well depths, and treated qanats as wells of depth 0. Towns in which no well depths were given were excluded from the study. I then noted whether Africans (not necessarily agriculturalists) were noted in each town, either by the *Gazetteer* or the travelogue literature. This process generated a master list of 172 towns, 16 of which were known to have been at least partially occupied by people of African ancestry. This data sample allows us to test the strength of the correlation between the presence of Africans in a given farming town and the depth of that town's wells, which I am using in this study as a proxy for malaria risk. The same data sample also allows us to test an alternative explanation for the distribution of African agriculturalists within the Arabian Peninsula: distance from Mecca, the commercial center of the African slave trade throughout the period of traditional Arabian history.

Turning first to the distance from Mecca, the data suggest that a given town's proximity to Mecca had relatively little impact on the presence, or absence, of African agriculturalists. The towns in which Africans are attested to in the sources were located at an average distance of approximately 602 kilometers from Mecca, while towns in which Africans are not mentioned were located on average 672 kilometers from Mecca. While on the face of it, this difference in distances seems to support the contention that the distribution of slaves in Arabia might have been influenced by distance from Mecca, the difference between the two means is nowhere near statistically significant, and the same result could have been obtained through any random sampling of sixteen villages about one-fifth of the time.

On the other hand, the correlation between shallow well depth and African agriculturalists is extremely strong. In villages where Africans are attested to either in the *Gazetteer* or the traveler's accounts, the average well depth was 7.2 meters. In areas where African agriculturalists are *not* mentioned, the well depth was much deeper on average: 13.31 meters, nearly twice the depth. Thus shallow wells, and presumably high water tables and more malarial conditions, correlate strongly with the presence of African laborers. This correlation is borne out by a statistical test, which revealed that the difference between well depths in African vs. non-African farming communities is significant to a very high degree ($t = 2.92$), indicating that a similar result could be obtained by random chance only .0025 percent of the time.

Although this correlation between well depth and African labor seems strong, a caveat could be raised: unlike distance from Mecca, which does not change except in geological time, well depth measurements do vary widely depending on the season, the volume of recent rain events, and the perspicacity of the observer. In Qusaibah, for example, the *Gazetteer* notes that the water table falls to 10.6 meters (35 feet) in the summer, but rises to the surface in the winter. Other variations are harder to explain, such as the dramatic increase in the well depth of the northern Najd town of Tabah, where, in 1875, the water level in the wells unexpectedly rose from 46 to 28 meters below the surface and stayed at that level for years afterwards. Not surprisingly, therefore, it was quite common for different observers active at different times to give widely variant results. The wells of Tharmida in Najd, for example, were estimated to be about 6 meters in depth by Leachman in 1912, but 15–18 meters in depth by the *Gazetteer*.[66] I am nonetheless confident that this study relies on enough data points to smooth out, on the aggregate, such statistical irregularities.

AS THIS chapter has repeatedly demonstrated, malaria has played an important role in the history of the Arabian Peninsula, most notably in mediating the relationship between traditional Arabian agriculture and

African servile labor. The Arabian Peninsula has long hosted both *falciparum* and *vivax* malaria, as well as a variety of *Anopheles* mosquito species, including several species (such as *An. arabiensis* and *An. gambiae*) that are highly anthropophilic and thus potent vectors of the disease. Rather than being equally distributed, however, the malaria risk is concentrated in wadis, oases, and other moist lowland landscapes, the same areas that are best suited for agricultural production. If cultivated, the intrinsic malaria problems of these landscapes are exacerbated by elevated water tables and waterlogging, the accumulation of stagnant water, and the creation of backwater swamps, all of which provide breeding habitats for *Anopheles* mosquitoes. Because of fear of disease, fear of jinn, or both, Arabs tended to avoid exploiting these fertile oasis environments directly, especially in areas with high groundwater. Rather, both the Bedouin and urban elites of the Arabian Peninsula, like the European planter class of the Atlantic world of the seventeenth through nineteenth centuries, often employed sub-Saharan African servile laborers endowed with intrinsic defenses against malaria plasmodia infection as proxy farmers in these highly malarial landscapes.

CHAPTER 5

Arabian Agricultural Slavery in the Longue Durée

AS THE previous chapters have amply documented, a system of African servile agriculture persisted in the Arabian Peninsula from at least 1800 into the middle of the twentieth century. But was this system of African slavery primarily a phenomenon of the nineteenth through the early twentieth centuries, or did the roots of this slave system lie deeper? In this chapter I will argue for the latter: While African agricultural slavery did flourish to an exceptional and perhaps unmatched degree in the nineteenth and twentieth centuries, African servile agriculturalists were almost certainly present in some numbers in earlier centuries in the Arabian Peninsula. In making this case, I will rely heavily on three sources of data: documentation of the "Oriental" slave trade, ethnographic studies of specific Arabian Peninsula rural populations, and genetic evidence. While the evidence from each of these sources is somewhat circumstantial, taken together they suggest that African slave colonies are a very old phenomenon in the Arabian Peninsula, though also an ephemeral one, as individual colonies have repeatedly disappeared due to assimilation into mainstream Arabian Peninsula society.

While the antiquity of African agricultural slavery in the Arabian Peninsula is a matter of some conjecture, we are on more solid ground when discussing the reasons for the abandonment of African servile agriculture in the twentieth century. Simply put, African agricultural slavery disappeared in the mid-1900s when the three pillars that sustained the system—cheap slaves, labor-intensive agricultural technology, and the risk of malaria—were no longer factors in Arabian agriculture. As a result of the decline of the slave trade, the importation of tube wells and other knowledge-intensive agricultural practices, and the gradual diminution of the malaria threat in the Arabian Peninsula, African slaves and servile laborers ceased to play a significant part in Arabian Peninsula agriculture by the middle of the twentieth century.

Problems with Traditional Sources

When conducting any historical investigation, historians generally prefer to work with archival data and with historical texts composed in and about the region. When it comes to the question of the antiquity of African agricultural slavery in the Arabian Peninsula, however, such materials are of little help. Due to the lack of large-scale, bureaucratic political structures, archival materials on the Arabian Peninsula are almost entirely lacking, except for some records produced during the fleeting moments when the Ottoman Empire was able to exert meaningful control over parts of the Peninsula. What is more, the Arabian Peninsula, in contrast to the Arab world as a whole, has produced relatively few native historians or chroniclers. Worse yet, from the standpoint of environmental history, the value of those historical documents that do exist is compromised by the pervasive urban bias of Arab elites, who wrote "little about non-elites in general and rural non-elites in particular," and for whom slavery was a matter of course rather than a subject worthy of comment.[1] The histories of the Arabian Peninsula that do exist are predominantly interested in religious and political affairs, not social or economic structures. Consider for example three of the most important Arabic sources on the early Saudi state, 'Uthman Ibn Bishr an-Najdi's *Tarikh Najd* [The History of Najd], Hussain Ibn Ghannam's *Tarikh Najd*, and the anonymously written *Kitab lam' al-shihab fi sirat Muhammad ibn 'Abd al-Wahhab* [The Book of the Brilliance of the Meteor in Mohammed ibn Abd al-Wahhab's Life]. All three are essentially biographies of the Wahhab, the religious reformer who gave his name to the Wahhabi movement, rather than histories in the classic sense, and while slaves appear occasionally in these texts, they are almost always combatants or victims in the warfare that accompanied the rise of the Saudi state.[2] These texts tell us next to nothing about Arabian agriculture in general, and nothing whatsoever about the phenomenon of African servile agriculture that is the specific subject of this book.

What is more, I also have found Arabic-language geographical texts and traveler's tales to be of little use in reconstructing the antiquity of African agricultural slavery in the Arabian Peninsula. The authors of these geographical texts, like Arab historians, tended to take slavery for granted, were uninterested in agriculture, and what is more prioritized the past rather than the present in their studies, drawing frequent connections to the time of the Prophet rather than presenting the modern-day status of the areas they described. Al-Muqaddasi's classic tenth-century world geography, *Ahsan al-Taqasim fi Ma'rifat al-Aqalim* [The Best Divisions for the Knowledge of the World], for example, begins its discussion of the Arabian Peninsula by noting that Arabia is the land of "the Sacred House of God, as also the City of the Prophet," and includes four pages of description of the *Kaba* and the pilgrimage rites. Nonetheless, while it does mention the existence of cultivated fields in some areas, and does acknowledge the frequency of fevers in some of the same areas (such as the vicinity of Medina), it has nothing to say as to who is doing the agricultural labor. In the thirty-seven pages dealing with the Arabian Peninsula, he mentions slavery only once, noting that Abyssinian slaves are one of the many goods traded in the southern Yemeni trading emporium of Aden. People of African ancestry are mentioned twice: he notes (based on a tradition of Abu- al-Fadlh bin Nahama of Shiraz) that in the Hijaz "there are many Blacks," and (more ambiguously) that the people of Hadramaut are "quite dark" in skin color.[3] Other Arab geographers are even less helpful. In his thirteenth-century world geography, Yaqut gives a detailed description of the Prophet's role in the siege of Khaybar's seven forts, but has nothing to say about either agricultural labor or slavery in Khaybar, despite the fact that Yaqut himself was a former slave of Greek origins.[4] Yaqut's description of Khaybar is in fact typical of his treatment of the Arabian Peninsula as a whole: while he does occasionally make note of palm trees and water sources, he obviously has little interest in either agriculture in general or agricultural labor in particular.

The work of Islamic travelers in the Arabian Peninsula is equally unhelpful, though with one notable exception. By and large, Islamic travelers into the Arabian Peninsula, who include al-Mujawir, Ibn al-Wardi, Ibn Jubayr, Nasir-I Khusraw, Ibn Tayyib, and Ibn Battuta, entered the peninsula in order to perform the Hajj, and in general strayed little from the well-trodden pilgrim's paths. What is more, while they are appreciative of the occasional patches of greenery they encountered along the way in the Arabian Peninsula, as a rule they displayed an urban elite's disdain for farmers and agricultural labor. Case in point is Ibn Tayyib, an eighteenth-century Moroccan traveler, who during his pilgrimage twice passed through the Wadi Safra of western Hijaz. Like T. E. Lawrence, whose description of the Wadi Safra was given in chapter 2, Ibn Tayyib is appreciative of its agricultural fertility: "We passed by al-Safra' and saw fruit orchards, gardens and running springs. All types of fruit are grown there, including dates, bananas, and melons. There is also a mosque."[5] Unlike Lawrence, however, Ibn Tayyib has nothing to say about the agricultural laborers that maintained the orchards and gardens, either in the Wadi Safra or elsewhere. Indeed, the only reference to agricultural labor I found in his entire text is the exception that proves the rule. Upon returning to Cairo after his pilgrimage, Ibn Tayyib and his companions attempted to sleep for the night in Cairo's Sindyun mosque, but were unable to do so "because it was full of farmers and uncivilized people."[6] If not for this inconvenience, neither farmers nor any other "uncivilized people" would have made it into Ibn Tayyib's text at all.

The only traveler's account that does give any substantial details concerning African agricultural slavery in Arabia is that of Nasir-I Khusraw, a Persian traveler and Shi'ite religious missionary who performed the Hajj four different times in the mid-eleventh century. When Khusraw finally decided to return to Persia, he eschewed the normal pilgrimage route and set out instead on what would prove to be a harrowing desert journey that took him through the eastern Hijaz, Najd, and Eastern Arabia. He eventually reached the al-Hasa oasis, where he found "thirty thousand Zanzibari and Abyssinian slaves working in the fields and orchards" of the rulers, who were of the Isma'ili Shi'ite sect.[7] Unfortunately, Khusraw's account is the only explicit historical reference concerning servile African agriculture in the Arabian Peninsula I have been able to discover for the entire premodern period. Indeed, African agricultural slavery in Arabia would not reemerge into the light of written history until British naval officer J. R. Wellsted began to survey the Red Sea coast of Arabia in the 1830s, almost a millennium after Khusraw's difficult journey from Mecca to al-Hasa.

Thus, when attempting to reconstruct the antiquity and scale of African agricultural slavery in the Arabian Peninsula, neither European nor Arabic historical and travel sources are of much help. Rather, I have had to turn to three untraditional sources that offer possible solutions to the puzzle: surveys of the changing scale of the Indian Ocean slave trade over time, ethnographic information concerning specific Arabian Peninsula agricultural groups, and genetic evidence, most notably studies of Arabian Peninsula Y-chromosome and mitochondrial DNA haplotypes. None of these sources are ideal, but as always, the study of Arabian Peninsula history obliges one to be as flexible and creative as possible with the relatively small amount of available evidence. The next three sections will consider the evidence from each of these data sources in turn.

The "Oriental" Slave Trade: Stability and Fluctuations

One way to measure the antiquity of agricultural slavery in the Arabian Peninsula is through logical inference. Based on information presented in the previous chapters, particularly chapters 1 and 4, I would argue that three crucial factors sustained the system of African agricultural slavery in nineteenth- through twentieth-century Arabia: (1) the highly malarial nature of Arabian agricultural landscapes, (2) the technologically unsophisticated, labor-intensive methods utilized for Arabian agriculture, and (3) the widespread availability of African slaves. It stands to reason, therefore, that the same factors that favored African agricultural slavery in the nineteenth and early twentieth centuries would also have favored it in the past, since these factors are necessary (though by no means sufficient) conditions for the existence of Arabian Peninsula African servile agriculture.

Of these three factors, two—the malarial nature of the landscape, and the unsophisticated, labor-intensive nature of the farming technology—were clearly constants throughout traditional Arabian history. As discussed by Potts and Varisco in chapter 1, Arabian bustan gardening and other agricultural systems changed very little over time, and genetic evidence suggests that these agricultural systems were highly malarial, and thus selected for malaria-protective genetic traits, since "early antiquity."[8] It may very well be that climate fluctuations over time influenced Arabian Peninsula agriculture. In periods of greater or lesser moisture, the area suitable to oasis agriculture would have increased or decreased accordingly, mainly as a result of changes in the groundwater level. This process is well documented elsewhere in the Arab world, such as in Syria and Palestine, which suffered from devastating tenth-century famines due to environmental fluctuations.[9] Recent works by Sam White and Alan Mikhail describe similar interactions between climate and human history in the Ottoman Empire and Egypt, respectively.[10] Most of the work conducted so far on climate change in the Arabian Peninsula, however, deals primarily with the prehistoric and early historic period, and focuses on long-term movements of the monsoon line rather than shorter-term climate fluctuations in more recent periods.[11] This focus on paleoclimate is probably a reflection of the lack of Arabian Peninsula trees that are suitable candidates for dendrochronology, the best tool available to paleoclimatologists studying shorter-term climate fluctuations. It also reflects the paucity of indigenous written records in the Arabian Peninsula: there are no Arabian equivalents to the monastic chronicles, grain price records, and meticulously kept diaries that have been used by climate scholars to chart weather fluctuations during Europe's Little Ice Age.[12] Thus, while in principle it cannot be doubted that climate fluctuations had an impact on Arabian Peninsula agriculture, it is impossible to say exactly what that impact might have been, and the little evidence currently available suggests overall continuity rather than discontinuity was the norm in Arabian agricultural systems.

The third factor—the ready availability of African slaves—is more open to question. From the standpoint of slave numbers, the nineteenth- to early twentieth-century era we have studied in the previous chapters was anything but typical. This period coincided with a golden age in "Oriental" slavery, the term used by Manning and others for slavery in the Old World, as opposed to the Western slave systems of the New World's European colonies. Indeed, the decline of the latter almost certainly led to a dramatic spike in the former, as existing slave trading networks reoriented themselves to the MENA (Middle East and North Africa) region following the progressive abolition of slavery and the slave trade in the Atlantic World. According to Patrick Manning, slave exports into the MENA region, which included the Arabian Peninsula, rose from about sixteen thousand to seventeen thousand a year c. 1800 to over forty thousand per year four decades later, and slave imports into MENA countries stayed above eighteenth-century levels until the 1880s, after which slave exports declined sharply, largely due to European colonization of Africa and the gradual suppression of slavery institutions within Africa itself.[13] Manning's data, therefore, suggest that the scale of African agricultural slavery in the 1800–1950 period was exceptional, and may reflect an anomalously high level of slave availability during that period.

That being said, the change in the MENA region's slave imports in the nineteenth century on one hand, and the pre-1800 period on the other, is one of degree rather than absolute difference. Data concerning the scale of the slave trade before 1800 are extremely speculative, in part because trans-Saharan and Indian Ocean slave traders left few written records and much of the information that does exist is, in the words of Edward A. Alpers, "haphazard" and "fragmentary."[14] Nonetheless, Paul Lovejoy has estimated that on average, 5,000 Sudan Africans a year entered the MENA region via the trans-Saharan slave trade from 650–1600 CE, with a high point of 8,700 per year in the period from 900–1100 CE.[15] What is more, on average, another 3,000 slaves entered the Middle East via the Indian Ocean and Red Sea coast in the years 800–1600 CE. As is clear from figure 5.1, which overlays Lovejoy's and Manning's statistics for the slave trade in the MENA region, this total trade of 8,000 slaves per year from 800–1600 CE is a far cry from the 40,000 or more slaves imported annually into the MENA region from the 1830s to the 1860s. Additionally, only a small fraction of these 8,000 slaves would have been sold to the Arabian

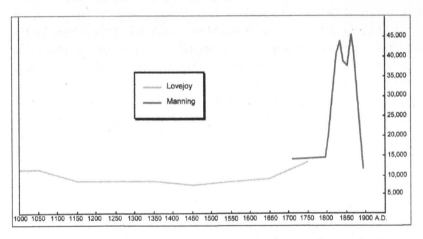

Figure 5.1. Average annual slave imports from trans-Sahara, Red Sea, and Indian Ocean trade, 1000–1900 CE

Sources: Paul E. Lovejoy, *Transformations in Slavery: A History of Slavery in Africa*, 2nd ed. (New York: Cambridge University Press, 2000), 26, 62; Patrick Manning, *Slavery and African Life: Occidental, Oriental, and African Slave Trades* (New York: Cambridge University Press, 1990), 83.

Peninsula, and only a fraction of those slaves, in turn, would have been employed as agriculturalists.[16] Although this steady trickle of slaves might have been harnessed to Arabian agriculture to some degree, the scale of such slave systems would have been far below that observed in the nine-teenth and early twentieth centuries.

That being said, it is difficult to reconcile Lovejoy's steady trickle of Sudan and East African slaves with some of the available evidence con-cerning agricultural slavery in the pre-modern Middle East. Consider for example the 30,000 Zanzibari slaves described by Khusraw in the eleventh-century al-Hasa oasis. Khusraw almost certainly exaggerated about the number of slaves, but even if the number was only a tenth as large, it is difficult to imagine how a population of even 3,000 slaves could have been built up and sustained in one relatively remote corner of the Arab world if the annual importation rate for African slaves into the entirety of that world was only 8,000 per year. Nor is the al-Hasa slave community unique. In the ninth century, large numbers of Zanj—African slaves—were employed in the marshes of lower Iraq to remove the natron-impregnated upper layer of the soil, pile it in heaps "as large as mountains," and establish vast sugarcane plantations on the reclaimed soil underneath. The Arab his-torian al-Tabari estimates their numbers at 15,000, and, unlike Khusraw's estimate, this was probably not an exaggeration: when the Zanj rebelled, they formed the core of a military force strong enough to sack the major city of Basra in 872 CE, and it would ultimately take fifteen years for the Abbasid state to fully suppress the Zanj rebellion, though this reflects the difficult (and almost certainly malarial) terrain of lower Iraq as much as the numbers and fighting prowess of the Zanj themselves.[17]

These short-term concentrations of slave numbers in a longue durée characterized by modest annual slave imports suggest that Lovejoy's statis-tics probably conceal dramatic and important short-term variations caused by war, drought, or increases in demand. Such fluctuations are clearly attested to in the eighteenth to twentieth centuries, a period in which some meager western documentation concerning the slave trade in the MENA region does exist. Lovejoy, for example, argues that horrific African fam-ines of the eighteenth century led to short-term spikes in slave exports due to the sale of children by hungry parents and even self-enslavement by Africans seeking to escape starvation.[18] Similarly, a devastating fam-ine that struck East Africa in the mid-1880s led to another pulse of cheap slaves flooding the market, as desperate people sold their "neighbors, their children, and even themselves in order to survive."[19] Other fluctuations in slave numbers had political causes. Between 1883 and 1885, for example, warfare in the Sudan disrupted overland travel, leading to a sharp decline in Sudan slaves and a smaller decline in the availability of slaves from Abyssinia.[20] Following the victory of the Sudanese Mahdi, however, the slave trade flourished anew, leading to a short-term spike in the late 1880s of slave numbers and a sharp drop in prices.[21] In addition, the market for agricultural slaves was in some cases affected by the commodity prices of the crop they cultivated. During the nineteenth century, the price of slaves in the Indian Ocean was strongly influenced by the current market price of cloves, which were grown and harvested in the Zanzibar and Pemba islands almost entirely by slave labor. The spike in slave imports into Egypt during the 1860s, was, in turn, driven largely by increases in cotton prices as a result of the American Civil War: according to Kenneth M. Cuno, Egypt may have imported between twenty-five thousand and thirty thousand slaves a year during the cotton boom.[22] Similarly, in Oman and the Gulf states, slave imports were closely linked to the current market prices of Gulf pearls, which slaves were often employed to harvest.[23]

Slave prices and numbers, therefore, were probably far more variable than Lovejoy's flat figures would have us believe. If this is true, it stands to reason that African agricultural colonies in Arabia would have been an intermittent phenomenon, established during occasional periods of high slave availability and corresponding low prices. But what would have happened to these African colonies when slave prices rose once again due to a decrease in supply?

Ethnographic Data on Arabian Agriculturalists: Slavery and Assimilation

In the Arabian Peninsula proper, the limitations of the available sources do not allow us to link the fate of any particular African colony with any particular pulse of surplus or decline in the international slave market. However, the example of Zanzibar in the nineteenth century does provide us with an interesting and perhaps instructive parallel. Prior to the mid-nineteenth century, the Omani-dominated island of Zanzibar served primarily as a trade entrepôt, a middle point for long-distance commodity exchanges, including slaves. By the 1860s, however, Zanzibar had retooled itself into a plantation economy, and thanks to the toil of its one hundred thousand to two hundred thousand African slaves, Zanzibar had become the most important exporters of cloves in the world.[24] According to Janet J.

Ewald, the crucial element of this transformation was the mid-nineteenth-century spike in slave availability, which created a new set of economic opportunities for Zanzibar's Omani elites.[25] Ewald argues that this increase in slave numbers was a side effect of increased slave raiding by the Egyptian and Ethiopian states at that time, but as we have already seen, the overall increase in slave supply that made Zanzibar's plantations possible also reflects the closure of the Atlantic slave trade and the redirection of slaves to the MENA region markets in the nineteenth century. In any case, based on manumission statistics, it appears that male slaves slightly outnumbered female slaves in Zanzibar, most likely because male slaves were cheaper and better suited to hard agricultural labor.[26]

The decline of Indian Ocean slave markets after the 1880s, at a time when British control over Zanzibar and German control over the adjacent mainland area was progressively choking off the slave supply, gradually but profoundly changed the character of Zanzibar's African servile population. Over time, the number of first-generation slaves from the interior, or *mtumwa mjinga*, shrank as a proportion of the slave population, while *mzalia*, or Africans born within the Swahili coast, grew in number. These mzalia generally became acculturated to Swahili coast traditions, embraced Islam, and even became Qu'ranic teachers or pilgrims to Mecca. Trusted mzalia slaves often rose to some positions of power either as overseers on plantations or as elected heads of villages "containing slaves owned by various masters."[27] In addition, as the supply of slaves was shut down, a growing proportion of the African servile population became free, since manumission of slaves by their masters was a common occurrence. As in Arabian society, however, freed slaves remained clients of their masters, who retained some legal rights over his or her former slave's property and had some claim on the freed slave's labor.[28] The clear overall trend is from a shift away from slave agriculture using mtumwa mjinga, and toward a system of servile agriculture, in which agricultural labor was carried out by a mixture of slave and freed Africans who were increasingly assimilated into the dominant Swahili culture.

The applicability of Zanzibar's example to agricultural slavery in the Arabian Peninsula is, of course, limited by a number of factors. Zanzibar's plantations were geared for market production, feeding an international demand for cloves, and in Zanzibar, people of African ancestry far outnumbered those of Arab ancestry. Furthermore, plantation owners in Zanzibar were able to oversee the labor of their servile African laborers far more efficiently than owners in the Arabian Peninsula, especially Bedouin owners, whose migratory lifestyle obliged them to spend most of the year in distant pastures. In addition, it is possible that the shift away from slave labor over time in Zanzibar had as much to do with the sharp decline of clove prices in the late nineteenth century as it did with the decline of slave availability during the same period.

Nonetheless, I would speculate that the example of nineteenth-century Zanzibar's clove plantations does help us understand the rise and decline of specific African slave colonies in the Arabian Peninsula. These colonies, like the plantations of Zanzibar, would have been founded when fluctuations in slave availability led to a glut of slaves available on the market. During such periods, Arabian Peninsula urban and Bedouin elites probably took advantage of the temporarily lowered slave prices and higher availability to acquire large numbers of slaves for agricultural purposes in the wadi environments of Arabia. The preferred slaves for this purpose were most likely male Sudan slaves, who were cheap, physically strong, and resistant to *falciparum* and *vivax* malaria.[29] So long as slave prices remained cheap, annual losses in slave numbers were made up with new purchases, and the relative lack of economically unproductive children in these African slave communities would have allowed maximum exploitation of African labor.

However, once slave prices rose, the cost of replacing existing agricultural slaves with new ones brought from the interior would have become prohibitive. Since these African servile communities would no longer have been sustained from outside, the only way to acquire more labor was through natural population growth of the servile population. This would have encouraged the manumission of slaves, since transferring a slave to mawla status would not only have been religiously beneficial to the slave owner, it would have allowed Arabian Bedouins and townsmen to avoid the direct costs of raising slave children, while at the same time allowing former owners continued access to the mawla's labor. What is more, since mortality rates in the unhealthy oasis environments would have remained high, Africans would likely have declined as a proportion of the oasis population, and Bedouin desert bankrupts and other relatively poor or low-status Arabs would have gravitated into the oasis environments in search of subsistence.[30] Taken together, these processes would have strongly influenced the culture and demographics of the former African colonies: the population would have become increasingly heterozygous, and locally born slaves and freedmen assimilated into Arab culture (the Arab equivalent of Zanzibari mzalia) would have come to predominate over first-generation African slaves.

Over time, the increasing assimilation and growing autonomy of these former African colonies would have led to profound changes in economic and social conditions. Direct supervision of African agricultural labor, which was never very practical in the Arabian Peninsula to begin with due to malaria risks and Bedouin transhumance, gave way over time to "squatter" or sharecropping systems, allowing servile Africans to produce a surplus for their owners while at the same time retaining enough to ensure their own survival and reproduction.[31] This process would no doubt have been furthered by active resistance of the slaves themselves against exploitation, and this resistance would undoubtedly have become more and more effective as the assimilating African agriculturalists became increasingly savvy concerning Arabian Peninsula cultural and political norms. In time, these African servile communities would even begin to intermarry with the surrounding Arab population, especially with low-status desert bankrupts and other marginalized Arab groups. By the end of this process, African slave colonies sustained by imports would have transformed themselves into subordinate but autonomous farming communities, sustained by local population growth as well as exogamous marriages with neighboring Arab groups, and distinguishable from other Arabian Peninsula farming towns only by the social stigma of African or servile ancestry.

The two paragraphs above are meant as a hypothetical explanatory model, based on the Zanzibari example as well as observations from the Arabian Peninsula ethnographic record, rather than statements of facts applicable to all places and times. Nonetheless, the degree to which this model approximates the reality of the Arabian Peninsula social situation is testable. If true, we would expect the Arabian Peninsula at any given point of time to contain servile groups at different stages in the assimilation process, from pure slave colonies to semi-free sharecropping settlements to fully autonomous settlements of some slave ancestry, each created by a different historical pulse in slave availability. And indeed, for the period of the nineteenth and early twentieth centuries described by the travelogue sources, this seems to be the case.

On one end of the spectrum are the Nakhawila, a Shi'ite community living in the palm gardens of Medina. In the nineteenth and twentieth centuries, the Nakhawila were predominantly "tenant farmers or farm laborers" who worked on the lands of others, principally the Sunni nobles of Medina, the powerful eunuch slaves who were custodians of the Prophet's Mosque in Medina, and the Bedouin Harb tribe. According to the eighteenth-century Medinan historian 'Abd al-Rahman al-Ansari, the Nakhawila were already an old community in the 1780s, and may date back as far back as the time of Yazid, who ruled the Umayyad state 680–83 CE. While al-Ansari ascribes their origins to rapes carried out by Yazid's troops during his sack of Medina, he also presents a more plausible origin story: that the Nakhawila have mixed racial origins, and are the result of intermarriage between Africans, who were brought into Medina's notoriously malarial palm groves as farmers, and Arabs, quite possibly lower-status Arabs drawn to Medina by poverty, pilgrimage, or both. Indeed, Werner Ende, who studied the Nakhawila in the 1980s, notes that the real Nakhawila—"the peasants, farmhands, gardeners, herdsmen, and workers of different trades living in the palm groves near Medina"—all share a "comparatively dark complexion."[32] The African ancestry of the Nakhawila is also attested to by genetic studies: Medina is "one of the major pockets of the sickle-cell gene" in the Arabian Peninsula, as might be expected of a region with significant and long-standing demographic ties to sub-Saharan Africa.[33] Nonetheless, Ende stresses that the "core of [the Nakhawila] community as it exists today has deep roots in the Hijaz and is basically of Arab origin."[34]

Much the same could be said of several other long-established agricultural populations of the Arabian Peninsula. As discussed in the last chapter, the Hasawiyah of the al-Hasa oasis also carry with them a set of antimalarial genes of sub-Saharan African origin which they likely inherited from the African slaves imported into al-Hasa in or before the tenth century. Indeed, in a 1976 study, medical researchers Gelpi and King found that 53 percent the population of al-Hasa was Duffy negative, and 25 percent of the population carried the sickle-cell trait.[35] This rate of sickle-cell trait, it should be noted, is even higher than that found in most areas of sub-Saharan Africa, and this probably reflects the high α-thalassemia rates in the al-Hasa population, since α-thalassemia has been shown clinically to reduce cell sickling in hemoglobin S patients and thus ameliorate the severity of sickle-cell disease.[36]

Another long-standing Arabian agricultural population with African roots was the Bani Khadhir, a large tribe scattered throughout the province of Najd. Although not as well studied as the Hasawiyah, who happened to live in the midst of ARAMCO's oil extraction operations, the small amount of data that exist suggest the Bani Khadhir were of mixed African Arab origins, the result of marriages between African tenants in the oasis gardens and low-status Arabs. Indeed, the term *Bani Khadhir* literally means "sons of the green one," which, according to British traveler Palgrave, was a reference to their intermediate skin tone, as "the colors green, black, and brown, are habitually confused in Arabic parlance." Palgrave notes that although the Bani Khadhir on the whole were of lower status, and did not "readily take their place among the nobles or upper ten thousand," their assimilated ancestors

> may end up doing even this in the process of time; and I have myself while in Arabia been honored by the intimacy of more than one handsome 'Green-man', with a silver-hilted sword at his side, and a rich dress on his dusky skin, but denominated Sheykh or Emeer [Emir], and humbly sued by Arabs of the purest . . . pedigree.[37]

Philby, on the other hand, describes the Bani Khadhir more prosaically as "of lower status than the true Arab folk of tribal descent," but notes that the Bani Khadhir, like the Nakhawila, considered themselves as true Arabs and "would be insulted by any suggestion of their slave origin."[38] The Bayasirah of Oman, an inferior social group of probable mixed African Arab origins, could perhaps be added to this list as well, though it is less clear that the Bayasirah caste was rooted in agricultural labor.[39]

While the Nakhawila, Hasawiyah, and Bani Khadhir were on one end of the spectrum, the African colony of the Wadi Safra, as described in chapter 2, is a clear example of the opposite end. According to Lawrence, the Wadi Safra was cultivated by African slaves, many of them of Takruri origin, though the slave population was already by Lawrence's day being thinned by manumission. These slaves were the property of tribesmen of the Harb, a Bedouin group that the British suspected to be involved in smuggling slaves into the Arabian Peninsula. Although the villages of the Wadi Safra had some autonomy by virtue of the nomadic lifeways of their Harb owners, who only occupied the wadi a few months of the year, the Wadi Safra Africans were clearly dependents of the Harb in both an economic and political sense, and there is no hint of any intermarriage between the Wadi Safra's Africans and the surrounding Arab tribes. Much the same was true of the Khaybara, as described in chapter 3, though the Khaybara seem to have been slightly farther along the road toward assimilation into Arabian society. Like the Africans of the Wadi Safra, the Khaybara included a number of recently enslaved Africans, though manumitted slaves and second- or third-generation Africans seem to have been the majority, and these Africans only rarely intermarried with Arabs. As in the Wadi Safra, the Khaybara enjoyed little political autonomy and

were tied economically to the dominant Bedouin tribes, who traditionally enjoyed a large share of the fruits of the Khaybara's labor. In addition,
the Khaybara, and presumably the Wadi Safra Africans as well, retained a
number of distinctive African cultural traditions that set them apart from
the mainstream Arab population. Thus, both the Wadi Safra and Khaybar
are typical African colonies, unassimilated or only partially assimilated
into wider Arabian Peninsula society, and are almost certainly of relatively
recent origins, though of course as we saw in chapter 3 Khaybar itself is
quite an old town.

Other nineteenth- and early twentieth-century farming groups of
clear African descent are of a more intermediate age. One such group is the
'Alowna, the inhabitants of the town of al-'Ula in northern Hijaz.[40] Al-'Ula
is primarily an agricultural town, famous for its springs, high water table,
good quality dates, and its fevers. Charles Huber notes that all visitors to
al-'Ula were expected to fall ill of fever, though the 'Alowna themselves did
"not feel the effects" of fever, or "if they [did] feel them, it [was] only to a
lesser degree."[41] Not surprisingly, given the malarial nature of the landscape, the 'Alowna were dark-skinned, "infected," in the racist thinking of
Charles Doughty, "with negro blood." Charles Huber tried to evaluate the
exact racial mixture in al-'Ula using a method outlined in the *Instructions
generals de la Société d'anthropologie de Paris*, and although such descriptions tell us more about nineteenth-century thoughts about race than the
people described, it is worth noting that, while he found the average skin
color in al-'Ula too light for the 'Alowna to be considered "properly black,"
he does note that the 'Alowna had a typically African "underbite." Huber
also notes that the lighter-skinned 'Alowna, who formed "the aristocracy
of the region," sometimes intermarried with surrounding Bedouin groups
including the 'Anaza tribe.[42] It should be noted that the 'Alowna community
was autonomous and self-governing, and while al-'Ula was subjected to
Bedouin raids, the 'Alowna (unlike the Khaybara) were apparently not subordinate sharecroppers of the surrounding Bedouin tribes, though some
powerful tribal chiefs did have large-scale land holdings in the town.[43]

Another partially assimilated African group of intermediate age is was
the Mutawalladeen of northern Hijaz. According to Wallin, who traveled
throughout the region in the 1840s, the Mutawalladeen were mawlas of
African origins who served mainly as agriculturalists in northern Hijaz,
though some followed the same pastoralist lifestyle as their former Bedouin owners, to whom "they generally remain attached from a feeling of
respect and gratitude." Although free, the Mutawalladeen nonetheless bore

the stigma of their African ancestry, and as a result the Bedouins "seldom, if ever condescend to take [one of the Mutawalladeen]" for a wife. However, "with the people in fixed abodes [the hadr] the feeling in favor of propagating a pure race is not so strong, and the [Mutawalladeen] in the towns and villages mix and intermarry with Arabs, and the children are produced in whose features it is often quite impossible to recognize the African type."[44] According to Charles Doughty, the same process was also underway in the Harrat Khaybar village of Hayat, where the predominantly African farmers "are become a whiter people of late years" due to intermarriage with poor Arab women of the relatively low-status Hataim and Juhainah Bedouin tribes.

The mini-histories of Arabian Peninsula agricultural populations given above are by necessity somewhat vague, as would be expected in a society where written records were nonexistent and genealogy was in any case highly contested. Nonetheless, taken together, they strongly, if indirectly, support the notion that the employment of African slaves in Arabian agricultural landscapes is of considerable pedigree. Even undeniably "Arab" populations, such as the Nakhawila and Hasawiyah, can ultimately trace at least a portion their ancestry—as well as their genetic resistance to malaria—to African agricultural populations established within Arabia in the distant past.

Arabian Peninsula Haplotypes: Y-Chromosome vs. Mitochondrial DNA

A third and final body of evidence concerning the Africa presence in the Arabian Peninsula is provided by recent studies of African haplotypes, distinctive genetic markers that can be used to trace the genetic origins of a particular population. In recent years, a number of haplotype studies of Arabian populations have been published in order to test two rival theories of human migrations out of the Arabian peninsula, one positing that Africans entered Eurasia via Egypt and the Sinai, the other arguing that they might instead have passed through the narrow Bab al-Mandab strait that separates Yemen from the horn of Africa.[45] These studies offer three main benefits to researchers of African agricultural slavery in the Arabian Peninsula. First, these studies allow us to quantify the overall African contribution to the modern Arabian Peninsula gene pool. Secondly, researchers have used these data to estimate when this genetic exchange began, which is of obvious relevance to the present study. Lastly, and most intriguingly, these data allow us to compare the relative female vs. male contribution from Africa to Arabian Peninsula genetics. This last point is of particular importance to the study of African agricultural slavery, as female and male slaves served somewhat different functions in Arabian slave systems, with female slaves being more commonly employed in domestic servitude and concubinage, while cheaper male slaves were more likely to be employed in tasks requiring crude physical labor, such as military service or agriculture. Male slaves were also employed as eunuchs, though for obvious reasons their genetic contribution to the Peninsula was nil and they can be discounted for the purposes of the present study.

Before delving into the data, a few words about the methodologies employed by the researchers are in order. Scientists who study haplotypes cannot employ regular DNA for this purpose, as the process of meiosis means such DNA is being rapidly swapped, transcripted, and randomized over time, making it too unstable to be useful to trace human ancestry. As a result, scientists seeking to trace human origins tend to study Y-chromosome DNA and mitochondrial DNA. Y-chromosomes are carried only by males, and unlike regular chromosomes (including the X-chromosome), they do not undergo meiosis, meaning that they do not split apart and recombine with other DNA during cell division. This means that Y-chromosomes change very slowly in relation to other DNA, and are therefore more useful as a source of haplotype markers. Mitochondrial DNA, in turn, is the DNA of our mitochondria, which are small organelles located with each cell in the body. Mitochondrial DNA does undergo meiosis, but only with itself, meaning that changes occur mainly by mutation. As a result, mitochondrial DNA is also very useful to researchers seeking to identify haplotype markers and trace the origins of human populations. Unlike Y-chromosome DNA, which by definition comes only from the father, all human mitochondrial DNA comes from the ova of the mother, since sperm mitochondria are lost during the fertilization process.

Using this mitochondrial DNA, medical researchers have come to a number of conclusions concerning the African contribution to Arabian Peninsula genetics. One is the age of these genetic exchanges. According to a 2003 study by Martin Richards and colleagues, large-scale gene flows out of Africa, at least for mitochondrial DNA, date back as far as 500 BCE.[46] Does this mean that African slavery in Arabia began around that date? Not necessarily. The slave trade was not the only route which could have carried these African genes into Arabia, after all. Some Africans came to Arabia not as slaves, but as conquerors, such as the Abyssinian troops who intervened in Yemen from the end of the second century to the later third century and then annexed Yemen in the sixth century CE.[47] What is more, the Tihamah coastal plain, which from the standpoint of climate and geology is an extension of Africa into the Arabian Peninsula, has long contained a free population of Africans whose ancestors probably crossed the Red Sea as voluntary migrants rather than slaves. Complicating matters further, the free Africans of Tihamah were themselves later tapped as a source of supply for the slave trade, presumably through the kidnapping of individual Africans or the sale of children by their parents.[48] The mere presence of numerous African haplotypes in a population, therefore, does not by itself prove the existence or the antiquity of the slavery in that population.

A more convincing argument for the antiquity of slavery in the Arabian Peninsula, at least in the opinion of some medical researchers, is provided by a comparison of Y-chromosome and mitochondrial DNA haplotypes in modern Arabian populations. As can be seen in figure 5.2, nations in and around the Arabian Peninsula all have substantial sub-Saharan African contributions to their gene pool. This is especially true in terms of mitochondrial DNA: in the countries listed in figure 5.2, African haplotypes accounted for 15.3 percent of all haplotypes in the region. The Y-chromosome DNA contribution from Africa, in contrast, appears on average to be much more modest: about 5.9 percent, roughly a third of the genetic contribution attested to in the mitochondrial DNA.

According to some researchers, this apparent disparity between the Y-chromosome and mitochondrial DNA evidence attests to the strong impact of the African slave trade on Arabian Peninsula genetics. Martin Richards and colleagues have argued that "the most likely explanation of predominantly female lineages of African origin . . . is that these trace back to women brought from Africa as part of the Arab slave trade, assimilated into the Arab population as a result of miscegenation and manumission."

	Yemen	Jordan	Egypt	Iraq	Qatar	Oman	Palestine	Syria	Saudi Arabia
Mitochondrial DNA haplotypes of African origin	37	12	22	9	Not available	Not available	14	7	7
Y-Chromosome DNA haplotypes of African origin	6.46	.68	7	.99	5.56	7	Not available	Not available	13.37

Figure 5.2. Y-chromosome vs. mitochondrial DNA haplotypes of African origin in Saudi Arabia and surrounding Arab populations

African women, these researchers hold, were more likely to transmit their genes to future generations since women "were imported specifically for the sexual gratification of male elites and for their reproductive potential." In contrast, the paucity of Y-chromosome haplotypes in Arab populations is explained by the fact that "relatively few men—mainly employed in manual labor and military service or castrated and employed as eunuchs—left descendants."[49] Although Martin Richards and colleagues do not make this point, the practice of polygamy in the Arabian Peninsula may have further selected against African Y-chromosome haplotypes in the Arabian Peninsula and its environs. Unlike Arabs, who by tradition could have up to four wives (not to mention an unlimited number of slave concubines), male African slaves in the Arabian Peninsula would likely have had much more restricted reproductive options, and their contribution consequently would have been much more limited than the Arab DNA contributions to the overall gene pool.

Richards and colleagues' argument seems quite plausible, and is consistent with what we know from the secondary literature about the use of slaves in the Islamic Middle East. However, the genetic data collected for Saudi Arabia present a notable exception to this rule. While in most countries, carriers of African mitochondrial DNA haplotypes greatly outnumber carriers of African Y-chromosome haplotypes, on average by a factor of 3–1, those statistics are nearly reversed in genetic studies of Saudi Arabian populations, where carriers of African mitochondrial DNA haplotypes are outnumbered by carriers of Y-chromosome haplotypes by a 1–2 margin. In a 2009 research article, Khaled Abu-Amero and colleagues note this discrepancy, arguing that they did not find "the strong sexual bias proposed by other authors for Arabian populations and attributed to the peculiarities of the recent slave-trade."[50]

It may be that the data collected on Saudi Arabia by Abu-Amero and colleagues are anomalous. The data sample they used in their 2009 paper is not very large—only 157 Saudi males—and they give no indication in their paper of where the samples were taken, which is somewhat surprising given the vast size of the Saudi state, which is five times the land area of California. Nonetheless, the information presented throughout this book offers a different explanation for Saudi Arabia's anomalously high African Y-chromosome DNA statistics. Richards and colleagues' argument depends on the notion that the demand for male and female slaves, and the uses they were put to, was consistent throughout the Arab Middle East. As this book has argued, however, the Arabian Peninsula was probably exceptional in the Arab world in its employment of African slaves. In the Arabian Peninsula, especially in the Hijaz and Najd regions where Bedouinism predominated, concubinage was probably less common an institution than elsewhere in the Arab world due to Bedouin disdain for intermarriage with Africans, and this would have reduced both the numbers of female slaves and their mitochondrial DNA legacy.[51] At the same time, Hijaz and Najd regions probably imported a higher proportion of male African slaves than elsewhere in the Arab world, since both the Bedouins and Arab townsmen of these regions used Africans as proxy farmers in the highly malarial wadi landscapes and bustan gardens of Arabia. The preferred proxy farmers in these agricultural zones would have been male sub-Saharan African (or Sudan) slaves, who would have combined lower prices, physical strength, and some genetic (and in the first generation, acquired) resistance to *falciparum* and *vivax* malaria. As we have seen in this chapter, such slave colonies would have gradually assimilated into Arab society and become a "whiter people" over time due to intermarriage with Arab women of low-status or subordinate tribes, but some trace of the original African Y-chromosome haplotypes would have remained in the Saudi gene pool.

Taken together, therefore, the Indian Ocean slave trade statistics, the ethnographic information dealing with specific Arabian Peninsula farming populations, and the African haplotype studies all give support to the notion that African agricultural slavery in the Arabian Peninsula had a long pedigree. Although it is clear that the nineteenth century was a period of uncommonly high slave availability in Arabia, the Indian Ocean slave trade data do not rule out the possibility of earlier short-term spikes in slave availability that might even have approached nineteenth century numbers, though probably for only a few years at a time. The slave communities created by these short-term spikes in slave availability, I would argue, were still visible in the Arabian Peninsula in the nineteenth to early twentieth centuries, though in fossilized form: the Nakhawila, Bani Khadhir, Mutawalladeen, and other farming communities were created originally through intermarriage between African agriculturalists and low-status Arabs. The size and number of such communities, finally, is attested to by genetic evidence. Based on the genetic data now available, the African genetic contribution to the Arabian Peninsula was not only substantial and long lasting, it was also disproportionately male, at least in the central Saudi Arabian portion of the Arabian Peninsula. This last piece of evidence strongly supports my contention that African agricultural slavery was far more common in the Arabian Peninsula in general, and the Hijaz and Najd regions in particular, than was true elsewhere in the Arab Middle East.

Modern Arabia and the End of African Agricultural Slavery

Early in this chapter I identified three crucial factors that, in the longue durée, sustained African agricultural slavery in the Arabian Peninsula: (1) widespread availability of African slaves, (2) labor-intensive agricultural practices, and (3) high rates of malaria in areas where agriculture was practiced. All three factors were in place at least until the end of the nineteenth century, if not much earlier, though as we have seen the price and availability of slaves probably fluctuated over time. However, the advent of the modern age in the Arabian Peninsula brought a new set of realities to bear on the Arabian agricultural sector. Slaves, who were plentiful and cheap in the earlier nineteenth century, became increasingly rare and expensive in the later nineteenth and twentieth centuries largely due to increased European supervision over African territory following the "scramble for Africa" in the 1880s. Secondly, over time, the traditional labor-intensive bustan gardens worked by servile labor gave way to mechanized agriculture superintended by skilled expatriate labor. Finally, antimalarial campaigns after 1950 sought to sever the traditional connection between agriculture and malaria, and although the progress of such campaigns was halting and not without setbacks, overall they greatly reduced the incidence of malaria within the Arabian Peninsula. The following section will consider each of these factors in turn.

Decline of the Slave Trade into Arabia

As mentioned before, statistics on the MENA region's slave trade are extremely speculative, since the slavers themselves kept few if any records. Nonetheless, it is abundantly clear from British archival records that the slave trade into Arabia was booming in the first half of the nineteenth century. Major Wilson, the Political Resident of the Gulf, wrote in 1831 that Muscat alone received 1,400–1,700 male and female slaves a year, including 10–15 eunuchs. Female slaves from sub-Saharan Africa, he wrote, "are usually sold at 25 to 45 German Crowns—males from 20 to 35," while Abyssinian slaves cost 35–150 Crowns.[52] Wilson's estimate may be a low one: another British official wrote to the Government of Bombay in 1842 that the annual importation of slaves to the Omani coast was 20,000 or even 30,000 souls.[53] Many more slaves were imported into Mocha, Hode-ida, and Jeddah on the Red Sea coast. Captain Davies, the Political Agent at Aden, wrote that he had "seen as many as 200 and 300 a month arrive at Mocha, and in landing they are immediately placed within a compound unclothed, and from whence they are drawn to a well for water twice a day like a flock of sheep, their food consisted of jowaise [millet] cake, and some sugar cane."[54] These slave flows were no doubt just the tip of the iceberg, since at this point the British were not yet actively involved in eliminating the Indian Ocean slave trade.

Britain's hands-off attitude toward the Indian Ocean slave trade changed in the late nineteenth century, in large part as a reaction to British missionary David Livingstone's reports concerning the brutality of the trade in the East African interior. In 1873, the British forced the sultan of Zanzibar to sign a treaty forbidding the trade of slaves into and within his possession, and British vessels began to actively interdict cargoes of slaves passing between Zanzibar and the mainland.[55] What is more, British cruisers were stationed in the Red Sea to intercept the passage of slaves between the Arabian Peninsula and the African mainland. At about the same time, British officials in Jeddah began to pressure the Ottoman Empire, which had seized control over much of the Hijaz in 1841, to enforce its own prohibitions against the slave trade. While the Ottomans in theory had abolished the slave trade in the 1850s, in practice these laws were little enforced, especially in the Hijaz, where taxes on slaves filled Ottoman coffers and where officials feared that an outright abolition of the trade would outrage local Arabs and weaken their already tenuous hold over this remote province.[56] As a result, despite being formally outlawed, the slave trade was "carried on with very little secrecy" as late as the 1860s, and Turkish troops seeking bribes actively protected and encouraged the trade on both sides of the Red Sea.[57]

A series of incidents occurring in Jeddah in 1879 illustrate the continued flow of slaves into the Hijaz, despite the technical illegality of these practices, as well as Britain's continued inability to stamp out the trade. In May of that year, Consul Zohrab, the ranking British official in Jeddah, complained to his superiors in London about "the remissness of the authorities here in regard to the Slave Trade, which is so active that at any time from 100 to 200 slaves can be bought without the least difficulty; not old, but newly imported ones."[58] Zohrab's complaints led to the arrest of 7 slavedealers and the manumission of 38 slaves, but he notes that only a few days later there were "between 200 and 300 newly-arrived slaves in the town, which could all be recaptured if we had honest officials and troops sufficient to prevent opposition."[59] As a result of these large-scale slave imports, Zohrab wrote, "the town is crowded with slaves for sale, nearly all being Abyssinians. The number was so great in Mecca . . . that prices have gone down from 100 dollars, the average price of last year, to 40 and 50 dollars."[60] A recent study of the Indian Ocean Red Sea trade estimates that, at the time Zohrab was writing, as many as 3,000 slaves per year were being smuggled into Arabia across the Gulf of Aden alone, plus another 1,500 or so from the Massawa area, 1,200 from Suakin, and 2,000 from the Danakil coast to the north of modern Djibouti.[61]

By the late nineteenth century, however, these large-scale slave imports were slowly becoming a thing of the past. Slave exports from East Africa to the Arabian Peninsula were already in decline by mid-century, in large part due to the absorption of many slaves into the Zanzibar clove and coconut plantation. By the 1870s, reinforced British naval interception efforts in East Africa further reduced the volume of this old slave trade. Crucial in this regard was the stationing of an old two-decker British warship, the *London*, in Zanzibari waters, along with its attendant "mosquito fleet" of small, highly mobile pinnaces and other vessels.[62] However, East African antislavery measures did not destroy the trade so much as shift it to over-land routes, and large numbers of slaves were still transported into Arabia across the Red Sea and the Gulf of Aden, where the narrowness of the seas combined with a large number of reefs and islands made the task of British naval interception nearly impossible.[63] Indeed, Martin Klein has argued that British naval suppression in East Africa actually stimulated the overland slave trade into Arabia, as British efforts ensured that the price of slaves in Africa remained cheap and thus created a dramatic price differential between African and Arabian slave markets.[64]

In the end, the death knell of the trade was sounded, not by British naval pressure, but by European colonization of Africa. As Suzanne Miers points out, European occupation of Africa did not immediately end slavery in Africa, but it did inhibit large-scale slave exports and as a result "the pathetic caravans of slaves, roped together . . . soon vanished from British Africa."[65] As a result of the closure of Africa, slave prices in Arabia, which had remained remarkably steady throughout the nineteenth century, spiked dramatically by the 1920s, reaching 200–250 percent of nineteenth-century high prices even after accounting for inflation of the pound.[66] Those slaves who were still smuggled in tended to be young children, who were no doubt far easier to smuggle across the Red Sea in small batches, and who could be passed off as children of the owner if the boat was stopped by British authorities.[67] In addition, Abyssinian slaves claimed an increasingly larger share of all slave exports to Arabia in the twentieth century, since Ethiopia remained independent of European control until 1936. According to Timothy Fernyhough, in fact, both slavery and the slave trade flourished in early twentieth-century Ethiopia despite occasional antislavery decrees by the Ethiopian government.[68] Slave traders also relied increasingly on the tactic of importing individual slaves via the Hajj pilgrimage, since it was fairly easy for African pilgrims to bring slaves along on the pilgrimage, in the guise of "sons" or "daughters," and then sell them into slavery upon reaching Mecca. Despite such tactics, British officials believed that, by 1929, "the import of slaves into [Arabia had] diminished considerably," and that the sale of an Abyssinian girl in Mecca that year was notable not only for its rarity, but for its high price: the girl sold for 136 pounds, the equivalent of 1,700 Maria Theresa thalers (MTT), well over ten times the price she would have fetched in the early nineteenth century.[69] Slave prices declined once again in the 1930s, which reflected not decreased demand, but the greatly diminished purchasing power of the Arabian Peninsula Arabs as a result of the Great Depression.[70] By the 1940s, slave prices had spiked once again, though now the demand for slaves was increasingly being met with slaves from the Makran region in what is now Persia and Baluchistan, not from traditional slave markets in Africa.[71]

As a result of reduced supply and consequently higher prices, African slaves in the late nineteenth to early twentieth centuries increasingly became a luxury commodity, with female slaves favored over male, child slaves favored over mature adults, and Abyssinian slaves increasingly dominating the market, a trend which probably reflects the increasing difficulty of smuggling Sudan slaves through British-controlled Egypt and (after 1899) Anglo-Egyptian Sudan. Since African agricultural slavery depended on a steady flow of inexpensive adult male slaves of sub-Saharan African origins, these changes would have disproportionally affected the Arabian agricultural sector. Well before the formal abolition of slavery in Saudi Arabia in 1962, therefore, agricultural slavery in the Arabian Peninsula was already undergoing a sharp decline.

The Transformation of Arabian Agriculture

At the same time that the price of slaves was rising, dramatic changes to Arabian Peninsula agricultural practices, especially in oil-rich Saudi

Arabia, were reducing the need for manual labor in Arabian agriculture. In traditional Arabia, agriculture gravitated toward water, and farming was limited to those areas where sufficient rainfall, ghayl, sayl, or groundwater permitted cultivation. What is more, in traditional Arabia, agriculture was one of the few sources of income in the Peninsula, along with trade, pastoralism, and the various fees extracted from Hajj pilgrims. With the advent of the oil age, however, the economic contribution of agriculture to the overall economy declined precipitously, falling to only 3 percent of GDP by the mid-1970s. Indeed, one side effect of the oil age was the large-scale reshuffling of the population to a few large urban areas, such as Dammam, Riyadh, and Jeddah, and the simultaneous depopulation of some established agricultural regions, such as the northern Hijaz and the Wadi Dawasir.

Saudi agriculture rebounded somewhat after 1960, but in an entirely different form. In response to high wheat prices of the 1980s, the Saudis invested their petroleum revenues into wheat production, creating huge circular wheat fields watered by self-propelled center-pivot sprinkler systems. While in traditional Arabia, agriculture had gravitated toward water supplies, in modern Arabia the reverse was true, and water was now drawn from deep underground aquifers and lavished upon agricultural lands using tube wells and diesel pumps. As a result of these new techniques, "the Najd landscape was completely transformed . . . as hundreds of startling green circles of wheat . . . appeared against the tawny desert."[72] During the same decade, wheat production skyrocketed from 4,000 tons to 4,100,000 tons, allowing Saudi Arabia to become a major wheat exporter. Production on this level was unsustainable however, as it was based on high government subsidies and the liberal use of finite groundwater reserves, and by 2005, wheat production had declined to an average of only 2,000,000 tons per year.[73]

In the meantime, dates, once the staple of Arabian Peninsula agriculture, declined drastically in importance to local economies. In much of Saudi Arabia, bustan gardens have largely disappeared: according to Colbert Held, "large areas of former date palm groves are now devoted to fruit trees and vegetable production in plastic greenhouses."[74] In other areas, bustan date gardens survived or even flourished, but changed their purpose entirely, becoming elite gardens maintained for display rather than for economic gain.[75] These new prestige date gardens were a side effect of the spread of drilling rigs and cheap diesel pumps into Arabia during World War II, and they "spread like wildfire" among the Arabian elite, first in the Riyadh area, later throughout the Arabian Peninsula.[76] These elite date gardens have even spread to Qatar, where bustan gardens were very rare in the premodern era. Unlike the date farms of traditional Arabia, which used renewable water resources, modern date gardens can only be sustained at a high cost and via heavy use of irreplaceable aquifer water, and thus exist despite, and not because of, current trends in the global economy.

Agricultural production in these new farms has required new types of farmers. Unlike Arabia's traditional date plantations, which were labor-intensive, the mechanized wheat farms of the modern Arabian Peninsula are knowledge-intensive, requiring workers with specialized skills. In one large farm built in the 1980s outside 'Unayzah, for example, researchers Altorki and Cole found an irrigation engineer, a civil engineer, a medical doctor, a geologist, a veterinary officer, a nursery and research supervisor, and a number of farm supervisors, some of whom had degrees in agriculture. Virtually all of these specialists were expatriate contract laborers, primarily from Egypt.[77] Unskilled labor on these farms was also performed by expatriate workers, in part because agriculture was traditionally a despised profession in Arabia, and in part because rising oil wealth drove up average Saudi wages, making expatriate workers much more financially attractive to employers. While some groups of African ancestry still served in agriculture in the late twentieth century, such as the muwalid of the Wadi Fatima, they were the exception that proved the rule: anthropologist Motoko Katakura notes that as early as the 1970s, many were taking advantage of educational opportunities to pursue other jobs, such as positions in the expanding Saudi bureaucracy.[78]

It would be going too far to say that the rise of oil wealth in modern Saudi Arabia has served only to replace one class of servile agriculturalists—African slaves and mawlas—with a new class of servile expatriate agriculturalists. Nonetheless, the plight of the modern expatriate farmer in the Arabian Peninsula is not an enviable one. During his travels in the Wadi Dawasir, Dutch diplomat and Bedouin poetry aficionado Marcel Kurpershoek recorded a vivid encounter with one such worker in the 1990s:

> An angry looking man in a pale blue tunic emerged from a cement-block hut. . . . "Who are you? What are you doing here? What is your job?" he barked at me.
>
> I decided to behave like a dandy in the desert. In a nonchalant tone I told him that I was a tourist visiting a friend in the Wadi,

that I had nothing to do and I didn't see the reason for working because I had enough money. "And you?" I asked in my turn. "How do you like it in the Wadi as an Egyptian?"

"*Zift*, life here is like black pitch, shit," he said bitterly. "At night I can't sleep for the mosquitoes. Everywhere there are flies, bedbugs, lizards, snakes. I was trained as an agricultural engineer and now I'm doing the work of an agricultural laborer. First I had a job at two hundred and forty dollars a month, at my level, but I was demoted by the owner of this business and now I only learn two hundred dollars." . . .

He invited me to sit down under the canopy of palm leaves in front of his hut. Inside I saw two meager beds and some cooking equipment. Washing was hanging on lines. Against the outside wall there were pans and a pot filled with water in which brown beans, the staple Egyptian food, were soaking. . . . He had left his wife and two children behind. He worked for part of the year as an immigrant labor in Saudi Arabia, then went home for six months, and so on. A dog's life.[79]

A dog's life, indeed. Yet still on the whole a more desirable life than that of the enslaved African agriculturalists that such expatriate laborers replaced.

The Taming of Malaria in the Arabian Peninsula

As for the third factor that sustained African agricultural labor in the traditional Arabian peninsula, the ubiquity of malaria in the Arabian Peninsula's fertile wadi landscapes, this too began to change dramatically (though not yet completely) as traditional Arabia gave way to Arabian modernity. The first steps toward getting malaria under control in the Arabian Peninsula were taken in the al-Hasa oasis, which served as the headquarters of sorts for ARAMCO as well as the home of many of ARAMCO's Arab workers. In order to protect the lives of these workers, starting in 1948, ARAMCO began an aggressive program of using DDT to eradicate al-Hasa and Qatif's resident *A. Stephensi* population. The results were fairly dramatic: within a year the morbidity rate from malaria dropped from a pre-spraying figure of 1,130 per 10,000 to only 86 per 10,000. By 1950, after two years of repeated spraying, Richard Daggy was proud to report that "for the first time in the history of the Aramco hospitals, no Saudi Arab employee cases were recorded in April and July."[80]

Unfortunately, in Arabia as elsewhere, DDT did not ultimately prove to be the magic bullet against malaria. By 1950, the first evidence of mosquito resistance to DDT was noted, but malaria rates remained low through 1954. However, by 1954, DDT mosquito resistance, plus a brief cessation of the antimalarial program due to financial squabbles between ARAMCO and the Saudi government, allowed the malaria rate to spike once again, reaching a rate of 311 per 10,000 in November 1954, and rising even higher in 1955. As a consequence, ARAMCO workers replaced DDT with another insecticide, dieldrin, which once again reduced both the mosquito and malaria rates in the al-Hasa oasis. Based on two years of spraying with dieldrin, Daggy felt confidence in announcing that, as of "the end of 1957 . . . malaria transmission had been stopped, for all practical purposes."[81] However, dieldrin was not the magic bullet either. By 1959, al-Hasa's mosquitoes were developing resistance to dieldrin as well, and in any case, like DDT, dieldrin was soon withdrawn from the market due to its toxic effects on humans and animals.[82]

In the end, the deciding factor in the gradual reduction of malaria throughout the Arabian Peninsula was the change in wealth and lifestyle. Starting in the 1960s, oil wealth funded the construction of a network of new hospitals in Saudi Arabia, greatly increasing the ability of the state to treat malaria infections as they occurred and thus cutting short chains of infection. In addition, these hospitals, combined with a rising standard of living, created a healthier and more malaria-resistant population. Oil wealth also allowed for the purchase of tube wells and fodder crops, allowing the Arabian Peninsula to maintain much larger herds of cattle, goats, and sheep than were previously possible given the technological limitations of the traditional Arabian Peninsula. This proliferation of livestock would have had the effect of reducing malaria infection, since it would have given zoophilic mosquitoes like *A. stephensi* a non-human food source, cutting the chain of transmission for malaria infection. The use of tube wells might have also lowered the malaria risk in some areas by creating "cones of depression"—localized drops in the water table—that would have diminished or dried up nearby springs and surface water.[83] What is more, the Saudis publicized antimalarial precautions via "films, pamphlets, [and] posters" in the burgeoning public school system, which once again was paid for by oil wealth. As a result of these measures, the al-Hasa region, "for all intents and purposes . . . saw few incidents of malaria after 1979."[84]

Perhaps most importantly, the influx of oil wealth contributed to the urbanization of the Saudi population, and with it, the abandonment of unhealthy rural areas where malaria traditionally predominated. The shifts of population within Khaybar described in chapter 3 are a case in point. Up until the nineteenth century, Khaybar's many villages were located in and among the palms themselves, though wealthier inhabitants might have lived in dwellings built upon the harrah, where the chance of malaria infection was lower, as *Anopheles* mosquitoes are poor uphill flyers. In the early twentieth century, with the first trickles of oil wealth, many people began to abandon the valleys of Khaybar, and population became concentrated in newer settlements built high upon the harrah to the south of town. By the end of the twentieth century, these settlements were in turn mostly abandoned, and Khaybar was rebuilt entirely several kilometers southeast of the old town in an area located outside of the Khaybar valley drainage system. Despite the construction of the new town, which has a modern population of about fifty-seven thousand, the predominant trend has been for population to leave the backwater town of Khaybar entirely and migrate to Saudi Arabia's burgeoning urban centers, such as Riyadh, Jeddah, Mecca, and Medina, all of which boasted over a million inhabitants by 2010. Other oil-rich Arabian Peninsula nations, such as the Gulf States and Oman, underwent similar transformations during the same period.

Largely as result of these demographic shifts, malaria infection has become increasingly rare in the modern Arabian Peninsula. In al-Hasa, once a hotbed of malaria infection, malaria has been decisively defeated: in a study examining malaria cases in al-Hasa from January 1994 to June 2005, a medical researcher for the Saudi ARAMCO medical services corporation found fifty-six cases of malaria in the Saudi Eastern province, but in all cases without exception the infection was imported into the province from outside, either from Saudi areas where malaria is still endemic, or from outside of the country, usually from Pakistan or India.[85] The only region of Saudi Arabia that still has significant levels of malaria today is southern Arabia, in the provinces of 'Asir, Najran, and Jizan. Malaria is still endemic in this relatively underdeveloped region, especially in rural communities, despite recent campaigns using "impregnated mosquito nets, vector control, training equipment, and surveillance teams."[86] Malaria eradication in southern Arabia is complicated by the fact that malaria is still largely uncontrolled in neighboring Yemen, which still suffers from seven hundred thousand to eight hundred thousand cases a year despite an antimalarial campaign launched in the early 2000s with significant financial help from the Saudi government.

AFRICAN AGRICULTURAL slavery had a long pedigree in the traditional Arabian Peninsula. Arabian Peninsula agriculture was highly labor intensive, and also very dangerous, due to the inherent malaria risk of wadi and other moist lowland landscapes. Thus, whenever slave prices were relatively cheap, Arabian townsmen and pastoralists acquired slaves for use in agriculture. Male sub-Saharan Africans, who were both cheap and often endowed with intrinsic antimalarial defenses, were most commonly employed in such tasks. The antiquity of this system is attested to in the ethnographic record, which records the existence of a number of partially or fully assimilated agricultural populations (such as the Khaybara, Bani Khadhir, etc.) with African roots. Genetic records tell a similar story, indicating that large-scale African genetic exchange with the Arabian Peninsula dates back to 500 BCE. What is more, the relative frequency of African Y-chromosome haplotypes in Saudi Arabia, compared to Saudi Arabia's relative deficiency in mitochondrial DNA haplotypes of African origin, suggests that northern and central Arabia were unique in the Arab world for employing large numbers of male slaves, presumably for agricultural purposes.

The same factors that sustained African agricultural slavery in the Arabian Peninsula over the longue durée also contributed to its relatively rapid decline in the modern era. By the beginning of the twentieth century, slaves were becoming increasingly expensive, as well as predominantly young, Abyssinian, and female, and these trends diminished the supply of cheap male slaves from sub-Saharan Africa necessary to sustain Arabian Peninsula agricultural slavery. By the twentieth century, agriculture itself had begun to change dramatically in the Arabian Peninsula, and the new mechanized reality favored skilled but low-paid expatriate labor rather than the semi-skilled or unskilled labor of increasingly rare and expensive slaves. Finally, the progressive taming of malaria within the Arabian Peninsula undercut the biological rationale for Arabian agricultural slavery, since farmers of African ancestry no longer enjoyed any comparative advantage in these increasingly malaria-free agricultural environments. While it is likely that some agricultural slaves still existed in the Arabian Peninsula up until the final, unconditional manumissions of the 1960s, such slaves were mere remnants of a traditional system of agricultural labor that had already unraveled by the middle of the twentieth century.

CHAPTER 6

Conclusions

AS THIS study has repeatedly demonstrated, African labor of slave origins played a significant, though previously unappreciated, role in agricultural production in the traditional Arabian Peninsula. This is not to say that servile African laborers ever amounted to more than a sizable minority of Arabian Peninsula farmers. The Arabian Peninsula has long hosted number of hadr (settled) tribes, such as the Bani Tamim of northern Najd, who specialized in agricultural production. Nor is this to say that the majority of these African agriculturalists were slaves, at least in the strict sense of the term. Rather, African agricultural populations seem to have been a mix of slaves and mawlas, with little distinction made between the two in the ethnographic texts. The dominant labor regime for both slaves and mawlas seems to have been sharecropping, with the slaves providing a set share of the produce of their date (or in Dhofar, coconut) palms to the masters in return for the right to keep the remainder and to grow crops for their own use under the shade of the palms. These findings should put to rest once and for all the often-cited adage that slavery in the Arab world was overwhelmingly consumptive rather than productive in character.

The importance of African servile labor in Arabian Peninsula agriculture was, to a large degree, a side-effect of high levels of endemic malaria in the arable zones of the Arabian Peninsula. The same Arabian wadi drainage channels and other lowland depressions that were suitable for agriculture were also well suited to the proliferation of *Anopheles* mosquitoes, the vector of the malaria plasmodium. Irrigation using jalibs, qanats, and other techniques only increased the malaria risk in these agricultural spaces by raising the water table and creating standing puddles, backwater swamps, and other habitats for *Anopheles* breeding. As a result, malaria was holoendemic in many Arabian agricultural zones, especially in bustan gardens, where a mix of crops were grown under a sheltering canopy of palms. Not surprisingly, native Arabs associated these agricultural zones with both jinn (malicious spirits) and fevers, and tended to avoid them. This aversion to palm plantations and other low-lying, moist places was particularly notable among Arabia's Bedouins, who avoided spending even a single night in a palm garden. The caution of the 'Anaza Bedouins, who camped on the elevated harrah surrounding the Khaybar oasis rather than in the oasis itself during the annual date harvest, was typical in this regard.

The high malaria risk inherent to the Arabian Peninsula's wadi and oasis environments, in turn, motivated Arabs to exploit these landscapes indirectly using African servile labor. Like the planters of the seventeenth-through the nineteenth-century Atlantic world, Bedouins and Arab townsmen preferred to farm the fertile but unhealthy wadis and other drainage basins in their midst by proxy, using Africans endowed with genetic or acquired resistance to malaria. The preferred slave for this endeavor was the male Sudan or Takruri (West African) slave, who would have combined relatively low price with high malaria resistance. Although present in large numbers and active in other professions in the Arabian Peninsula, most notably domestic and military service, Abyssinian slaves were rarely used as agriculturalists. Most likely, this was a consequence both of their higher price and their relative lack of hemoglobin S and the Duffy-negative antigen, the main genetic defenses possessed by sub-Saharan Africans against *falciparum* and *vivax* malaria respectively. Obviously, Arab slaveowners did not understand the genetic protections possessed by sub-Saharan Africans in modern terms, but relied instead on folk beliefs derived from practical experience. Conventional wisdom held that sub-Saharan Africans were more resilient to disease, for example, and could drink from water sources, such as the supposedly poisoned wells of Khaybar, which would cause fatal fevers in Arabs.

Although the picture is far from clear, indirect evidence, such as slave trade studies, ethnographic accounts of particular Arab tribal groups, and genetic studies, all suggest that African servile agriculturalists have been a factor in Arabian history from a very early period. Genetic evidence suggests that large-scale African migration into the Arabian Peninsula has been occurring since at least 500 BCE. Of course, not all of these Africans were agricultural slaves, but the relative frequency of Y-chromosome African haplotypes in the modern Arabian population compared to African haplotypes carried by mitochondrial DNA suggests that the African migration into the Hijaz and Najd was disproportionally male, as might be expected if the region included a large number of enslaved African agriculturalists. The antiquity of African agriculturalists in Arabia is also clear from the ethnographic literature, which indicates that, despite Arab prejudices against intermarrying with people of African ancestry, a number of important Arabian Peninsula farming communities, including the Nakhawila of Medina and the Bani Khadhir of Najd, were partially African in origin. Slave trade studies, in turn, suggest that the African contribution to Arabian agriculture probably reached a peak in the nineteenth century, at a time when the Atlantic slave trade was dying out and slaves were being rerouted toward Eastern slave markets. This nineteenth-century spike, however, does not preclude the possibility that large numbers of African agriculturalists were purchased during pre-nineteenth-century gluts in the slave markets caused by wars, famines, or other calamities in Africa.

As might be expected, this large and sustained forced migration of Africans into Arabia left important imprints on the Arabian Peninsula. One such legacy was the zar possession ritual cult, a healing ritual of African origins that flourished in many parts of Arabia before falling into disuse in the modern era, in large part due to repression by the Wahhabi Saudis in the mid-twentieth century. One other important legacy that African agriculturalists bequeathed to the Arabian Peninsula was their genetic defenses against malaria, which passed over time from African agriculturalists to Arab farming communities. Case in point are the Hasawiyah of the al-Hasa oasis in eastern Arabia, an Arab agricultural community which nonetheless has African-level frequencies of hemoglobin S and Duffy negativity, probably bequeathed to them by the large African slave

colony established in al-Hasa by the Shi'ite Qarmatians in the tenth century. A case could be made, in fact, that the importation of large numbers
of African agricultural laborers, and their malaria-protective genes, probably hastened the creation of later Arab agricultural communities.

While the evidence concerning the antiquity of African agricultural
slavery is somewhat speculative, we are on much more solid ground
when describing the end of African agricultural slavery in Arabia in the
mid-twentieth century. The decline of the African slave trade into Arabia,
which was a direct consequence of the imposition of European control over
African territory during the post-1880s "scramble for Africa," caused the
price of slaves to rise sharply. Perhaps more importantly, twentieth-century
slave smugglers increasingly shipped cargoes of slaves that were young,
female, and Abyssinian, which were precisely the wrong type of slave for
Arabian farming. At the same time, new technologies like the diesel pump
and central pivot irrigation transformed Arabian agriculture. While the
labor-intensive practices of traditional Arabian farming had made African
slaves desirable, the new agricultural practices demanded technical exper-
tise and professional skills that only expatriate laborers could provide.
Finally, the taming of malaria in most of the Arabian Peninsula, with the
exception of Yemen, has undermined the genetic logic that once encouraged the use of servile African labor in Arabia's unhealthy wadi landscapes.

Notes

Preface

1. For the state of environmental history as a subdiscipline, as well as its geographical strengths and weaknesses, see J. R. McNeill, "Observations on the Nature and Culture of Environmental History," *History and Theory* 42, no. 4 (December 2003): 5–43.

Introduction

1. Alan Mikhail, ed., *Water on Sand: Environmental Histories of the Middle East and North Africa* (New York: Oxford University Press, 2013), 1.

2. Portions of this section appeared previously in my article "*Mutawalladeen* and Malaria: African Slavery in Arabian Wadis," *Journal of Social History* 47, no. 4 (2014): 1–19.

3. Bernard Lewis, *Race and Slavery in the Middle East* (New York: Oxford University Press, 1990), iv.

4. Orlando Patterson, *Slavery and Social Death: A Comparative Study* (Cambridge, MA: Harvard University Press, 1982), 11; Phillip Curtin, *The Rise and Fall of the Plantation Complex: Essays in Atlantic History* (London: Cambridge University Press, 1976), 41. For more recent echoes of this attitude see also Paul E. Lovejoy, *Transformations in Slavery: A History of Slavery in Africa*, 2nd ed. (New York: Cambridge University Press, 2000), 32; and Ronald Segal, *Islam's Black Slaves* (New York: Farrar, Straus, and Giroux, 2001), 107. Ironically, Patterson does note elsewhere in *Slavery and Social Death* that "one should be careful not to underestimate the non-domestic and rural uses of slaves in [Muslim] societies" (159) and even acknowledges that the employment of agricultural slaves among Arabian Bedouins was an ancient practice that "long predated Muhammed" (277).

5. See Gwyn Campbell, "Servitude and the Changing Face of the Demand for Labor in the Indian Ocean World, c. 1800–1900," in *Indian Ocean Slavery in the Age of Abolition*, ed. Robert Harms, Bernard K. Freamon, and David W. Blight (London: Yale University Press, 2013), 30.

6. Alexandre Popovic, *The Revolt of African Slaves in Iraq*, trans. Léon King (Princeton, NJ: Markus Wiener Publishers, 1999), 23–24. Ghada Hashem

Talhami has argued convincingly that the term *Zanj*, often used to refer specifically to East Africans, in this case was used to describe all blacks irrespective of origins, and that in fact the bulk of the "Zanj" were imported from across the Sahara or from the horn of Africa. See Ghada Hashem Talhami, "The Zanj Rebellion Reconsidered," *International Journal of African Historical Studies* 10, no. 3 (1977): 443-461.

7. Nasir-I Khusraw, *Book of Travels*, ed. and trans. Wheeler M. Thackston (Costa Mesa, CA: Mazda Publishers, 2001), 112.

8. Trabelsi, for example, uses the rebellion of Medina's African slaves in 762 CE as an example of the widespread nature of African agricultural slavery in the Early Islamic world, but a closer examination of the facts does not support this contention. Arab historian al-Tabari, who is Trabelsi's source, quite unambiguously describes this revolt as being led by urban blacks associated with the marketplace, and not as a rural uprising. See Salah Trabelsi, "L'esclavage domanial dans le paysage agraire musulman au Moyen Age," in *Esclavage et dependences serviles*, ed. M. Cottias, A. Stella, and B. Vincent (Paris: L'Harmattan, 2006), 305-24; and Abu Ja'far Muhammad ibn Jarir al-Tabari, *The History of al-Tabari*, vol. 28, '*Abbāsid Authority Affirmed*, trans. Jane Dammen McAuliffe (Albany: State University of New York Press, 1995), 231-37.

9. J. H. Galloway, "The Mediterranean Sugar Industry," *Geographical Review* 67, no. 2 (April 1977): 177-94; and Thomas Vernet, "Slave Trade and Slavery on the Swahili Coast, 1500-1750," in *Slavery, Islam, and Diaspora*, ed. Behnaz A. Mirzai, Ismael Musah Montana, and Paul E. Lovejoy (Trenton, NJ: Africa World Press, 2009), 55.

10. Gabriel Baer, "Slavery in Nineteenth Century Egypt," *Journal of African History* 8, no. 3 (1967): 420.

11. Ibid., 421; Kenneth M. Cuno, "African Slaves in Nineteenth-Century Rural Egypt: A Preliminary Assessment," in *Race and Slavery in the Middle East*, ed. Terence Walz and Kenneth M. Cuno (New York: American University of Cairo Press, 2010), 77-98.

12. Ehud R. Toledano, *Slavery and Abolition in the Ottoman Middle East* (Seattle: University of Washington Press, 1998), 81-110.

13. See Abdul Sheriff, *Slaves, Spices, and Ivory in Zanzibar* (Athens: Ohio University Press, 1987); Sheriff, "The Slave Mode of Production Along the East African Coast, 1810-1873," in *Slaves and Slavery in Muslim Africa*, ed. John Ralph Willis (London: F. Cass, 1985), 2:164, 175; and Frederick Cooper, *Plantation Slavery on the East Coast of Africa* (Portsmouth, NH: Heinemann, 1997).

14. Omar A. Eno, "The Abolition of Slavery and the Aftermath Stigma: The Case of the Bantu/Jareer People on the Benadir Coast of Southern Somalia," in *Abolition and Its Aftermath in the Indian Ocean Africa and Asia*, ed. Gwyn Campbell (New York: Routledge, 2005), 83-93.

15. See Willem Floor, *The Persian Gulf: A Political and Economic History of Five Port Cities, 1500-1730* (Washington, DC: Mage Publishers, 2006), 337;

Mathew S. Hopper, "Slaves of One Master: Globalization and the African Diaspora in Arabia in the Age of Empire," in Harms, Freamon, and Blight, *Indian Ocean Slavery*, 223–40; and Hopper, "Globalization and the Economics of African Slavery in Arabia in the Age of Empire," *Journal of African Development* 12, no. 1 (2010): 155–84.

16. See for example Benjamin Claude Brower, "The Servile Populations of the Algerian Sahara, 1850–1900," in Mirzai, Montana, and Lovejoy, *Slavery, Islam and Diaspora*, 169–91; Stephen Baier and Paul E. Lovejoy, "The Tuareg of the Central Sudan: Gradations in Servility at the Desert Edge (Niger and Nigeria)," in *Slavery in Africa: Historical and Anthropological Perspectives*, ed. Suzanne Miers and Igor Kopytoff (Madison: University of Wisconsin Press, 1977), 391–441; Segal, *Islam's Black Slaves*, 139; and for a more general view, James L. A. Webb, Jr., *Desert Frontier: Ecological and Economic Change along the Western Sahel, 1600–1850* (Madison: University of Wisconsin Press, 1995).

17. Murray Gordon, *Slavery in the Arab World* (New York: New Amsterdam Books, 1989), 50.

18. John Hunwick and Eve Trout Powell, comps. and eds., *The African Diaspora in the Mediterranean Lands of Islam* (Princeton, NJ: Markus Wiener Publishers, 2002), 35.

19. William Ochsenwald, "Muslim-European Conflict in the Hijaz: The Slave Trade Controversy, 1840–1895," *Middle Eastern Studies* 16 (January 1980): 118.

20. Suzanne Miers, *Slavery in the Twentieth Century: The Evolution of a Global Problem* (New York: AltaMira Press, 2003), 89; Abdussamad H. Ahmad, "Ethiopian Slave Exports at Matamma, Massawa, and Tajura c. 1830 to 1885," in *The Economics of the Indian Ocean Slave Trade in the Nineteenth Century*, ed. William Gervase Clarence-Smith (London: Frank Cass, 1989), 99; Beatrice Nicolini, "The Makran-Baluch-African Network in Zanzibar and East Africa during the XIXth Century," *African and Asian Studies* 5, no. 3 (2006): 356; and 'Abd al-'Alīm 'Ali Abd al-Wahhāb Abū Haykal, "Al-Raqīq al-Afrīqī bi-l-Hijāz khilāl al-Nisf al-Awwal min al-Qarn al-'Ishrin," *Al-Majalla al-Tārīkhiyya al-Misriyya* 39 (1989): 336.

21. See Carsten Niebuhr, *Travels through Arabia and other Countries in the East*, trans. Robert Heron, 2 vols. (Farmington Hills, MI: Thomson Gale, 2005); Hugh Scott, *In the High Yemen* (London: Paul Kegan, 2002), 185; and Francine Stone, ed., *Studies on the Tihāmah: The Report of the Tihāmah Expedition 1982 and Related Papers* (Harlow, UK: Longman, 1985).

22. Robin Bidwell, *Travelers in Arabia* (Reading, UK: Garnet Publishing, 1994), 179.

23. Ruthven W. Pike, "Land and Peoples of the Hadhramaut, Aden Protectorate," *Geographical Review* 30, no. 4 (October 1940): 627–48.

24. Jörg Janzen, *Nomads in the Sultanate of Oman: Tradition and Development in Dhofar* (Boulder, CO: Westview Press, 1986), 24, 30, 37.

25. S. B. Miles, *The Countries and Tribes of the Persian Gulf* (London: Harrison and Sons, 1919), 2:85. Pagination based on reprinted volume by General Books.

26. J. R. Wellsted, *Travels in Arabia* (London: John Murray, 1838), 2:188–89.

27. See Frederick F. Anscombe, "An Anational Society: Eastern Arabia in the Ottoman Period," in *Transnational Connections and the Arab Gulf,* ed. Madawi Al-Rasheed (New York: Routledge, 2005), 21–38.

28. See Lawrence G. Potter, ed., *The Persian Gulf In History* (New York: Palgrave Macmillan, 2009), 1–12.

29. See for example Charles E. Davies, *The Blood-Red Arab Flag: An Investigation into Qasimi Piracy 1797–1820* (Exeter, UK: University of Exeter Press, 1997).

30. E. B. Banning, "Peasants, Pastoralists, and 'Pax Romana': Mutualism in the Southern Highlands of Jordan," *Bulletin of the American Schools of Oriental Research* 261 (February 1986): 29.

31. Ernest Gellner, "Tribalism and the State in the Middle East," in *Tribes and State Formation in the Middle East,* ed. Philip S. Khoury and Joseph Kostiner (Los Angeles: University of California Press, 1990), 111.

32. Ibid., 119–20.

33. See M. A. Hiyari, "The Origins and Development of the Amirate of the Arabs during the Seventh/Thirteenth and Eighth/Fourteenth Centuries," *Bulletin of the School of Oriental and African Studies* 38, no. 3 (1975): 509–24.

34. See for example John L. Meloy, "Imperial Strategy and Political Exigency: the Red Sea Spice Trade and the Mamluk Sultanate in the Fifteenth Century," *Journal of the American Oriental Society* 123, no. 1 (January–March 2003): 1–19; Beate Dignas and Engerbert Winter, *Rome and Persia in Late Antiquity: Neighbors and Rivals* (New York: Cambridge University Press, 2007); and Patricia Crone, *Meccan Trade and the Rise of Islam* (Princeton, NJ: Princeton University Press, 1987).

35. See Fernand Braudel, *The Mediterranean and the Mediterranean World in the Age of Philip II* (Berkeley: University of California Press, 1996).

36. R. B. Serjeant, "The Cultivation of Cereals in Mediaeval Yemen," *Arabian Studies* 1 (1974): 39.

37. D. T. Potts, "Date Palms and Date Consumption in Eastern Arabia During the Bronze Age," in *The Date Palm: From Traditional Resource to Green Wealth* (Abu Dhabi, UAE: The Emirates Center for Strategic Studies and Research, 2003), 50.

38. Joseph Kostiner, "Transforming Dualities: Tribe and State Formation in Saudi Arabia," in *Tribes and State Formation in the Middle East,* ed. Philip S. Khoury and Joseph Kostiner (Los Angeles: University of California Press, 1990), 242.

39. Trabelsi, "L'esclavage domanial," 307. My translation.

40. Serge Cleuziou, Maurizio Tosi, and Juris Zarins, eds., *Essays on the Prehistory of the Arabian Peninsula* (Rome: Instituto Italiano per l'Africa e l'Orient, 2002), 9; and J. Alexander, "Islam, Archaeology, and Slavery in Africa," *World Archeology* 33, no. 1 (June 2001): 57.

41. I have borrowed the term "undeclared empire" from John Darwin, "An Undeclared Empire: The British in the Middle East, 1918–39," *Journal of Imperial and Commonwealth History* 27, no. 2 (1999): 159–76. See also James Onley, *The Arabian Frontier of the British Raj: Merchants, Rulers, and the British in the Nineteenth-Century Gulf* (New York: Oxford University Press, 2007), 32

42. Michael Christopher Low, "Empire and the Hajj: Pilgrims, Plagues, and Pan-Islam under British Surveillance, 1865–1908," *International Journal of Middle East Studies* 40, no. 2 (May 2008): 269–90; and F. E. Peters, *The Hajj: The Muslim Pilgrimage to Mecca and the Holy Places* (Princeton, NJ: Princeton University Press, 1994), 301–2, 326–31.

43. Onley, *Arabian Frontier*, 21–25.

44. Sheila A. Scoville, "Historiography on the 'Gazetteer of Arabia': Vol. I," *Proceedings of the Seminar for Arabian Studies* 12 (1982): 74.

45. *Gazetteer of Arabia* (Simla, India: General Staff of India, 1917), 2:536.

46. Sheila A. Scoville, ed., *Gazetteer of Arabia: A Geographical and Tribal History of the Arabian Peninsula*, 2 vols. (Austria: Akademische Druk- u. Verlagsanstalt, 1979).

47. Madawi al-Rasheed, *Politics in an Arabian Oasis: The Rashidis of Saudi Arabia* (New York: I. B. Tauris Publishers, 1991), 8.

48. See Peters, *Hajj*; Norman Lewis, *Nomads and Settlers in Syria and Jordan, 1800–1980* (New York: Cambridge University Press, 1987); and Alexei Vassiliev, *The History of Saudi Arabia* (New York: New York University Press, 2000).

49. See Jibrail S. Jabbur, *The Bedouins and the Desert: Aspects of Nomadic Life in the Arab East* (Albany: State University of New York Press, 1995); Soraya Altorki and Donald Cole, *Arabian Oasis City: The Transformation of 'Unayzah* (Austin: University of Texas Press, 1989); and Raouf Sa'd Abujaber, *Pioneers over Jordan: The Frontier of Settlement in Transjordan, 1850–1914* (London: I. B. Tauris and Company, 1989).

50. G. Wyman Bury, *Arabia Infelix: Or the Turks in Yamen* (Reading, UK: Garnet Publishing, 1998), xi.

51. R. E. Cheesman, *In Unknown Arabia* (London: Macmillan, 1926).

52. Good biographies of the main Arabian travelers can be found in Bidwell, *Travelers in Arabia*, and Richard Trench, *Arabian Travelers* (Topsfield, MA: Salem House, 1986). Unfortunately, both of these sources are highly Anglocentric and shortchange important French language travelers, including Charles Huber and Maurice Tamisier. See also Benjamin Reilly, "Arabian Travelers, 1800-1950: An Analytical Bibliography," *British Journal of Middle Eastern Studies*, 2015, doi:10.1080/13530194.2015.1060155.

53. Charles Huber, "Voyage dans L'Arabie Centrale: Hamâd, Šammar, Qaçîm, Hedjâz," *Bulletin de la Société de Géographie,* 1884: 327, 485.

54. See Edward Said, *Orientalism* (New York: Vintage Books, 1978).

55. Ameen Rihani, *Maker of Modern Arabia* (New York: Houghton Mifflin, 1928), 6.

56. Mohamad Ali Hachicho, "English Travel Books about the Arab Near East in the Eighteenth Century," *Die Welt des Islams* 9, no. 1 (1964): 199–200.

Chapter 1: Traditional Arabian Agriculture

1. J. R. Wellsted, "Narrative of a Journey into the Interior of Oman, in 1835," *Journal of the Royal Geographical Society of London* 7 (1837): 107.

2. Joy McCorriston, "Breaking the Rain Barrier and the Tropical Spread of Near Eastern Agriculture into Southern Arabia," in *Behavioral Ecology and the Transition to Agriculture,* ed. Douglas J. Kennett and Bruce Winterhalder (Berkeley: University of California Press, 2006), 217–36.

3. Joy McCorriston et al., "Cattle Cults of the Arabian Neolithic and Early Territorial Societies," *American Anthropologist* 114, no. 1 (2012): 45–63.

4. McCorriston, "Breaking the Rain Barrier," 129.

5. Potts, "Date Palms and Date Consumption," 33–50.

6. J. R. Wellsted, *Travels in Arabia* (London: John Murray, 1838), 1:99.

7. H. St. J. B. Philby, *The Heart of Arabia: A Record of Travel and Exploration* (London: Constable and Company, 1922), 2:263.

8. Ibid., 76.

9. G. A. Wallin, *Travels in Arabia (1845 and 1848)* (Cambridge, UK: Falcon-Oleander, 1979), 178.

10. K. S. Twitchell, *Saudi Arabia: With an Account of the Development of Its Natural Resources* (Princeton, NJ: Princeton University Press, 1953), 18.

11. D. T. Potts, "Contributions to the Agrarian History of Eastern Arabia I. Implements and Cultivation Techniques," *Arabian Archaeology and Epigraphy* 5 (1994): 158–68.

12. Charles M. Doughty, *Travels in Arabia Deserta* (Cambridge, UK: Cambridge University Press, 1888), 2:389.

13. Barclay Raunkiaer, *Through Wahhabiland on Camelback* (New York: Frederick A. Praeger, 1969), 145.

14. J. Theodore Bent and Mabel Bent, *Southern Arabia* (London: Smith, Elder and Co., 1900), 41.

15. Daniel van der Meulen and H. von Wissmann, *Ḥaḍramaut: Some of Its Mysteries Unveiled,* photomechanical reprint of 1932 ed. (Leiden, NL: E. J. Brill, 1964), 29; and Freya Stark, "Two Months in the Hadhramaut," *Geographical Journal* 87, no. 2 (February 1936): 115.

16. For more information on the usefulness and the limitations of the 1917 *Gazetteer* as a primary source, see Scoville, "Historiography," 73–78.

17. Another source of ambiguity was the difference in language and terminology used by the different contributors to the *Gazetteer*. While some authors gave raw population data for town populations, others gave only the number of houses, and the estimates of population-per-house used by the text ranged wildly. Thus, when only the number of houses was given by the informant, I used a middling estimate of nine people per house to convert to population numbers. Given that it is unknown how many houses in each settlement were unoccupied, this has probably yielded inflated population numbers for locales where only the number of houses was mentioned. Nonetheless, since this bias was consistent throughout the regions of Arabia, it does not invalidate the impression given by figure 1.2 concerning population clustering in the Arabian Peninsula.

18. Neil Roberts, "Water Conservation in Ancient Arabia," *Proceedings of the Seminar of Arabian Studies* 7 (1977): 135.

19. F. W. Holland, "On the Peninsula of Sinai," *Journal of the Royal Geographical Society of London* 38 (1868): 248–49.

20. Michael J. Harrower, "Hydrology, Ideology, and the Origins of Irrigation in Ancient Southwest Arabia," *Current Anthropology* 49, no. 3 (June 2008): 499. See also Harrower, "Mapping and Dating Incipient Irrigation in Wadi Sana, Hadramawt (Yemen)," *Proceedings of the Seminar for Arabian Studies* 38 (2008): 187–202.

21. Francisco G. Fedele, "Man, Land, and Climate: Emerging Interactions from the Holocene of the Yemen Highlands," in *Man's Role in Shaping the Eastern Mediterranean Landscape*, ed. S. Bottema, G. Entjes-Nieborg, and W. Van Zeist (Rotterdam: A. A. Balkema, 1990), 39.

22. Hubert Chanson, *The Hydraulics of Open Channel Flow: An Introduction* (New York: Elsevier, 2004), 533.

23. Vincenzo Maria Francaviglia, "Some Remarks on the Irrigation Systems of Ancient Yemen," in Cleuziou, Tosi, and Zarins, *Late Prehistory of the Arabian Peninsula*, 137.

24. I. Hehmeyer, "Irrigation Farming in the Ancient Oasis of Marib," *Proceedings of the Seminar for Arabian Studies* 19 (1989): 36.

25. Chanson, *Open Channel Flow*, 533–34; and Francaviglia, "Irrigation Systems," 119.

26. U. Brunner and H. Haefner, "The Successful Floodwater Farming System of the Sabeans, Yemen Arab Republic," *Applied Geography* 6, no. 1 (1986): 82.

27. Ibid., 84.

28. John Peter Oleson, "Water Supply in Jordan through the Ages," in *The Archeology of Jordan*, ed. Burton MacDonald, Russel Adams, and Piotr Bienkowski (London: Continuum International Publishing Group, 2001), 603.

29. M. Evenari, L. Shanan, and N. H. Tadmor, "'Runoff Farming' in the Desert. I. Experimental Layout," *Agronomy Journal* 69 (January–February 1968): 29–30.

30. Ibid., 31; and Steven Mithen, *Thirst: Water and Power in the Ancient World* (London: Weidenfeld and Nicolson, 2012), 111–12.

31. John Peter Oleson, "The Origins and Design of Nabataean Water-Supply Systems," in *Studies in the History and Archaeology of Jordan V*, ed. Khairieh 'Amr, Fawzi Zayadine, and Muna Zaghloul (Amman, JO: Department of Antiquities, 1995), 713; and Vernon L. Scarborough, *The Flow of Power: Ancient Water Systems and Landscapes* (Santa Fe, NM: SAR Press, 2003), 77.

32. Bent and Bent, *Southern Arabia*, 127–28.

33. H. St. J. B. Philby, *The Heart of Arabia: A Record of Travel and Exploration* (London: Constable and Company, 1922), 1:212.

34. Daniel van der Meulen, *Aden to the Hadramaut: A Journey in South Arabia* (London: John Murray, 1947), 32.

35. Charles J. Cruttenden, "Narrative of a Journey from Mokha to San'a by the Tarik-esh-Sham, or Northern Route, in July and August, 1936," *Journal of the Royal Geographical Society of London* 8 (1838): 279–80.

36. H. St. J. B. Philby, "The Land of Sheba," *Geographical Journal* 92, no. 1 (July 1938): 10.

37. Norman N. Lewis, "Lebanon: The Mountain and Its Terraces," *Geographical Review* 43, no. 1 (January 1953): 2–4.

38. Horst Vogel, "Impoundment-Type Bench Terracing with Underground Conduits in Jibal Haraz, Yemen Arab Republic," *Transactions of the Institute of British Geographers*, n.s., 13, no. 1 (1988): 30.

39. Horst Vogel, "Terrace Farming in Yemen," *Journal of Soil and Water Conservation* 42, no. 1 (1987): 19.

40. Daniel Martin Varisco, "The Ard in Highland Yemeni Agriculture," *Tools and Tillage* 4, no. 3 (1982): 157–72.

41. Vogel, "Impoundment-Type Bench Terracing," 33–36.

42. F. S. Vidal, *The Oasis of Al-Hasa* (N.p.: Arab-American Oil Company, 1955), 14.

43. Ibid., 15.

44. Cheesman, *In Unknown Arabia*, 52, 56–57.

45. Paul Ward English, "The Origin and Spread of Qanats in the Old World," *Proceedings of the American Philosophical Society* 112, no. 3 (June 1968): 175; and Dale R. Lightfoot, "The Origin and Diffusion of Qanats in Arabia: New Evidence from the Northern and Southern Peninsula," *Geographical Journal* 166, no. 3 (September 2000): 223.

46. A. S. Alsharhan et al., *Hydrogeology of an Arid Region: The Arabian Gulf and Adjoining Areas* (New York: Elsevier, 2001), 131.

47. George B. Cressy, "Qanats, Karez, and Foggaras," *Geographical Review* 48, no. 1 (January 1958): 30–36.

48. Wallin, *Travels in Arabia*, 140.

49. H. St. J. B. Philby, *Arabia of the Wahhabis*, reprint with additional materials (London: Franck Cass, 1977), 241. The number given here is based on

Philby's statement that a typical well could irrigate 300–500 *haudhs* (small rectangular plots of land about 4 paces by 5 in area).

50. Philby, *Heart of Arabia*, 1:76–77. Note that for simplicity's sake I have omitted some of the specialized terminology used by Philby.

51. Michael A. Sells, *Desert Tracings: Six Classic Arabian Odes by 'Alqama, Shánfara, Labíd, 'Antara, Al'A'sha, and Dhu al-Rúmma* (Middletown, CT: Wesleyan University Press, 1989), 14, 74.

52. van der Meulen, *Aden to the Hadhramaut*, 149.

53. Philip Ward, *Ha'il: Oasis City of Saudi Arabia* (New York: Oleander Press, 1983), 473.

54. Charles Huber, *Journal d'un Voyage en Arabie* (1883–1884) (Paris: Imprimerie Nationale, 1891), 382. Charles Doughty mentions that the going price for the rent of a camel from the Bedouins for one month was 100 measures of dates for each beast, or five riyals cash; see Doughty, *Travels in Arabia Deserta* (Cambridge, UK: Cambridge University Press, 1888), 1:543.

55. Bertram Thomas, *Alarms and Excursions in Arabia* (Indianapolis: Bobbs-Merrill Company, 1931), 126.

56. Philby, *Heart of Arabia*, 1:115–16.

57. Andrew Thompson, *Origins of Arabia* (Chicago: Fitzroy Dearborn Publishers, 2000), 54–55.

Chapter 2:"Diggers and Delvers"

1. Anonymous, *The Romance of 'Antar: An Epitome of the First Part*, trans. Terrick Hamilton (UK: Dodo Press, 2008), 56–57.

2. Bernard Lewis, "The Crows of the Arabs," *Critical Inquiry* 12, no. 1 (Autumn 1985): 92; and Akbar Muhammad, "The Image of Africans in Arabic Literature: Some Unpublished Manuscripts," in *Slaves and Slavery in Muslim Africa*, ed. John Ralph Willis (London: F. Cass, 1985), 1:50.

3. Lewis, *Race and Slavery*, 6.

4. Ibid.

5. Patterson, *Slavery and Social Death*, 202–3.

6. T. G. Otte, "'A Course of Unceasing Remonstrance:' British Diplomacy and the Suppression of the Slave Trade in the East, 1852–1898," in *Slavery, Diplomacy, and Empire: Britain and the Suppression of the Slave Trade, 1807–1975*, ed. Keith Hamilton and Patrick Salmon (Portland, OR: Sussex Academic Press, 2009), 94.

7. Gordon, *Slavery in the Arab World*, 19.

8. Eldon Rutter, "Slavery in Arabia," *Journal of the Royal Central Asian Society* 20, no. 3 (1933): 317–18.

9. Lewis, *Race and Slavery*, 7.

10. Daniel Pipes, "Mawlas: Freed Slaves and Converts in Early Islam," in Willis, *Slaves and Slavery* (New York: Frank Cass, 1985), 1:203–4, 221. See also

Mohammed Ennaji, *Slavery, the State, and Islam* (New York: Cambridge University Press, 2013), 190–96.

11. See Benjamin Reilly, "Revisiting Consanguineous Marriage in the Greater Middle East: Milk, Blood, and Bedouins," *American Anthropologist* 115, no. 3 (2013): 374–87.

12. Toledano, *Slavery and Abolition*, 7.

13. William Gervase Clarence-Smith, *Islam and the Abolition of Slavery* (New York: Oxford University Press, 2006), 131–32.

14. Najwa Adra, "The Concept of Tribe in Rural Yemen," in *Arab Society: Social Science Perspectives*, ed. Saad Eddin Ibrahim and Nicholas S. Hopkins (Cairo: American University in Cairo Press, 1985), 275, 280.

15. Scott, *In the High Yemen*, 182–83.

16. F. J. G. Mercadier, *L'esclave de Timimoun* (Paris: Editions France-Empire, 1971), 140–41. Note that I have converted the French term coudée, which means "cubit," into meters using the common conversion rate of .45 meters = 1 cubit. My translation.

17. Ibid., 141–42.

18. Philby, *Heart of Arabia*, 2:103.

19. Antonin Jaussen and Raphaël Savignac, *Mission archéologique en Arabie* (Paris: Ernest Leroux, 1909), 66.

20. Altorki and Cole, *Arabian Oasis City*, 55–56.

21. Ibid., 40.

22. Ibid., 41.

23. Huber, *Journal d'un voyage en Arabie*, 385; and van der Meulen, *Aden to the Hadhramaut*, 149.

24. Portions of this section have been drawn from my earlier article on the subject: Reilly, "*Mutawalladeen* and Malaria," 1–19.

25. Gordon, *Slavery in the Arab World*, 50.

26. *Gazetteer of Arabia* (Simla, India: General Staff of India, 1917) 1:354, 760; *Gazetteer of Arabia*, 2:1517. Thomas M. Ricks notes in his study of slavery in the eighteenth- and nineteenth-century Gulf that some African slaves were used "as farm laborers" in Bahrain as well as Basra and Muscat, but gives no indication as to the scale of this phenomenon, nor does he list his sources; see Thomas M. Ricks, "Slaves and Slave Traders in the Persian Gulf, 18th and 19th Centuries: An Assessment," in Clarence-Smith, *Indian Ocean Slave Trade*, 65.

27. *Gazetteer of Arabia*, 354

28. L. Luca Cavalli-Sforza, Paolo Menozzi, and Alberto Piazza, *The History and Geography of Human Genes* (Princeton, NJ: Princeton University Press, 1994), 129–30, 146–48.

29. Alan de Lacy Rush, ed., *Ruling Families of Arabia: Qatar, the Ruling Family of Al-Thani* (Slough, UK: Archive Editions, 1991), 137.

30. *Gazetteer of Arabia*, 2:1512.

31. Ibid., 1:271–72.

32. Ibid., 276.

33. Wilfred Thesiger, "A Journey through the Tihama, the 'Asir, and the Hijaz Mountains," *Geographical Journal* 110, no. 4/6 (October–December 1947): 192, 196. A similar but more superficial description of the Tihamah African population is provided by R. B. Serjeant, "Société et gouvernement en Arabie du Sud," *Arabica* 14, no. 3 (October 1967): 287.

34. Thesiger, "Journey," 192.

35. *Gazetteer of Arabia*, 1:46.

36. G. Wyman Bury, *The Land of Uz* (London: Macmillan, 1911), 11.

37. Ibid., 32–33.

38. Joseph Halévy, *Rapport sur une mission archéologique dans le Yémen* (Paris: Imprimerie Nationale, 1872), 25; and Halévy, "Voyage au Nedjran," *Bulletin de la Société de Géographie*, July–December 1873: 594.

39. Halévy, "Voyage au Nedjran," 271–72.

40. Floor, *Persian Gulf*, 377.

41. Sheriff, *Slaves, Spices, and Ivory in Zanzibar*, 35–37.

42. Cooper, *Plantation Slavery*, 37.

43. Hopper, "Economics of African Slavery," 116.

44. A. L. P. Burdett, ed., *The Slave Trade into Arabia: 1820–1973* (Slough, UK: Archive Editions, 2006), 6:271–72.

45. Thomas, *Alarms and Excursions in Arabia*, 238.

46. Bertram Thomas, *Arabia Felix: Across the Empty Quarter of Arabia* (London: Reader's Union, 1938), 9.

47. Ibid., 29–30.

48. Ibid., 194–97. C. Snounk Hurgronje, who describes the zar possession cult in Mecca in some depth, ascribes this ritual primarily to Abyssinian slaves, though he also notes that the cult had a "Maghrebin [North-West African], a Sudanese, an Abyssinian, and a Turkish method." C. Snouck Hurgronje, *Mekka in the Latter Part of the 19th Century*, trans. J. H. Monahan (Leiden, NL: E. J. Brill, 2007), 112–16.

49. Janzen, *Nomads*, 149–50.

50. Bent and Bent, *Southern Arabia*, 79–80.

51. van der Meulen and von Wissmann, *Ḥaḍramaut*, 69.

52. Freya Stark, *A Winter in Arabia: A Journey Through Yemen* (New York: Overlook Press, 2002), 72.

53. Ibid., 264.

54. Ibid., 295.

55. Harold Ingrams, *Arabia and the Isles* (London: John Murray, 1943), 280–81.

56. *Gazetteer of Arabia*, 2:1019; *Gazetteer of Arabia* (Simla, India: General Staff of India, 1917), 3:1829.

57. *Gazetteer of Arabia*, 3:1717.

58. Ibid., 2:1582.

59. Philby, *Arabia of the Wahhabis*, 179, 181.

60. Ibid., 337.

61. *Gazetteer of Arabia*, 3:1784.

62. G. Leachman, "A Journey through Central Arabia," *Geographical Journal* 43, no. 5 (May 1914): 513.

63. Philby, *Arabia of the Wahhabis*, 136.

64. *Gazetteer of Arabia*, 2:1452.

65. Alois Musil, *Northern Neğd: A Topographical Itinerary* (New York: American Geographical Society, 1928), 239–40.

66. Musil, *Northern Neğd*, 85.

67. Philby, *Heart of Arabia*, 2:12–13.

68. *Gazetteer of Arabia*, 1:533. The *Gazetteer* seems to imply, implausibly, that Jau-as-Sabaini is a satellite town of Dhurma, which lies about 60 kilometers away from Riyadh and the Wadi Hanifa, across a mountainous escarpment.

69. Philby, *Heart of Arabia*, 2:92–94.

70. *Gazetteer of Arabia*, 1:118.

71. Ibid., 163.

72. Philby, *Heart of Arabia*, 2:189.

73. Marcel Kurpershoek, *Arabia of the Bedouins*, trans. Paul Vincent (London: Saqi Books, 1995), 180.

74. *Gazetteer of Arabia*, 2:949. See also Wallin, *Travels in Arabia*, 115.

75. Gottlieb Schumacher, *Across the Jordan: An Exploration and Survey of Part of Hauran and Jaulan* (London: Alexander Watt, 1889), 154–55, 187–93.

76. H. B. Tristram, *The Land of Moab: Travels and Discoveries on the East Side of the Dead Sea and the Jordan* (London: John Murray, 1873), 303.

77. Abujaber, *Pioneers over Jordan*, 85.

78. William Lancaster, *The Rwala Bedouin Today*, 2nd ed. (Long Grove, IL: Waveland Press, 1997), 108.

79. J. R. Wellsted, "Observations on the Coast of Arabia between Ras Mohammed and Jiddah," *Journal of the Royal Geographical Society of London* 6 (1836): 55.

80. Wallin, *Travels in Arabia*, 115–16.

81. *Gazetteer of Arabia*, 2:1022.

82. Doughty, *Travels in Arabia Deserta*, 2:183.

83. *Gazetteer of Arabia*, 2:1021.

84. The term "Takruri" (also written Takruzi or Takrasi) was a general term for slaves of West African origins, whether they were from "Nigeria, the Congo, the Cameroons, French West Africa, or elsewhere." See British Consulate of Jeddah to the Foreign Office, "Note on Slavery in the Hejaz, with suggestions for Checking it," 9 June 1925, in *The Slave Trade into Arabia: 1820–1973*, ed. A. L. P. Burdett (Slough, UK: Archive Editions, 2006), 5:565.

85. T. E. Lawrence, *Seven Pillars of Wisdom: A Triumph*, 1st Anchor Books ed. (New York: Anchor Books, 1991), 89.

86. Ibid.

87. Philby, *Heart of Arabia*, 1:213–15.

88. Motoko Katakura, *Bedouin Village: A Study of a Saudi Arabian People in Transition* (Tokyo: University of Tokyo Press, 1977), 55, 59.

89. Philby, *Heart of Arabia*, 1:170–73.

90. *Gazetteer of Arabia*, 3:1615–16.

91. Philby, *Heart of Arabia*, 1:168–69.

92. Maurice Tamisier, *Voyage en Arabie* (Paris: Louis Desessart, 1840), 1:258. My translation.

93. Tamisier, *Voyage en Arabie*, 2:62, 107, 124. My translation.

94. See Onn Winckler, "The Surprising Results of the Saudi Arabian 2004 Demographic Census," *International Journal of Middle East Studies* 40, no. 1 (2008): 13.

95. Suzanne Miers, "Slavery and the Slave Trade in Saudi Arabia and the Arab State of the Persian Gulf, 1921–1963," in Campbell, *Abolition and Its Aftermath*, 120.

96. Sir A. Ryan to the Foreign Office, "Memorandum on Slavery in Saudi Arabia," 15 May 1934, in Burdett, *Slave Trade into Arabia*, 6:683.

97. Alaine S. Hutson, "Enslavement and Manumission in Saudi Arabia, 1926–38," *Critique: Critical Middle Eastern Studies* 11, no. 1 (Spring 2002): 60–66.

98. In 1848, for example, British officials estimated that female slaves imported into Muscat outnumbered men by a ratio of 6 to 5, while in 1894 a British official in Jeddah estimated the ratio of imports was 2 females to 1 male. See Letter from H. D. Robertson, Officiating Resident, Persian Gulf, Karrack, to Lt.-Col. Sheil, 9 July 1842, in *The Slave Trade into Arabia: 1820–1973*, ed. A. L. P. Burdett (Slough, UK: Archive Editions, 2006), 1:320–21; and "Notes on slaves, answers by Dr. Abdul Razzack, to queries by Commander Paget," 12 June 1894, in *The Slave Trade into Arabia: 1820–1973*, ed. A. L. P. Burdett (Slough, UK: Archive Editions, 2006), 4:764.

99. British Embassy in Jeddah to the Earl of Home, 12 September 1963, in *The Slave Trade into Arabia: 1820–1973*, ed. A. L. P. Burdett (Slough, UK: Archive Editions, 2006), 8:404–5.

100. Ibid.

101. Suzanne Miers, "The Anti-Slavery Game: Britain and the Suppression of Slavery in Africa and Arabia, 1890–1875," in Hamilton and Salmon, *Slavery, Diplomacy, and Empire*, 198; and Benjamin Reilly, "A Well-Intentioned Failure: British Antislavery Measures and the Arabian Peninsula, 1820–1940," *Journal of Arabian Studies*, forthcoming.

102. Webb, *Desert Frontier*, 25.

Chapter 3: Case Study: Khaybar

1. Doughty, *Travels in Arabia Deserta*, 2:92.

2. Thompson, *Origins of Arabia*, 51.

3. H. St. John Bridger Philby, *The Land of Midian* (London: Ernest Benn Limited, 1957), 37.

4. Ibid., 198.

5. Abdullah al-Nasif has suggested that water was supplied to Khaybar via qanats, though I know of no evidence that supports this claim. See al-Nasif, "Al-'Ula (Saudi Arabia): A Report on a Historical and Archaeological Survey," *Bulletin of the British Society for Middle Eastern Studies* 8, no. 1 (1981): 31–32.

6. Huber, "Voyage dans L'Arabie Centrale," 525. My translation.

7. Irfan Shahîd, *Byzantium and the Arabs in the Sixth Century* (Washington, DC: Dumbarton Oaks, 2010), 322.

8. Yāqūt [Yāqūt ibn-'Abdullah al-Rūmī al-Hamawī], *Kitāb mu'jam al-buldān*, trans. Raji Kitabe (Beirut: Dar Beirut, 1955.), 55.

9. al-Tabari [Abu Ja'far Muhammad ibn Jarir al-Tabari], *The History of al-Tabari*, vol. 8, *The Victory of Islam*, trans. Michael Fishbein (Albany: State University of New York Press, 1997), 116; and Ibn Isḥāq [Muḥammad ibn Isḥāq ibn Yasār ibn Khiyār], *Sīrat Rasūl Allāh*, trans. A. Guillaume (London: Oxford University Press, 2012), 511.

10. Martin Lings, *Muhammad: His Life Based on the Earliest Sources*, 2nd US ed. (Rochester, VT: Inner Traditions, 2006), 273.

11. See Ibn Isḥāq, *Sīrat Rasūl Allāh*, 525.

12. C. E. Bosworth, "The 'Protected Peoples' (Christians and Jews) in Medieval Egypt and Syria," *Bulletin of the John Rylands University Library of Manchester* 62, no. 1 (1979): 24.

13. al-Muqaddasi [Muḥammad ibn Aḥmad Shams al-Dīn al-Muqaddasī], *The Best Divisions for Knowledge of the Regions*, trans. Basil Anthony Collins (Reading, UK: Garnet Publishing, 1994), 81–82.

14. *The Itinerary of Benjamin of Tudela*, trans. Marcus N. Adler (Charleston, SC: BiblioBazaar, 2008), 60, 111–12.

15. *The Travels of Ludovico di Varthema* (Lexington, KY: Elibron Classics, 2005), 22–24, 33. Alternatively, Varthema may have meant the northern Yemeni town of Tin'am, which Franco-Ottoman traveler Halévy describes as a ruined town once "famous for its large population of warrior Jews"; see Halévy, *Rapport sur une mission archéologique*, 59.

16. Clinton Bailey, *A Culture of Desert Survival: Bedouin Proverbs from Sinai and the Negev* (New Haven, CT: Yale University Press, 2004), 192.

17. Huber, "Voyage dans L'Arabie Centrale," 529.

18. Carlo Guarmani, *Northern Najd: A Journey from Jerusalem to Anaiza in Qasim*, trans. Muriel Capel-Cure (London: The Argonaut Press, 1938), 26.

19. Doughty, *Travels in Arabia Deserta*, 2:75.

20. Huber, "Voyage dans L'Arabie Centrale," 518, 530. My translation.

21. Doughty, *Travels in Arabia Deserta*, 2:171.

22. Ibid., 114.

23. Ibid.

24. Gerald de Gaury, *Review of the 'Anizah Tribe* (Beirut, Lebanon: Kutub, 2005, originally compiled 1932), 14–15. See also Touvia Ashkenazi, "Social and Historical Problems of the 'Anazeh Tribes," *Journal of the Economic and Social History of the Orient* 8, no. 1 (August 1965): 93–100.

25. Albrecht Noth, "Isfahan-Nihawand: A Source-critical Study of Early Islamic Historiography" in *The Expansion of the Early Islamic State*, ed. Fred M. Donner (Burlington, VT: Ashgate Publishing, 2008), 241–62.

26. Guarmani, *Northern Najd*, 82.

27. Hurgronje, *Mekka*, 18–19.

28. Report by Lynedock N. Moncrieff, Jeddah, "Memorandum on the Slave Traffic in the Red Sea during 1882," 30 February 1883, in *The Slave Trade into Arabia: 1820–1973*, ed. A. L. P. Burdett (Slough, UK: Archive Editions, 2006), 3:659.

29. Guarmani, *Northern Najd*, 29.

30. Doughty, *Travels in Arabia Deserta*, 2:80.

31. Charles M. Doughty, *Travels in Arabia Deserta* (N.p.: Elibron Classics, 2006), 1:553.

32. Doughty, *Travels in Arabia Deserta*, 2:85.

33. Ibid., 90, 94.

34. Ibid., 117.

35. Mercadier, *L'esclave de Timimoun*, 132–33. My translation.

36. Ibid.

37. Doughty, *Travels in Arabia Deserta*, 2:199.

38. Ibid.

39. Ibid.

40. Philby, *Land of Midian*, 42.

41. Ibid., 92.

42. Ibid.

43. Huber, "Voyage dans L'Arabie Centrale," 530. My translation.

44. Doughty, *Travels in Arabia Deserta*, 2:140.

45. Mercadier, *L'esclave de Timimoun*, 171–75. My translation.

46. Doughty, *Travels in Arabia Deserta*, 2:199.

47. Philby, *Land of Midian*, 18.

48. Ibid., 34.

49. Doughty, *Travels in Arabia Deserta*, 2:113–14.

50. Reilly, "Revisiting Consanguineous Marriage," 374–87.

51. Alois Musil, *In the Arabian Desert* (New York: Horace Liveright, 1930), 206–7.

52. Doughty, *Travels in Arabia Deserta*, 2:115.

53. Ibid., 93–94.

54. Ibid., 107.

55. Ibid., 191.

56. Anne Meneley, for example, notes the existence of the zar possession cults in the Yemeni town of Zabid well into the twentieth century. As in Khaybar, zar ceremonies were associated primarily with ex-slaves and other lower-class populations of African descent. See Anne Meneley, *Tournaments of Value: Sociability and Hierarchy in a Yemeni Town* (Toronto: University of Toronto Press, 1996), 15, 151–52.

57. Ehud Toledano, *As if Silent and Absent: Bonds of Enslavement in the Islamic Middle East* (New Haven, CT: Yale University Press, 2007), 33, 259.

58. Ibid., 220.

59. Ibn Isḥāq, *Sīrat Rasūl Allāh*, 67–68.

60. Philby, *Land of Midian*, 33.

61. Doughty, *Travels in Arabia Deserta*, 2:77.

62. Ibid., 110.

63. Ibid., 143.

64. Ibid., 34.

65. Ibid., 42.

66. Ibid., 34.

67. Ibid., 44.

Chapter 4: "Oasis Fever"

1. Mabel Bent, "Exploration in the Yafei and Fadhli Countries," *Geographical Journal* 12, no. 1 (July 1898): 44–45, 62.

2. Rihani, *Maker of Modern Arabia*, 141.

3. Dale F. Eickelman, *The Middle East and Central Asia: An Anthropological Approach* (Upper Saddle River, NJ: Prentice Hall, 2002), 30.

4. A. J. Lysenko and I. N. Semashko, "Geography of Malaria. A Medico-geographic Profile of an Ancient Disease," in *Itogi Nauki: Medicinskaja Geografija*, ed. A. W. Lebedew (Moscow: Academy of Sciences USSR, 1968), 25–146. For those of us unable to read Russian, these findings are summarized in Peter W. Gething et al., "Climate Change and the Global Malaria Recession," *Nature* 465 (20 May 2010): 342.

5. B. Anderson and C. Vullo, "Did Malaria Select for Primary Adult Lactase Deficiency?" *Gut* 35, no. 19 (1994): 1487.

6. W. H. Schoff, trans. and ed., *The Periplus of the Erythraean Sea: Travel and Trade in the Indian Ocean by a Merchant of the First Century* (London: Longman, Green and Company, 1912), 29.

7. Ibn Isḥāq, *Sīrat Rasūl Allāh*, 280.

8. Lings, *Muhammad: His Life*, 356.

9. Sells, *Desert Tracings*, 28.

10. C. E. Bosworth, "A note on taʿarrub in early Islam," *Journal of Semitic Studies* 34, no. 2 (1989): 360–61.

11. Ibid.

12. Anderson and Vullo, "Adult Lactase Deficiency," 1487. Anderson and Vullo's contention that malaria influenced observed global LP gene distributions has been questioned: see A. Inkeri Lokki et al., "Lactase Persistence Genotypes and Malaria Susceptibility in Fulani of Mali," *Malaria Journal* 10, no. 6 (2011): 5; and E. Ingram et al., "Lactose Digestion and the Evolutionary Genetics of Lactase Persistence," *Human Genetics* 124 (2009): 588.

13. van der Meulen, *Aden to the Hadhramaut*, 121.

14. Bertram Thomas, "The South-Eastern Borderlands of Rub' al Khali," *Geographical Journal* 73, no. 3 (March 1929): 205.

15. Stark, *Winter in Arabia*, 236. French geographer J. Passama notes that the Wadi Najran in Yemen had a similar reputation for fevers "after the flowering of the dates"; see J. Passama, "Notice géographique sur quelques parties de l'Yémen," *Bulletin de la Sociéte de Géographie*, January 1843: 227. My translation.

16. R. E. Cheesman, "The Deserts of Jafra and Jabrin," *Geographical Journal* 65, no. 2 (February 1925): 131.

17. See for example Alois Musil, *The Northern Hegaz: A Topographical Itinerary* (New York: American Geographical Society, 1926), 129; and Cheesman, *In Unknown Arabia*, 113.

18. Musil, *In the Arabian Desert*, 116.

19. Albertine Jwaidah and J. W. Cox, "The Black Slaves of Turkish Arabia during the 19th Century," *Slavery and Abolition* 9, no. 3 (1988): 48.

20. Wellsted, *Travels in Arabia*, 1:311.

21. Stephen E. Sidebothham, "Aelius Gallus and Arabia," *Latomus* 45, no. 3 (July–September 1986): 590.

22. *Narrative of the Life and Adventures of Giovanni Finati* (London: John Murray, 1830), 2:42

23. Vassiliev, *History of Saudi Arabia*, 220–21.

24. Musil, *The Northern Hegaz*, 84.

25. Margaret Humphreys, *Malaria: Poverty, Race, and Public Health in the United States* (Baltimore: John Hopkins University Press, 2001), 11.

26. Randall M. Packard, *The Making of a Tropical Disease: A Short History of Malaria* (Baltimore: John Hopkins University Press, 2007), 23.

27. Margaret Humphreys gives the figure of 20–40%, while James L. A. Webb, Jr., provides the statistic of 25–50%. See James L. A. Webb, Jr., *Humanity's Burden: A Global History of Malaria* (Cambridge, UK: Cambridge University Press, 2009), 5.

28. James L. A. Webb, Jr., *The Long Struggle against Malaria in Tropical Africa* (New York: Cambridge University Press, 2014), 5.

29. Ibid., 1.

30. Humphreys, *Poverty, Race, and Public Health*, 9–10.

31. Webb, *Humanity's Burden*, 2.

32. E. I. Khater et al., "Ecology and Habitat Characterization of Mosquitoes in Saudi Arabia," *Tropical Biomedicine* 30, no. 3 (2013): 420.

33. F. Mattingly and K. L. Knight, "The Mosquito of Arabia," *International Bulletin of the British Museum (Entomology)* 4, no. 3 (1956): 89–141; and Azzam Mohammed Alahmed, "Mosquito Fauna (Diptera: Culicidae) of the Eastern Region of Saudi Arabia and Their Seasonal Abundance," *Journal of King Saud University—Science* 24 (2012): 57.

34. Alahmed, "Mosquito Fauna (Diptera: Culicidae)," 57. See also Ashraf M. Ahmed et al., "Mosquito Vectors Survey in the Al-Ahsaa District of Eastern Saudi Arabia," *Journal of Insect Science* 11 (2011): 1–11.

35. A-M. M. O. Abdoon and A. M. Alshahrani, "Prevalence and Distribution of Anopheline Mosquitoes in Malaria Endemic Areas of Asir Region, Saudi Arabia," *La Revue de Santé de la Méditerranée Orientale* 9, no. 3 (2003): 240.

36. Khater, "Ecology and Habitat," 421; and Abdulsalam M. Q. al-Mekhlafi et al., "Clinical Situation of Endemic Malaria in Yemen," *Tropical Biomedicine* 27, no. 3 (2010): 551.

37. Colbert C. Held, *Middle East Patterns: Places, People, and Politics* (Boulder, CO: Westview Press, 2006), 47.

38. Julius Euting, *Tagbuch Einer Reise in Inner-Arabien* (Leiden, NL: E. J. Brill, 1896). Quoted in Ward, *Ha'il*, 473. Ward's translation.

39. Wilfrid Scawen Blunt, "A Visit to Jebel Shammar (Nejd). New Routes Through Northern and Central Arabia," *Proceedings of the Royal Geographical Society and Monthly Record of Geography* 2, no. 2 (February 1880): 84.

40. Marianne E. Sinka et al., "The Dominant *Anopheles* Vectors of Human Malaria in the Asia-Pacific Region: Occurrence Data, Distribution Maps and Bionomic Précis," *Parasites and Vectors* 4 (2011), doi: 10.1186/1756-3305-4-89.

41. Norman N. Lewis, "Malaria, Irrigation, and Soil Erosion in Central Syria," *Geographical Review* 39, no. 2 (April 1949): 287.

42. Ibid.

43. Ibid., 287–88.

44. Huber, "Voyage dans L'Arabie Centrale," 500. My translation. Huber's "Qeçeïbah," as he spelled it, is undoubtedly the same town as Qusaibah from the *Gazetteer of Arabia*, and is probably identical to the present-day town of Qasr 'Ali, which lies about 8–9 kilometers north-northwest of 'Unaizah.

45. Richard H. Daggy, "Malaria in Oases of Eastern Saudi Arabia," *American Journal of Tropical Medicine and Hygiene* 8 (1959): 225.

46. Ibid., 237.

47. Ibid., 235.

48. Ibid., 235, 236, 249.

49. Ibid., 243–46.

50. Laila Zahed, "The Spectrum of β-thalassemia Mutations in the Arab Populations," *Journal of Biomedicine and Biotechnology* 1, no. 3 (2001): 130.

51. Baker H. al-Awamy, "Thalassemia Syndromes in Saudi Arabia: Meta-analysis of Local Studies," *Saudi Medical Journal* 21, no. 1 (2000): 15.

52. Cavalli-Sforza, Menozzi, and Piazza, *Human Genes*, 150.

53. Ibid., 160.

54. O. S. Platt et al., "Mortality in Sickle Cell Disease: Life Expectancy and Risk Factors for Early Death," *New England Journal of Medicine* 330 (1994): 1639–43.

55. Webb, *Humanity's Burden*, 28.

56. James H. Mielke et al., *Human Biological Variation*, 2nd ed. (New York: Oxford University Press, 2011), 162.

57. Ibid., 37.

58. Kenneth F. Kiple, *The Caribbean Slave: A Biological History* (Cambridge, UK: Cambridge University Press, 1984), 9.

59. Ibid., 12, 178.

60. John Lewis Burckhardt, *Travels in Nubia* (London: John Murray, 1819), 312. It should be noted that Burckhardt defines the "Nubian" slaves as a distinct subclass of Africans, differentiated both from the Abyssinians to the north of them and the "true Negroe" of the south, "whose hands, when touched feel like wood."

61. Ahmad Alawad Sikainga, "Comrades in Arms or Captives in Bondage: Sudanese Slaves in the Turko-Egyptian Army, 1821–1865," in *Slave Elites in the Middle East and Africa*, ed. Toru Miamura and John Edward Philips (New York: Kegan Paul International, 2000), 206.

62. See for example Major Wilson, Resident of Bushire, "Comprehensive Survey of the Extent and Nation of the Slave trade in Trucial Oman in 1831," in Burdett, *Slave Trade into Arabia*, 1:40–42; Wellsted, *Travels in Arabia*, 1:389; "Memorandum on the Slave Traffic in the Red Sea during 1882," Report by Lynedock N. Moncrieff, Jeddah 30 February 1883 in Burdett, *Slave Trade into Arabia*, 3:659–60; and "Notes on slaves, answers by Dr. Abdul Razzack, to queries by Commander Paget," 12 June 1894 in Burdett, *Slave Trade into Arabia*, 4:764.

63. Cavalli-Sforza, Menozzi, and Piazza, *Human Genes*, 147, and plate 160.

64. Hutson, "Enslavement and Manumission," 61.

65. Miers, "Anti-Slavery Game," 204.

66. *Gazetteer of Arabia*, 2:1538; and *Gazetteer of Arabia*, 3:1727, 1846.

Chapter 5: Arabian Agricultural Slavery in the Longue Durée

1. Chase F. Robinson, *Islamic Historiography* (New York: Cambridge University Press, 2003), 124; and Trabelsi, "L'esclavage domanial," 307.

2. 'Uthman Ibn Bishr an-Najdi, *'Unwān al-majd fī Tārīkh Najd* [The History of Najd] (Al-Riyadh, SA: Daar al-Habeeb, 1999); Husain Ibn Ghannam, *Tarīkh Najd* [The History of Najd], ed. Nāṣir al-Dīn Asad (Al-Riyadh, SA: 'Abd al-'Aziz ibn Muhammad ibn Ibrahim al-Shaykh, 1982); and Anonymous, *Kitab*

lam' al-shihāb fī sīrat Muḥammad ibn 'Abd al-Wahhāb, ed. Ahmad Mustafa Abu-Hakima (Beirut: Dar al-Thaqafah, 1967).

3. al-Muqaddasi, Knowledge of the Regions, 67–103.

4. Yāqūt, Kitāb mu'jam al-buldān.

5. Muhammad Ibn al-Tayyib al-Sharaqī, The Travels of Ibn al-Ṭayyib: The Forgotten Journey of an Eighteenth Century Traveller to the Ḥijāz, trans. El Mustapha Lahlali, Salah Al-Dihan, and Wafa Abu Hatab (New York: I. B. Tauris, 2010), 102.

6. Ibid., 114.

7. Khusraw, Book of Travels, 112. Note that Khusraw's "Zanzibaris" were most likely East African or Sudan slaves of sub-Saharan Africa rather than slaves from Zanzibar proper: see Popovic, Revolt of African Slaves, 20; and Talhami, "Zanj Rebellion Reconsidered," 461.

8. A. Gelpi, "Agriculture, Malaria, and Human Evolution: A Study of Genetic Polymorphisms in the Saudi Oasis Population," Saudi Medical Journal 4, no. 3 (July 1983): 234.

9. Ronnie Ellenblum, The Collapse of the Eastern Mediterranean: Climate Change and the Decline of the East, 950–1072 (New York: Cambridge University Press, 2012), 214.

10. Sam White, The Climate of Rebellion in the Early Modern Ottoman Empire (New York: Cambridge University Press, 2011); White, "The Little Ice Age Crisis of the Ottoman Empire: A Conjuncture in Middle East Environmental History," in Mikhail, Water on Sand, 71–90; and Alan Mikhail, Nature and Empire in Ottoman Egypt: An Environmental History (New York: Cambridge University Press, 2011).

11. See for example Juris Zarins, "Environmental Disruption and Human Response: An Archaeological-Historical Example from South Arabia," in Environmental Disaster and the Archeology of Human Response, ed. Garth Bawden and Richard M. Reycraft (Albuquerque: University of New Mexico, Maxwell Museum of Anthropology, 2000), 35–49; Jean-François Berger et al., "Rivers of the Hadramawt Watershed (Yemen) during the Holocene: Clues of Late Functioning," Quaternary International 266 (2012): 142–61; Dominik Fleitmann et al., "Palaeoclimatic Interpretation of High-Resolution Oxygen Isotope Profiles Derived from Annually Laminated Speleothems from Southern Oman," Quaternary Science Reviews 23 (2004): 935–45; Markus Fuchs and Andreas Buerkert, "A 20 ka Sediment Record from the Hajar Mountain Range in N-Oman, and Its Implication for Detecting Arid-Humid Periods on the Southeastern Arabian Peninsula," Earth and Planetary Science Letters 265 (2008): 546–58; B. Urban and A. Buerkert, "Palaeoecological Analysis of a Late Quaternary Sediment Profile in Northern Oman," Journal of Arid Environments 73 (2009): 296–305; and G. W. Preston et al., "From Nomadic Herder-hunters to Sedentary Farmers: The Relationship between Climate Change and Ancient Subsistence Strategies in South-Eastern Arabia," Journal of Arid Environments 86 (2012): 122–30.

12. See Brian Fagan, *The Little Ice Age: How Climate Made History, 1300–1850* (New York: Basic Books, 2000), 51–52.

13. Patrick Manning, *Slavery and African Life: Occidental, Oriental, and African Slave Trades* (New York: Cambridge University Press, 1990), 83.

14. Edward A. Alpers, "The African Diaspora in the Northwestern Indian Ocean: Reconsideration of an Old Problem, New Directions for Research," *Comparative Studies of South Asia, Africa and the Middle East* 17, no. 2 (1997): 63.

15. These statistics do not include slaves who were carried through the Indian Ocean on European ships, a traffic that became quite considerable from 1700–1850: see Richard B. Allen, "Satisfying the 'Want for Labouring People': European Slave Trading in the Indian Ocean, 1500–1850," *Journal of World History* 21, no. 1 (March 2010): 68.

16. Lovejoy, *Transformations in Slavery*, 26.

17. Popovic, *Revolt of African Slaves*, 24.

18. Lovejoy, *Transformations in Slavery*, 72–73.

19. Cooper, *Plantation Slavery*, 126. This famine may have been the same as the "Evil Days" famine of Ethiopian History, in which up to a third of the Ethiopian population is said to have died; see Alex de Waal, *Evil Days: 30 Years of War and Famine in Ethiopia* (New York: Human Rights Watch, 1991), 29–30.

20. Consul Jago to the Marquis of Salisbury, London, July 9, 1887, in Burdett, *Slave Trade into Arabia*, 4:256.

21. Gordon, *Slavery in the Arab World*, 181.

22. Cuno, "African Slaves," 81.

22. Ibid., 89, 96.

24. Cooper, *Plantation Slavery*, 56–61. Similar statistics are given by Sheriff, *Slaves, Spices, and Ivory in Zanzibar*, 59–60.

25. Janet J. Ewald, "Crossers of the Sea: Slaves, Freedmen, and other Migrants in the Northwestern Indian Ocean c. 1750–1914," *American Historical Review* 105, no. 1 (February 2000): 77.

26. Cooper, *Plantation Slavery*, 222.

27. Ibid., 228, 216.

28. Ibid., 242–52.

29. Although the sex ratio of slaves imported for agriculture vs. other professions in the Arab word has not been systematically studied, Cuno ("African Slaves," 83) found that 71–85 percent of slaves in rural Egyptian villages were male, which stands in direct contrast with slave ownership in cities and towns, where the majority were female.

30. The issue of relative demographic trends within desert and oasis environments has not been extensively studied, but J. R. Wellsted argued, sensibly, that Arabian oasis environments generally had a net annual population loss, since the oasis laborers are "less healthy than the hardy inhabitants of the Desert." As a result, "in order to supply these deficiencies, a regular progressive migration [to the oases environments] must be kept up, or when it fails . . .

large tracks of cultivated lands become abandoned." See Wellsted, *Travels in Arabia*, 1:363–64.

31. Sheriff, "Slave Mode of Production," 161. I should note that I am making use of Sheriff's broader analytical framework rather than his specific conclusions, which relate to slavery on the East African coast rather than the Arabian Peninsula.

32. Werner Ende, "The Nakhāwila, a Shiite Community in Medina Past and Present," *Die Welt des Islams* 37, no. 3 (November 1997): 303, 310.

33. Zakaria M. Al Hawsawi and Ghousia A. Ismail, "Stroke Among Sickle-Cell Disease Patients in Madina Maternity and Children's Hospital," *Annals of Saudi Medicine* 18, no. 5 (1998): 472.

34. Ende, "Nakhāwila, a Shiite Community," 310.

35. A. Gelpi and M. C. King, "Association of Duffy Blood Groups with the Sickle Cell Trait," *Human Genetics* 32 (1976): 66.

36. Stephen H. Embury et al., "Concurrent Sickle-Cell Anemia and α-thalassemia: Effect on Pathological Properties of Sickle Erythrocytes," *Journal of Clinical Investigation* 73 (January 1984): 121.

37. W. G. Palgrave, *Personal Narrative of a Year's Journey Through Central and Eastern Arabia (1862–63)* (London: Macmillan and Co., 1868), 271–72.

38. H. St. J. B. Philby, "African Contacts with Arabia," *Journal of the Royal African Society* 38, no. 150 (January 1939): 41. For geographic distribution of the Bani Khadhir, see *Gazetteer of Arabia*, 2:1019.

39. A. M. H. Sheriff, "The Slave Trade and Its Fallout in the Persian Gulf," in Campbell, *Abolition and Its Aftermath*, 110.

40. Al-'Ula is also spelled al-'Ali; the *Gazetteer of Arabia* (1:149) notes that the name is written al-'Ula but it is never so pronounced, but always as "al-Ali." Doughty called the town "el-Ally," and Huber called it "El 'Alâ."

41. Huber, "Voyage dans L'Arabie Centrale," 517–18.

42. Ibid., 518.

43. Ibid.

44. Wallin, *Travels in Arabia*, 115.

45. Khaled K. Abu-Amero et al., "Saudi Arabian Y-Chromosome Diversity and Its Relationship with Nearby Regions," *BMC Genetics* 10, no. 59 (September 2009): 2.

46. Martin Richards et al., "Extensive Female-Mediated Gene Flow from Sub-Saharan Africa into Near Eastern Arab Populations," *American Journal of Human Genetics* 72 (2003): 1062.

47. G. W. Bowersock, *The Throne of Adulis: Red Sea Wars on the Eve of Islam* (New York: Oxford University Press, 2013), 15, 92.

48. Philby, "African Contacts with Arabia," 41.

49. Richards et. al., "Female-Mediated Gene Flow," 1062.

50. Abu-Amero et al., "Saudi Arabian Y-Chromosome Diversity," 7.

51. Reilly, "Revisiting Consanguineous Marriage," 393–94.

52. Major Wilson, Resident of Bushire, "Comprehensive Survey of the Extent and Nation of the Slave trade in Trucial Oman in 1831," in Burdett, *Slave Trade into Arabia*, 1:40–42. Wilson's "crowns" are undoubtedly the Maria Theresa thalers, the ubiquitous currency of the Arabian Peninsula from the eighteenth century onwards.

53. Letter from the Political Department, Kharrack, to J. Willoughby, Secretary to the Government of Bombay, 4 March 1842, in Burdett, *Slave Trade into Arabia*, 1:305–6.

54. Letter from Captain Davies, Political Agent of Aden, to J. Willoughby, Secretary to the Government of Bombay, 3 July 1841, in Burdett, *Slave Trade into Arabia*, 1:292.

55. Richard B. Allen, "Suppressing a Nefarious Traffic: Britain and the Abolition of Slave Trading in India and the Western Indian Ocean, 1770–1830," *William and Mary Quarterly* 66, no. 4 (October 2009): 893.

56. Ochsenwald, "Slave Trade Controversy," 119.

57. Dr. Schimper of Adwa, "On the Red Sea slave trade," 1868, in *The Slave Trade into Arabia: 1820–1973*, ed. A. L. P. Burdett (Slough, UK: Archive Editions, 2006), 2:390.

58. Consul Zohrab to the Marquis of Salisbury, May 14, 1879, in Burdett, *Slave Trade into Arabia*, 3:454.

59. Consul Zohrab to the Marquis of Salisbury, May 3, 1879, in Burdett, *Slave Trade into Arabia*, 3:459–60.

60. Consul J. Zohrab, Jedda to the Earl of Granville, 9 December 1880, in Burdett, *Slave Trade into Arabia*, 3:587–88.

61. Henri Médard, "La plus ancienne et la plus récente des traites: panorama de la traite de l'esclavage en Afrique orientale et dans l'océan Indien," in *Traites et esclavages en Afrique oriental et dans l'océan Indien*, ed. Henri Médard et al. (Paris: Karthala et Ciresc, 2013): 115.

62. R. W. Beachey, *The Slave of Eastern Arabia* (New York: Harper and Row Publishers, 1976), 119. For details on the British Navy's East African slave trade suppression see also Christopher Lloyd, *The Navy and the Slave Trade: The Suppression of the African Slave Trade in the Nineteenth Century* (New York: Longmans, Green and Co., 1949); and Raymond C. Howell, *The Royal Navy and the Slave Trade* (New York: St. Martin's Press, 1987).

63. Howell, *Royal Navy and the Slave Trade*, 100.

64. Martin A. Klien, "The Emancipation of Slaves in the Indian Ocean," in Campbell, *Abolition and Its Aftermath*, 200–1.

65. Miers, "Antislavery Game," 198. See also Miers, *Slavery in the Twentieth Century*, 18–24. It should be noted that European control over the African coast and interior was uneven, however, and in some areas poor surveillance meant that slaves were still being smuggled into Arabia in large numbers into the twentieth century. Collett Dubois, in fact, argues that the slave trade in the French colony of Tadjoura only ended in 1936; see Colette Dubois, "Un traite

tardive en mer Rouge méridionale: la route des esclaves du golf de Tadjoura (1880–1936)," in Médard et al., *Traites et esclavages*, 221.

66. Reilly, "A Well-Intentioned Failure."

67. Ryan, "Memorandum on Slavery," 670.

68. Timothy Derek Fernyhough, *Serfs, Slaves, and Shifta; Modes of Production and Resistance in Pre-Revolutionary Ethiopia* (Addis Ababa, Ethiopia: Shama Books, 2010), 120–21, 157–59. See also Richard Pankhurst, "The Ethiopian Slave Trade in the Nineteenth and Early Twentieth Centuries: A Statistical Inquiry," *Journal of Semitic Studies* 9, no. 1 (1964): 220–28.

69. Mr. Jakins, Jeddah, to the Foreign Secretary Sir Austin Chamberlain, June 8, 1929, in Burdett, *Slave Trade into Arabia*, 6:302.

70. Ryan, "Memorandum on Slavery," 674.

71. Miers, *Slavery in the Twentieth Century*, 309.

72. Held, *Middle East Patterns*, 421.

73. Ibid.

74. Ibid.

75. Altorki and Cole, *Arabian Oasis City*, 176–77.

76. Daniel van der Meulen, *The Wells of Ibn Sa'ud* (New York: Kegan Paul International, 2000), 221.

77. Ibid., 169, 127.

78. Katakura, *Bedouin Village*, 55.

79. Kurpershoek, *Arabia of the Bedouins*, 248.

80. Daggy, "Malaria in Oases," 272.

81. Ibid., 276.

82. Chad H. Parker, "Controlling Man-Made Malaria: Corporate Modernisation and the Arabian American Oil Company's Malaria Control Program in Saudi Arabia, 1947–1956," *Cold War History* 12, no. 3 (August 2012): 485.

83. Gwyn Rowley, "Irrigation Systems in the Holy Land: A Comment," *Transactions of the Institute of British Geographers* 11, no. 3 (1986): 356–59.

84. Ibid., 486.

85. Jaffar A. Al-Tawfiq, "Epidemiology of Travel-related Malaria in a Non-malarious Area in Saudi Arabia," *Saudi Medical Journal* 27, no. 1 (2006): 86.

86. May Meleigy, "Arabian Peninsula States Launch Plan to Eradicate Malaria." *British Medical Journal* 334 (2007): 117.

Glossary

'Abid (عبد)   A slave. Also used more generally to refer to anyone of African descent.

Ard   Also known as the scratch plow, an ard is a light plow that cuts and aerates but does not turn over the soil.

Bustan (بستان)   Literally "garden," in the Arabian Peninsula this referred to the practice of growing secondary crops under the shade of a palm orchard.

Deera (ديرة)   A Bedouin tribe's customary pasture grounds, through which the tribe cycles during its seasonal migrations. The world derives from the verb dara, meaning rotation or cycle.

Fellaheen (فلاحين)   Plural; peasants, farmers, or agricultural workers.

Galla   A member of a commonly enslaved ethnic group found in southern and eastern Abyssinia. In common use, Galla could also refer to all slaves of Abyssinian origins.

Ghayl (غيل)   A natural flowing spring.

Habash (حبش)   An Abyssinian or Ethiopian.

Harrah or Harrat (حرة)   A lava field, consisting mainly of naked basalt rock. By Arabic grammatical convention, harrah is generally spelled "harrat" when used as a modifying adjective, as in "Harrat Khaybar."

Hadr (حضر)   An adjective used for settled, as opposed to Bedouin, populations.

Jalib (جلب)   A draw well, worked with animal power, consisting of a well, a wooden frame, wheels or pulleys, and a ramp or trench for the draft animals. Also called a zijrah.

Jinn (الجن)   Spirits, often harmful or capricious. Singular is jinee.

Khayabira   Descendants of the Jews in Khaybar.

Khaybara   Collective name given to the African farmers of Khaybar.

Mawla (مولى)   Literally an inheritor, but generally used as a term for a manumitted slave.

Muwallad (مولدون)   Generally used to describe a slave born into captivity, though the term can also be applied to offspring of mixed racial backgrounds. Plural is muwalladeen.

Qanat (قناة)   An artificial spring, consisting of a horizontal underground channel connected to the surface by a chain of vertical wells. Also called fogarra or falaj.

Sadaa (سادة)   "Descendants of the Prophet," nobles. Singular is sayyid.

Sayl (سال)   A flash flood.

Sharif (شريف)   "High" or "noble." Amongst Bedouins, sharif refers to the "noble" camel-breeding tribes. The term was also used for descendants of the Prophet. Plural is ashraf.

Sudan (سودان)   A sub-Saharan African. The term derives from the Arabic term aswad, meaning black or dark-colored.

Takruri   A sub-Saharan African of West African descent. Sometimes spelled "Takrusi" or "Takruzi" in the sources.

Wadi (وادي)   A seasonal watercourse or flood channel.

Zanj (زنج)   Technically Africans from Zanzibar in East Africa, also used more generally to refer to people of African descent.

Zar   A healing ritual involving the exorcism of evil spirits, imported into the Arabian Peninsula from Africa.

Bibliography

Primary Sources

Nineteenth- through Twentieth-Century Geographical Journal Articles and Traveler's Accounts

Arnaud, M. "Relation d'un voyage a Mareb (Saba) dans l'Arabie Méridionale, entrepris en 1843." *Journal Asiatique*, 4th ser., 5 (1845): 208–45, 309–45.

Bell, Gertrude. *The Desert and the Sown: Travels in Palestine and Syria.* New York: Dover Publications, 2008.

Bent, J. Theodore, and Mabel Bent. *Southern Arabia.* London: Smith, Elder and Co., 1900.

Bent, Mabel. "Exploration in the Yafei and Fadhli Countries." *Geographical Journal* 12, no. 1 (July 1898): 41–63.

Bent, Theodore. "Exploration of Frankincense Country, Southern Arabia." *Geographical Journal* 6, no. 2 (August 1895): 109–33.

Bertou, J. de. "Depression de la vallée du Jourdain et du lac Asphaltite." *Bulletin de la Société de Géographie*, September–October 1839: 113–65.

———. "Itinéraire de la mer Morte à Akaba par les Wadys-el-Ghor, el-Araba, et el-Akaba, et retour à Hébron par Petra." *Bulletin de la Société de Géographie*, January 1839: 274–331.

Bey, Ali. *Travels of Ali Bey.* 2 vols. London: Longman, Hurst, Rees, Orme and Brown, 1816.

Blunt, Lady Anne. *A Pilgrimage to Nejd.* Piscataway, NJ: Gorgias Press, 2002.

Blunt, Wilfrid Scawen. "A Visit to Jebel Shammar (Nejd). New Routes Through Northern and Central Arabia." *Proceedings of the Royal Geographical Society and Monthly Record of Geography* 2, no. 2 (February 1880): 81–102.

Botta, M. "Extraits de la relation d'une excursion au mont Saber dans l'Arabie méridionale." *Bulletin de la Société de Géographie*, September–October 1839: 369–82.

Burckhardt, John Lewis. *Travels in Arabia.* 2 vols. London: Henry Colburn, 1829.

———. *Travels in Nubia.* London: John Murray, 1819.

Burton, Richard F. *Pilgrimage to El Medinah and Meccah*. 2 vols. London: Longman, Brown, Green, Longmans, and Roberts, 1857.

——. *The Land of Midian*. 2 vols. London: C. Kegan Paul and Co., 1879.

Bury, G. Wyman. *The Land of Uz*. London: Macmillan and Co., 1911.

——. *Arabia Infelix: Or the Turks in Yamen*. New ed. Reading, UK: Garnet Publishing, 1998.

Butler, S. S. "Baghdad to Damascus viâ El Jauf, Northern Arabia." *Geographical Journal* 33, no. 5 (May 1909): 517–33.

Caraman, Adolphe de. "Voyage de Homs a Palmyre et retour." *Bulletin de la Société de Géographie*, June 1840 : 321–45.

Carruthers, Douglas. "A Journey in North-Western Arabia." *Geographical Journal* 35, no. 3 (March 1910): 225–45.

——. *Arabian Adventure: To the Great Nafud in Quest of the Oryx*. London: H. F. G. Witherby, 1935.

Cheesman, R. E. "The Deserts of Jafra and Jabrin." *Geographical Journal* 65, no. 2 (February 1925): 112–37.

——. *In Unknown Arabia*. London: Macmillan, 1926.

Cox, Percy. "Some Excursions in Oman." *Geographical Journal* 66, no. 3 (September 1925): 193–221.

Cruttenden, Charles J. "Narrative of a Journey from Mokha to San'a by the Tarik-esh-Sham, or Northern Route, in July and August, 1936." *Journal of the Royal Geographical Society of London* 8 (1838): 267–89.

Doughty, Charles M. *Travels in Arabia Deserta*. 2 vols. Cambridge, UK: Cambridge University Press, 1888.

——. "Travels in North-Western Arabia and Nejd." *Proceedings of the Royal Geographical Society and Monthly Record of Geography* 6, no. 7 (July 1884): 382–99.

Euting, Julius. *Tagbuch Einer Reise in Inner-Arabien*. Leiden, NL: E. J. Brill, 1896.

Finati, Giovanni. *Narrative of the Life and Adventures of Giovanni Finati*. 2 vols. London: John Murray, 1830.

Forbes, Rosita. "A Visit to the Idrisi Territory in 'Asir and Yemen." *Geographical Journal* 62, no. 4 (October 1923): 271–78

Forder, A. "To the Jof and Back." *Geographical Journal* 20, no. 6 (December 1902): 619–24.

——. *With the Arabs in Tent and Town*. London: Marshall Brothers, 1902.

Gaury, Gerald de. *Arabia Phoenix: An Account of a Visit to Ibn Saud*. London: George G. Harrap, 1946.

——. *Arabian Journey and other Desert Travels*. London: George G. Harrap, 1950.

Gervais-Courtellemont, Jules. *Mon voyage à Mecque*. Paris: Librairie Hachette, 1897.

Grilhon, d'Alciati de. "Résume d'un voyage en Arabie et en Égypt, exécuté en 1844–1845." *Bulletin de la Société de Géographie*, October 1845: 185–208.

Guarmani, Carlo. *Northern Najd: A Journey from Jerusalem to Anaiza in Qasim.* Translated by Muriel Capel-Cure. London: The Argonaut Press, 1938.

Haines, Stafford Bettesworth. "Memoir of the South and East Coasts of Arabia. Part II." *Journal of the Royal Geographical Society of London* 15 (1845): 104–16.

Halévy, Joseph. *Rapport sur une mission archéologique dans le Yémen.* Paris: Imprimerie Nationale, 1872.

———. "Voyage au Nedjran." *Bulletin of the Société de Géographie*, July–December 1873: 5–31, 249–73, 581–606.

Helfritz, Hans. "The First Crossing of Southwestern Arabia." *Geographical Review* 25, no. 3 (July 1935): 395–407.

Hirsch, Leo. *Reisen in Sud-Arabien, Mahra-Land und Hadramut.* Leiden, NL: E. J. Brill, 1897.

Holland, F. W. "On the Peninsula of Sinai." *Journal of the Royal Geographical Society of London* 38 (1868): 237–57.

Huber, Charles. *Journal d'un Voyage en Arabie* (1883–1884). Paris: Imprimerie Nationale, 1891.

———. "Voyage dans L'Arabie Centrale: Hamâd, Šammar, Qaçîm, Hedjâz." *Bulletin de la Société de Géographie*, 1884: 304–63, 468–530.

Hurgronje, C. Snouck. *Mekka in the Later Part of the 19th Century.* Translated by J. H. Monahan. Leiden, NL: E. J. Brill, 2007.

Ingrams, Harold. "Hadhramaut: A Journey to the Sei'ar Country and Through the Wadi Maseila." *Geographical Journal* 88, no. 6 (December 1936): 524–51.

———. *Arabia and the Isles.* London: John Murray, 1943.

Jaussen, Antonin, and Raphaël Savignac. *Mission archéologique en Arabie.* Paris: Ernest Leroux, 1909.

Keane, John F. T. *Six Months in the Hijaz: Journeys to Makkah and Madinah 1877–1878.* 1st Barzan ed. Manchester, UK: Barzan Publishing, 2006.

Lawrence, T. E. *Seven Pillars of Wisdom: A Triumph.* 1st Anchor Books ed. New York: Anchor Books, 1991.

Leachman, G. "A Journey in North-Eastern Arabia." *Geographical Journal* 37, no. 3 (March 1911): 265–74.

———. "A Journey Through Central Arabia." *Geographical Journal* 43, no. 5 (May 1914): 500–20.

Malmignati, D. *Through The Inner Deserts to Medina.* London: Philip Allan, 1925.

Mauss, Christophe, and Henri Sauvaire. "De Karak au Chaubak: Extrait du Journal de Voyage." *Bulletin de la Société de Géographie*, November 1867: 449–552.

Merrill, Selah. *East of the Jordan: A Record of Travel and Observation in the Countries of Moab, Gilead, and Bashan During the Years 1875–1877.* New York: Charles Scribner's Sons, 1883.

Meryon, C. L. *Travels of Lady Hester Stanhope.* 3 vols. N.p.: Elibron Classics, 2005.

Meulen, Daniel van der. *Aden to the Hadramaut: A Journey in South Arabia.* London: John Murray, 1947.

———. *The Wells of Ibn Sa'ud.* New York: Kegan Paul International, 2000, originally published 1957.

Meulen, Daniel van der, and Hermann von Wissmann. *Ḥaḍramaut: Some of Its Mysteries Unveiled.* Photomechanical reprint of 1932 ed. Leiden, NL: E. J. Brill, 1964.

Miles, S. B. "Account of an Excursion into the Interior of Southern Arabia." *Proceedings of the Royal Geographical Society of London* 15, no. 5 (1870–71): 319–28.

———. "Across the Green Mountains of Oman." *Geographical Journal* 18, no. 5 (November 1901): 465–98.

———. "On the Border of the Great Desert: A Journey in Oman." *Geographical Journal* 36, no. 2 (October 1910): 159–78.

———. *The Countries and Tribes of the Persian Gulf.* Vol. 2. London: Harrison and Sons, 1919. Pagination based on reprinted volume by General Books.

Milligen, Charles. "Notes of a Journey in Yemen." *Journal of the Royal Geographical Society of London* 44 (1874): 118–26.

Müller, Victor. *En Syrie avec les Bédouins: Les Tribus du Désert.* Paris: Libraire Ernest Leroux, 1931.

Musil, Alois. *In the Arabian Desert.* New York: Horace Liveright, 1930.

———. *The Northern Hegaz: A Topographical Itinerary.* New York: American Geographical Society, 1926.

———. *Northern Negd: A Topographical Itinerary.* New York: American Geographical Society, 1928.

Nolde, Eduard. *Reis nach Innerarabien, Kurdistan, und Armenien.* Braunschweig, Germany: Druck und Verlag von Vriedrich Vieweg und Sohn, 1895.

Palgrave, W. G. "Observations Made in Central, Eastern, and Southern Arabia during a Journey Through That County in 1862 and 1863." *Journal of the Royal Geographical Society of London* 34 (1864): 111–154.

———. *Personal Narrative of A Year's Journey Through Central and Eastern Arabia (1862–63).* London: Macmillan and Co., 1868.

Passama, J. "Notice géographique sur quelques parties de l'Yémen." *Bulletin de la Sociéte de Géographie,* January 1843: 219–36.

Pelly, Lewis. "A Visit to the Wahabee Capital, Central Arabia." *Journal of the Royal Geographical Society of London* 35 (1865): 169–91.

Philby, H. St. J. B. "Across Arabia: From the Persian Gulf to the Red Sea." *Geographical Journal* 56, no. 6 (December 1920): 446–63.

———. "African Contacts with Arabia." *Journal of the Royal African Society* 38, no. 150 (January 1939): 33–46.

———. *Arabia of the Wahhabis*. Reprinted with additional material. London: Frank Cass and Co., 1977.

———. *Arabian Jubilee*. London: Robert Hale Limited, 1952.

———. *The Empty Quarter*. London: Century, 1986.

———. *The Heart of Arabia: A Record of Travel and Exploration*. 2 vols. London: Constable and Company, 1922.

———. *The Land of Midian*. London: Ernest Benn Limited, 1957.

———. "The Land of Sheba." *Geographical Journal* 92, no. 1 (July 1938): 1–21.

———. "The Land of Sheba (continued)." *Geographical Journal* 92, no. 2 (August 1938): 107–28.

———. *Sheba's Daughters: A Record of Travel in Southern Arabia*. London: Methuen and Co., 1939.

Prax, M. "Notice sur la Mekke et sur les femmes musulmanes." *Bulletin de la Société de Géographie*, January 1841: 245–59.

Raswan, Carl R. *Black Tents of Arabia*. 1st Hungry Minds Press ed. Saint Paul, MN: Hungry Minds Press, 1998.

Raunkiaer, Barclay. *Through Wahhabiland on Camelback*. New York: Frederick A. Praeger, 1969.

Rihani, Ameen. *Arabian Peak and Desert: Travels in Al-Yaman*. Reprint. Delmar, NY: Caravan Books, 1983.

———. *Around the Coasts of Arabia*. Reprint. Delmar, NY: Caravan Books, 1983.

———. *Maker of Modern Arabia*. New York: Houghton Mifflin, 1928.

Roches, Léon. *Trente-Deux Ans à Travers l'Islam: 1832–1864*. Vol. 2. Paris: Librairie de Firmin-Didot, 1885.

Sadlier, George Forster. *Diary of a Journey Across Arabia: From El Khatif In the Persian Gulf, to Yambo in the Red Sea, During the Year 1819*. Bombay: Education Society's Press, Byculla, 1866.

Schumacher, Gottlieb. *Across the Jordan: An Exploration and Survey of Part of Hauran and Jaulan*. London: Alexander Watt, 1889.

Scott, Hugh. *In the High Yemen*. London: Paul Kegan, 2002.

Seetzen, Ulrich Jasper. *A Brief Account of the Countries Adjoining the Lake of Tiberias, the Jordan, and the Dead Sea*. London: Hatchard, Piccadilly, 1810.

———. *Reisen durch Syrien, Palästina, Phönicien, die Transjordan-Länder, Arabia Petraea und Unter-Aegypten*. Edited by Hinrichs Kruse and Herman Müller. Berlin: G. Reimer, 1854.

Skene, James [attributed]. *Rambles in the Deserts of Syria and Among the Turkomans and Bedaweens*. London: John Murray, 1864.

Stark, Freya. "An Exploration in the Hadhramaut and Journey to the Coast." *Geographical Journal* 93, no. 1 (January 1939): 1–14.

——. *Seen in the Hadhramaut*. New York: E. Dutton, 1939.

——. *The Southern Gates of Arabia: A Journey in the Hadhramaut*. J. P. Tarcher ed. Los Angeles: J. Tarcher, 1983.

——. "In Southwestern Arabia in Wartime." *Geographical Review* 34, no. 3 (July 1944): 349–64.

——. "Two Months in the Hadhramaut." *Geographical Journal* 87, no. 2 (February 1936): 113–24.

——. *A Winter in Arabia: A Journey Through Yemen*. New York: Overlook Press, 2002.

Stevens, G. J. "Report on the Country around Aden." *Journal of the Royal Geographical Society of London* 43 (1873): 206–40.

Tamisier, Maurice. *Voyage en Arabie*. 2 vols. Paris: Louis Desessart, 1840.

Thesiger, Wilfred. *Arabian Sands*. New ed. New York: Penguin Classics, 2007.

——. "The Badu of Southern Arabia." *Journal of the Royal Central Asian Society* 38, no. 1 (January 1950): 53–61.

——. "Desert Borderlands of Oman." *Geographical Journal* 116, no. 4/6 (October–December 1950): 137–68.

——. "A Further Journey across the Empty Quarter." *Geographical Journal* 113 (January–June 1949): 21–44.

——. "A Journey through the Tihama, the 'Asir, and the Hijaz Mountains." *Geographical Journal* 110, no. 4/6 (October–December 1947): 188–200.

——. "A New Journey in Southern Arabia." *Geographical Journal* 108, no. 4/6 (October–December 1946): 129–45.

Thomas, Bertram. *Alarms and Excursions in Arabia*. Indianapolis: Bobbs-Merrill Company, 1931.

——. "Anthropological Observations in South Arabia." *Journal of the Royal Anthropological Institute of Great Britain and Ireland* 62 (January–June 1932): 83–103.

——. *Arabia Felix: Across the Empty Quarter of Arabia*. London: Reader's Union, 1938.

——. "The South-Eastern Borderlands of Rub' al Khali." *Geographical Journal* 73, no. 3 (March 1929): 193–212.

Thomas, Bertram, and B. K. N. Wyllie. "A Camel Journey across the Rub' Al Khali." *Geographical Journal* 78, no. 3 (September 1931): 209–38.

Tristram, H. B. *The Land of Moab: Travels and Discoveries on the East Side of the Dead Sea and the Jordan*. London: John Murray, 1873.

Wallin, G. A. *Travels in Arabia (1845 and 1848)*. Cambridge, UK: Falcon-Oleander, 1979.

Wavell, A. J. B. *A Modern Pilgrim in Mecca and a Siege in Sanaa*. London: Constable and Company, 1913.

Wellsted, J. R. "Narrative of a Journey from the Tower of Ba-'l-haff, on the Southern Coast of Arabia, to the Ruins of Nakab al Hajar, in April, 1835." *Journal of the Royal Geographical Society of London* 7 (1837): 20–34.

——. "Narrative of a Journey into the Interior of Oman, in 1835." *Journal of the Royal Geographical Society of London* 7 (1837): 102–113.

——. "Observations on the Coast of Arabia between Ras Mohammed and Jiddah." *Journal of the Royal Geographical Society of London* 6 (1836): 51–96.

——. *Travels in Arabia.* 2 vols. London: John Murray, 1838.

Wrede, Adolphe Baron. "Account of an Excursion into Haudramaut." *Journal of the Royal Geographical Society of London* 14 (1844): 107–112.

Zwemer, S. M. "Oman and Eastern Arabia." *Bulletin of the American Geographical Society* 39, no. 10 (1907): 597–606.

Other Primary Source Materials

Anonymous. *The Romance of Antar: An Epitome of the First Part.* Translated by Terrick Hamilton. UK: Dodo Press, 2008.

——. *Kitab lam' al-shihāb fī sīrat Muḥammad ibn 'Abd al-Wahhāb.* Edited by Ahmad Mustafa Abu-Hakima. Beirut: Dar al-Thaqafah, 1967.

Bailey, Clinton. *A Culture of Desert Survival: Bedouin Proverbs from Sinai and the Negev.* New Haven, CT: Yale University Press, 2004.

Benjamin of Tudela. *The Itinerary of Benjamin of Tudela.* Translated by Marcus N. Adler. Charleston, SC: BiblioBazaar, 2008.

Burdett, A. L. P., ed. *Records of the Hijaz.* 8 vols. London: Archive Editions, 1996.

——, ed. *Slave Trade into Arabia: 1820–1973.* 9 vols. Slough, UK: Archive Editions, 2006.

Gazetteer of Arabia. 3 vols. Simla, India: General Staff of India, 1917.

Ibn Battuta. *The Travels of Ibn Battuta in the Near East, Asia, and Africa 1325–1354.* Translated by Samuel Lee. New York: Dover Publications, 2004.

Ibn Bishr an-Najdi, 'Uthman. *'Unwān al-majd fī Tārīkh Najd* [The History of Najd]. 2 vols. Al-Riyadh, SA: Daar al-Habeeb, 1999.

Ibn Ghannam, Hussain. *Tarīkh Najd* [The History of Najd]. Edited by Nāṣir al-Dīn Asad. Al-Riyadh, SA: 'Abd al-'Aziz ibn Muhammad ibn Ibrahim al-Shaykh, 1982.

Ibn Isḥāq [Muḥammad ibn Isḥāq ibn Yasār ibn Khiyār]. *Sīrat Rasūl Allāh.* [Life of the Prophet of God]. Translated by A. Guillaume. New York: Oxford University Press, 2002.

Ibn Jubayr al-Kinānī, Abū'l Ḥusain Muḥammad ibn Ahmad. *The Travels of Ibn Jubayr.* Edited by William Wright. 2nd ed. London: Luzac and Co., 1907.

Ibn al-Mujawir, Yūsuf ibn Ya'qūb. *Tarikh al-Mustabsir: A Traveller in Thirteenth-Century Arabia*. Edited and translated by G. Rex Smith. London: The Hakluyt Society, 2008.

Ibn al-Wardi, Umar ibn Muzaffar. *Kharidat al-'Aja'ib wa Faridat al-Ghara'ib* [The Pearl of Wonders and the Uniqueness of Things Strange]. Cairo: Maktabat al Thakafa al Deeneya, 2008.

Ibn Ya'qūb al-Hamdānī, Abū Muhammad al-Hasan ibn Ahmad. *Sīfat Jazirat ul-Arab* [Geography of the Arabian Peninsula]. Amsterdam: Brill, 1884.

Khusraw, Nasir-i. *Book of Travels*. Edited and translated by Wheeler M. Thackston. Costa Mesa, CA: Mazda Publishers, 2001.

Mercadier, F. J. G. *L'Esclave de Timimoun*. Paris: Editions France-Empire, 1971.

al-Muqaddasi [Muhammad ibn Ahmad Shams al-Dīn al-Muqaddasī]. *The Best Divisions for Knowledge of the Regions*. Translated by Basil Anthony Collins. Lebanon: Garnet Publishing, 1994.

Niebuhr, Carsten. *Travels through Arabia and other Countries in the East*. Translated by Robert Heron. 2 vols. Farmington Hills, MI: Thomson Gale, 2005.

al-Rasheed, Madawi. *Politics in an Arabian Oasis: The Rashidis of Saudi Arabia*. New York: I. B. Tauris Publishers, 1991.

Rush, Alan de L., ed. *Ruling Families of Arabia: Qatar, the Ruling Family of Al-Thani*. Slough, UK: Archive Editions, 1991.

Scoville, Sheila A., ed. *Gazetteer of Arabia: A Geographical and Tribal History of the Arabian Peninsula*. 2 vols. Graz, AT: Akademische Druk- u. Verlagsanstalt, 1979.

al-Tabari [Abu Ja'far Muhammad ibn Jarir al-Tabari]. *The History of al-Tabari*. Vol. 8, *The Victory of Islam*. Translated by Michael Fishbein. Albany: State University of New York Press, 1997.

———. *The History of al-Tabari*. Vol. 28, *'Abbāsid Authority Affirmed*. Translated by Jane Dammen McAuliffe. Albany: State University of New York Press, 1995.

Tayyib al-Sharaqī, al-Muhammad Ibn. *The Travels of Ibn al-Tayyib: The Forgotten Journey of an Eighteenth Century Traveller to the Hijāz*. Translated by El Mustapha Lahlali, Salah Al-Dihan, and Wafa Abu Hatab. New York: I. B. Tauris, 2010.

Twitchell, K. S. *Saudi Arabia: With an Account of the Development of Its Natural Resources*. Princeton, NJ: Princeton University Press, 1953.

Varthema, Ludovico di. *The Travels of Ludovico di Varthema*, translated by John Winter Jones. Facsimile of edition published in 1863 by The Hakluyt Society, London. Lexington, KY: Elibron Classics, 2005.

Yāqūt [Yāqūt ibn-'Abdullah al-Rūmī al-Hamawī]. *Kitāb mu'jam al-buldān* [Dictionary of Countries]. Beirut: Dar Beirut, 1955.

Secondary Sources

Abdoon, A-M. M. O. and A. M. Alshahrani. "Prevalence and Distribution of Anopheline Mosquitoes in Malaria Endemic Areas of Asir Region, Saudi Arabia." *La Revue de Santé de la Méditerranée Orientale* 9, no. 3 (2003): 240–47.

Abu-Amero, Khaled K., Ana M. González, Jose M. Larruga, Thomas M. Bosley, and Vicente M. Cabrera. "Eurasian and African Mitochondrial DNA Influences in the Saudi Arabian Population." *BMC Evolutionary Biology* 7, no. 32 (March 2007). doi: 10.1186/1471-2148-7-32.

———. "Saudi Arabian Y-Chromosome Diversity and Its Relationship with Nearby Regions." *BMC Genetics* 10, no. 59 (September 2009). doi: 10.1186/1471-2156-10-59.

Abū Haykal, 'Abd al-'Alīm 'Ali Abd al-Wahhāb. "Al-Raqīq al-Afrīqī bi-l-Hijāz khilāl al-Nisf al-Awwal min al-Qarn al-'Ishrin." *Al-Majalla al-Tārīkhiyya al-Misriyya* 39 (1989): 336.

Abujaber, Raouf Saʿd. *Pioneers over Jordan: The Frontier of Settlement in Transjordan, 1850–1914.* London: I. B. Tauris and Company, 1989.

Adra, Najwa. "The Concept of Tribe in Rural Yemen." In *Arab Society: Social Science Perspectives*, edited by Saad Eddin Ibrahim and Nicholas S. Hopkins, 275–85. Cairo: American University in Cairo Press, 1985.

Ahmad, Abdussamad H. "Ethiopian Slave Exports at Matamma, Massawa, and Tajura c. 1830 to 1885." In Clarence-Smith, *Indian Ocean Slave Trade*, 93–102.

Ahmed, Ashraf M., Essam A. Shaalan, Mourad A. M. Aboul-Soud, Frédéric Tripet, and Abdulaziz A. al-Khedhairy. "Mosquito Vectors Survey in the Al-Ahsaa District of Eastern Saudi Arabia." *Journal of Insect Science* 11 (2011): 1–11.

Alahmed, Azzam Mohammed. "Mosquito Fauna (Diptera: Culicidae) of the Eastern Region of Saudi Arabia and their Seasonal Abundance." *Journal of King Saud University—Science* 24 (2012): 55–62.

Alexander, J. "Islam, Archaeology, and Slavery in Africa." *World Archeology* 33, no. 1 (June 2001): 44–60.

Allen, Richard B. "Satisfying the 'Want for Labouring People': European Slave Trading in the Indian Ocean, 1500–1850." *Journal of World History* 21, no. 1 (March 2010): 45–73.

———. "Suppressing a Nefarious Traffic: Britain and the Abolition of Slave Trading in India and the Western Indian Ocean, 1770–1830." *William and Mary Quarterly* 66, no. 4 (October 2009): 873–94.

Alpers, Edward A. "The African Diaspora in the Northwestern Indian Ocean: Reconsideration of an Old Problem, New Directions for Research." *Comparative Studies of South Asia, Africa and the Middle East* 17, no. 2 (1997): 62–81.

Alsharhan, A. S., Z. A. Rizk, A. E. M. Nairn, D. W. Bakhit, and S. A. Alhajari. *Hydrogeology of an Arid Region: The Arabian Gulf and Adjoining Areas.* New York: Elsevier, 2001.

Altorki, Soraya, and Donald Cole. *Arabian Oasis City: The Transformation of 'Unayzah.* Austin: University of Texas Press, 1989.

Anderson, B., and C. Vullo. "Did Malaria Select for Primary Adult Lactase Deficiency?" *Gut* 35, no. 19 (1994): 1487–89.

Anscombe, Frederick F. "An Anational Society: Eastern Arabia in the Ottoman Period." In *Transnational Connections and the Arab Gulf,* edited by Madawi al-Rasheed, 21–38. New York: Routledge, 2005.

Ashkenazi, Touvia. "Social and Historical Problems of the 'Anazeh Tribes." *Journal of the Economic and Social History of the Orient* 8, no. 1 (August 1965): 93–100.

al-Awamy, Baker H. "Thalassemia Syndromes in Saudi Arabia: Meta-analysis of Local Studies." *Saudi Medical Journal* 21, no. 1 (2000): 8–17.

Baer, Gabriel. "Slavery in Nineteenth Century Egypt." *Journal of African History* 8, no. 3 (1967): 417–41.

Baier, Stephen, and Paul E. Lovejoy. "The Tuareg of the Central Sudan: Gradations in Servility at the Desert Edge (Niger and Nigeria)." In *Slavery in Africa: Historical and Anthropological Perspectives,* edited by Suzanne Miers and Igor Kopytoff, 391–441. Madison: University of Wisconsin Press, 1977.

Banning, E. B. "Peasants, Pastoralists, and 'Pax Romana': Mutualism in the Southern Highlands of Jordan." *Bulletin of the American Schools of Oriental Research* 261 (February 1986): 25–50.

Beachey, R. W. *The Slave Trade of Eastern Africa.* New York: Harper and Row Publishers, 1976.

Beaumont, Peter, Gerald H. Blake, and J. Malcolm Wagstaff. *The Middle East: A Geographical Study.* New York: Halsted Press, 1988.

Berger, Jean-François, Jean-Paul Bravard, Louise Purdue, Anne Benoist, Michel Mouton, and Frank Braemer. "Rivers of the Hadramawt Watershed (Yemen) During the Holocene: Clues of Late Functioning." *Quaternary International* 266 (2012): 142–61.

Bidwell, Robin. *Travelers in Arabia.* Reading, UK: Garnet Publishing, 1994.

Bosworth, C. E. "The 'Protected Peoples' (Christians and Jews) in Medieval Egypt and Syria." *Bulletin of the John Rylands University Library of Manchester* 62, no. 1 (1979): 11–36.

———. "A note on ta'arrub in early Islam." *Journal of Semitic Studies* 34, no. 2 (1989): 355–62.

Bowersock, G. W. *The Throne of Adulis: Red Sea Wars on the Eve of Islam.* New York: Oxford University Press, 2013.

Brower, Benjamin Claude. "The Servile Populations of the Algerian Sahara, 1850–1900." In Mirzai, Montana, and Lovejoy, *Slavery, Islam, and Diaspora,* 169–91.

Braudel, Fernand. *The Mediterranean and the Mediterranean World in the Age of Philip II*. Berkeley: University of California Press, 1996.

Brunner, U., and H. Haefner. "The Successful Floodwater Farming System of the Sabeans, Yemen Arab Republic." *Applied Geography* 6, no. 1 (1986): 77–86.

Campbell, Gwyn, ed. *Abolition and Its Aftermath in the Indian Ocean Africa and Asia*. New York: Routledge, 2005.

———. "Servitude and the Changing Face of the Demand for Labor in the Indian Ocean World, c. 1800–1900." In Harms, Freamon, and Blight, *Indian Ocean Slavery*, 23–44.

Cavalli-Sforza, L. Luca, Paolo Menozzi, and Alberto Piazza. *The History and Geography of Human Genes*. Princeton, NJ: Princeton University Press, 1994.

Chanson, Hubert. *The Hydraulics of Open Channel Flow: An Introduction*. New York: Elsevier, 2004.

Clarence-Smith, William Gervase, ed. *The Economics of the Indian Ocean Slave Trade in the Nineteenth Century*. London: Frank Cass, 1989.

———. *Islam and the Abolition of Slavery*. New York: Oxford University Press, 2006.

Cleuziou, Serge, Maurizio Tosi, and Juris Zarins, eds. *Essays on the Prehistory of the Arabian Peninsula*. Rome: Instituto Italiano per l'Africa e l'Orient, 2002.

Cooper, Frederick. *Plantation Slavery on the East Coast of Africa*. Portsmouth, NH: Heinemann, 1997.

Cressy, George B. "Qanats, Karez, and Foggaras." *Geographical Review* 48, no. 1 (January 1958): 27–44.

Crone, Patricia. *Meccan Trade and the Rise of Islam*. Princeton, NJ: Princeton University Press, 1987.

Cuno, Kenneth M. "African Slaves in Nineteenth-Century Rural Egypt: A Preliminary Assessment." In *Race and Slavery in the Middle East*, edited by Terence Walz and Kenneth M. Cuno, 77–98. New York: American University of Cairo Press, 2010.

Curtin, Phillip. *The Rise and Fall of the Plantation Complex: Essays in Atlantic History*. London: Cambridge University Press, 1976.

Daggy, Richard H. "Malaria in Oases of Eastern Saudi Arabia." *American Journal of Tropical Medicine and Hygiene* 8 (1959): 223–91.

Darwin, John. "An Undeclared Empire: the British in the Middle East, 1918–39." *Journal of Imperial and Commonwealth History* 27, no. 2 (1999): 159–76.

Davies, Charles E. *The Blood-Red Arab Flag: An Investigation into Qasimi Piracy 1797–1820*. Exeter, UK: University of Exeter Press, 1997.

Dignas, Beate, and Engerbert Winter. *Rome and Persia in Late Antiquity: Neighbors and Rivals*. New York: Cambridge University Press, 2007.

Donner, Fred M., ed. *The Expansion of the Early Islamic State*. Burlington, VT: Ashgate Publishing, 2008.

Dubois, Colette. "Un traite tardive en mer Rouge méridionale: la route des esclaves du golf de Tadjoura (1880–1936)." In *Traites et esclavages en Afrique oriental et dans l'océan Indien*, edited by Henri Médard, Marie-Laure Derat, Thomas Vernet, and Marie Pierre Ballarin, 197–222. Paris: Karthala et Ciresc, 2013.

Eickelman, Dale F. *The Middle East and Central Asia: An Anthropological Approach*. Upper Saddle River, NJ: Prentice Hall, 2002.

Ellenblum, Ronnie. *The Collapse of the Eastern Mediterranean: Climate Change and the Decline of the East, 950–1072*. New York: Cambridge University Press, 2012.

Embury, S. H., M. R. Clark, G. Monroy, and N. Mohandas. "Concurrent Sickle-Cell Anemia and α-thalassemia: Effect on Pathological Properties of Sickle Erythrocytes." *Journal of Clinical Investigation* 73 (January 1984): 116–23.

Ende, Werner. "The Nakhāwila, a Shite Community in Medina Past and Present." *Die Welt des Islams* 373 (November 1997): 263–348.

English, Paul Ward. "The Origin and Spread of Qanats in the Old World." *Proceedings of the American Philosophical Society* 112, no. 3 (June 1968): 170–81.

Ennaji, Mohammed. *Slavery, the State, and Islam*. New York: Cambridge University Press, 2013.

Eno, Omar A. "The Abolition of Slavery and the Aftermath Stigma: The Case of the Bantu/Jareer People on the Benadir Coast of Southern Somalia." In Campbell, *Abolition and Its Aftermath*, 83–93.

Evenari, M., L. Shanan, and N. H. Tadmor. "'Runoff Farming' in the Desert. I. Experimental Layout." *Agronomy Journal* 69 (January–February 1968): 29–32.

Ewald, Janet J. "Crossers of the Sea: Slaves, Freedmen, and Other Migrants in the Northwestern Indian Ocean c. 1750–1914." *American Historical Review* 105, no. 1 (February 2000): 69–91.

Fagan, Brian. *The Little Ice Age: How Climate Made History, 1300–1850*. New York: Basic Books, 2000.

Fedele, Francisco G. "Man, Land, and Climate: Emerging Interactions from the Holocene of the Yemen Highlands." In *Man's Role in Shaping the Eastern Mediterranean Landscape*, edited by S. Bottema, G. Entjes-Nieborg, and W. van Zeist. Rotterdam, BE: A. A. Balkema, 1990.

Fernyhough, Timothy Derek. *Serfs, Slaves, and Shifta: Modes of Production and Resistance in Pre-Revolutionary Ethiopia*. Addis Ababa, ET: Shama Books, 2010.

Fleitmann, Dominik, Stephen J. Burns, Ulrich Neff, Manfred Mudelsee, Augusto Mangini, and Albert Matter. "Palaeoclimatic Interpretation of High-resolution Oxygen Isotope Profiles Derived from Annually Laminated

Speleothems from Southern Oman." *Quaternary Science Reviews* 23 (2004): 935–45.

Floor, Willem M. *The Persian Gulf: A Political and Economic History of Five Port Cities, 1500–1730.* Washington, DC: Mage Publishers, 2006.

Francaviglia, Vincenzo Maria. "Some Remarks on the Irrigation Systems of Ancient Yemen." In Cleuziou, Tosi, and Zarins, *Late Prehistory of the Arabian Peninsula,* 111–44.

Fuchs, Markus, and Andreas Buerkert. "A 20 ka Sediment Record from the Hajar Mountain Range in N-Oman, and Its Implication for Detecting Arid-Humid Periods on the Southeastern Arabian Peninsula." *Earth and Planetary Science Letters* 265 (2008): 546–58.

Galloway, J. H. "The Mediterranean Sugar Industry." *Geographical Review* 67, no. 2 (April 1977): 177–94.

Gaury, Gerald de. *Review of the 'Anizah Tribe.* Beirut: Kutub, 2005. Originally compiled 1932.

Gellner, Ernest. "Tribalism and the State in the Middle East." In Khoury and Kostiner, *Tribes and State Formation,* 109–26.

Gelpi, A. "Agriculture, Malaria, and Human Evolution; A Study of Genetic Polymorphisms in the Saudi Oasis Population." *Saudi Medical Journal* 4, no. 3 (July 1983): 229–34.

Gelpi, A., and M. C. King. "Association of Duffy Blood Groups with the Sickle Cell Trait." *Human Genetics* 32 (1976): 65–67.

Gething, Peter W., David L. Smith, Anand P. Patil, Andrew J. Tatem, Robert W. Snow, and Simon I. Hay. "Climate Change and the Global Malaria Recession." *Nature* 465 (May 20, 2010): 342–46.

Gordon, Murray. *Slavery in the Arab World.* New York: New Amsterdam Books, 1989.

Hachicho, Mohamad Ali. "English Travel Books about the Arab Near East in the Eighteenth Century." *Die Welt des Islams* 9, no. 1 (1964): 1–206.

Hamilton, Keith, and Patrick Salmon, eds. *Slavery, Diplomacy, and Empire: Britain and the Suppression of the Slave Trade, 1807–1975.* Portland, OR: Sussex Academic Press, 2009.

Harms, Robert, Bernard K. Freamon, and David W. Blight, eds. *Indian Ocean Slavery in the Age of Abolition* (London: Yale University Press, 2013).

Harrower, Michael J. "Hydrology, Ideology, and the Origins of Irrigation in Ancient Southwest Arabia." *Current Anthropology* 49, no. 3 (June 2008): 497–510.

———. "Mapping and Dating Incipient Irrigation in Wadi Sana, Hadhramawt (Yemen)." *Proceedings of the Seminar for Arabian Studies* 38 (2008): 187–202.

Al Hawsawi, Zakaria M., and Ghousia A. Ismail. "Stroke among Sickle Cell Disease Patients in Madina Maternity and Children's Hospital." *Annals of Saudi Medicine* 18, no. 5 (1998): 472–74.

Hehmeyer, I. "Irrigation Farming in the Ancient Oasis of Marib." *Proceedings of the Seminar for Arabian Studies* 19 (1989): 33–44.

Held, Colbert C. *Middle East Patterns: Places, People, and Politics.* Boulder, CO: Westview Press, 2006.

Hiyari, M. A. "The Origins and Development of the Amirate of the Arabs during the Seventh/Thirteenth and Eighth/Fourteenth Centuries." *Bulletin of the School of Oriental and African Studies* 38, no. 3 (1975): 509–24.

Hopper, Mathew S. "Globalization and the Economics of African Slavery in Arabia in the Age of Empire." *Journal of African Development* 12, no. 1 (2010): 155–84.

——. "Slaves of One Master: Globalization and the African Diaspora in Arabia in the Age of Empire." In Harms, Freamon, and Blight, *Indian Ocean Slavery*, 223–40.

Howell, Raymond C. *The Royal Navy and the Slave Trade.* New York: St. Martin's Press, 1987.

Humphreys, Margaret. *Malaria: Poverty, Race, and Public Health in the United States.* Baltimore: John Hopkins University Press, 2001.

Hunwick, J. O., and Eve Trout Powell, comps. and eds. *The African Diaspora in the Mediterranean Lands of Islam.* Princeton, NJ: Markus Wiener Publishers, 2002.

Hutson, Alaine S. "Enslavement and Manumission in Saudi Arabia, 1926–38." *Critique: Critical Middle Eastern Studies* 11, no. 1 (Spring 2002): 49–70.

Ingram, Catherine J. E., Charlotte A. Mulcare, Yuval Itan, Mark G. Thomas, and Dallas M. Swallow. "Lactose Digestion and the Evolutionary Genetics of Lactase Persistence." *Human Genetics* 124 (2009): 579–91.

Jabbur, Jibrail S. *The Bedouins and the Desert: Aspects of Nomadic Life in the Arab East.* Albany: State University of New York Press, 1995.

Janzen, Jörg. *Nomads in the Sultanate of Oman: Tradition and Development in Dhofar.* Boulder, CO: Westview Press, 1986.

Jwaidah, Albertine, and J. W. Cox. "The Black Slaves of Turkish Arabia during the 19th Century." *Slavery and Abolition* 9, no. 3 (1988): 45–59.

Katakura, Motoko. *Bedouin Village: A Study of a Saudi Arabian People in Transition.* Tokyo: University of Tokyo Press, 1977.

Khater, E. I., M. M. Sowilem, M. F. Sallam, and A. M. Alahmed. "Ecology and Habitat Characterization of Mosquitoes in Saudi Arabia." *Tropical Biomedicine* 30, no. 3 (2013): 409–27.

Khoury, Philip S., and Joseph Kostiner, eds. *Tribes and State Formation in the Middle East.* Los Angeles: University of California Press, 1990.

Kiple, Kenneth F. *The Caribbean Slave: A Biological History.* Cambridge, UK: Cambridge University Press, 1984.

Klien, Martin A. "The Emancipation of Slaves in the Indian Ocean." In Campbell, *Abolition and Its Aftermath*, 198–218.

Kostiner, Joseph. "Transforming Dualities: Tribe and State Formation in Saudi Arabia." In Khoury and Kostiner, *Tribes and State Formation*, 226–51.

Kurpershoek, Marcel. *Arabia of the Bedouins*. Translated by Paul Vincent. London: Saqi Books, 1995.

Lancaster, William. *The Rwala Bedouin Today*. 2nd ed. Long Grove, IL: Waveland Press, 1997.

Landen, Robert G. *Oman Since 1856: Disruptive Modernization in a Traditional Society*. Princeton, NJ: Princeton University Press, 1967.

Lewis, Bernard. "The Crows of the Arabs." *Critical Inquiry* 12, no. 1 (Autumn 1985): 88–97.

———. *Race and Slavery in the Middle East*. New York: Oxford University Press, 1990.

Lewis, Norman N. "Lebanon: The Mountain and Its Terraces." *Geographical Review* 43, no. 1 (January 1953): 1–14.

———. "Malaria, Irrigation, and Soil Erosion in Central Syria." *Geographical Review* 39, no. 2 (April 1949): 278–90.

———. *Nomads and Settlers in Syria and Jordan, 1800–1980*. New York: Cambridge University Press, 1987.

Lightfoot, Dale R. "The Origin and Diffusion of Qanats in Arabia: New Evidence from the Northern and Southern Peninsula." *Geographical Journal* 166, no. 3 (September 2000): 215–66.

Lings, Martin. *Muhammad: His Life Based on the Earliest Sources*. 2nd US ed. Rochester, VT: Inner Traditions, 2006.

Lloyd, Christopher. *The Navy and the Slave Trade: The Suppression of the African Slave Trade in the Nineteenth Century*. New York: Longmans, Green and Co., 1949.

Lokki, A. Inkeri, Irma Järvelä, Elisabeth Israelsson, Bakary Maiga, Marita Troye-Blomberg, Amagana Dolo, Ogobara K Doumbo, Seppo Meri, and Ville Holmberg. "Lactase Persistence Genotypes and Malaria Susceptibility in Fulani of Mali." *Malaria Journal* 10, no. 6 (2011). http://www.malariajournal.com/content/10/1/9.

Lovejoy, Paul E. *Transformations in Slavery: A History of Slavery in Africa*. 2nd ed. New York: Cambridge University Press, 2000.

Low, Michael Christopher. "Empire and the Hajj: Pilgrims, Plagues, and Pan-Islam under British Surveillance, 1865–1908." *International Journal of Middle East Studies* 40, no. 2 (May 2008): 269–90.

Lysenko, A. J., and I. N. Semashko. "Geography of Malaria. A Medico-Geographic Profile of an Ancient Disease." In *Itogi Nauki: Medicinskaja Geografija*, edited by A. W. Lebedew, 25–146. Moscow: Academy of Sciences USSR, 1968.

Manning, Patrick. *Slavery and African Life: Occidental, Oriental, and African Slave Trades*. New York: Cambridge University Press, 1990.

Mattingly, F., and K. L. Knight. "The Mosquito of Arabia." *International Bulletin of the British Museum (Entomology)* 4, no. 3 (1956): 89–141.

McCorriston, Joy. "Breaking the Rain Barrier and the Tropical Spread of Near Eastern Agriculture into Southern Arabia." In *Behavioral Ecology and the Transition to Agriculture*, edited by Douglas J. Kennett and Bruce Winterhalder, 217–36. Berkeley: University of California Press, 2006.

McCorriston, Joy, Michael Harrower, Louise Martin, and Eric Oches. "Cattle Cults of the Arabian Neolithic and Early Territorial Societies." *American Anthropologist* 114, no. 1 (2012): 45–63.

McNeill, J. R. "Observations on the Nature of Environmental History." *History and Theory* 42, no. 4 (December 2003): 5–43.

Médard, Henri. "La plus ancienne et la plus récente des traites: panorama de la traite de l'esclavage en Afrique orientale et dans l'océan Indien." In Médard, Derat, Vernet, and Ballarin, *Traites et esclavages en Afrique oriental et dans l'océan Indien*, 65–118.

Médard, Henri, Marie-Laure Derat, Thomas Vernet, and Marie Pierre Ballarin. *Traites et esclavages en Afrique oriental et dans l'océan Indien*. Paris: Karthala et Ciresc, 2013.

al-Mekhlafi, Abdulsalam M. Q., Mohammed A. K. Mahdy, Ahmed A. Azazy, and M. Y. Fong. "Clinical Situation of Endemic Malaria in Yemen." *Tropical Biomedicine* 27, no. 3 (2010): 551–58.

Meleigy, May. "Arabian Peninsula States Launch Plan to Eradicate Malaria." *British Medical Journal* 334 (2007): 117.

Meloy, John L. "Imperial Strategy and Political Exigency: The Red Sea Spice Trade and the Mamluk Sultinate in the Fifteenth Century." *Journal of the American Oriental Society* 123, no. 1 (January–March 2003): 1–19.

Meneley, Anne. *Tournaments of Value: Sociability and Hierarchy in a Yemeni Town*. Toronto: University of Toronto Press, 1996.

Mielke, James H., Lyle W. Konigsberg, and John H. Relethford. *Human Biological Variation*. 2nd ed. New York: Oxford University Press, 2011.

Miers, Suzanne. *Slavery in the Twentieth Century: The Evolution of a Global Problem*. New York: AltaMira Press, 2003.

———. "Slavery and the Slave Trade in Saudi Arabia and the Arab State of the Persian Gulf, 1921–1963." In Campbell, *Abolition and Its Aftermath*, 120–36.

———. "The Anti-Slavery Game: Britain and the Suppression of Slavery in Africa and Arabia, 1890–1875." In Hamilton and Salmon, *Slavery, Diplomacy, and Empire*, 196–214.

Mikhail, Alan, ed. *Nature and Empire in Ottoman Egypt: An Environmental History*. New York: Cambridge University Press, 2011.

———, ed. *Water on Sand: Environmental Histories of the Middle East and North Africa*. New York: Oxford University Press, 2013.

Mirzai, Behnaz A., Ismael Musah Montana, and Paul E. Lovejoy, eds. *Slavery, Islam, and Diaspora*. Trenton, NJ: Africa World Press, 2009.

Mithen, Steven. *Thirst: Water and Power in the Ancient World*. London: Weidenfeld and Nicolson, 2012.

Muhammad, Akbar. "The Image of Africans in Arabic Literature: Some Unpublished Manuscripts." In Willis, *Slaves and Slavery in Muslim Africa*, 1:47–74.

al-Nasif, Abdulla. "Al-'Ula (Saudi Arabia): A Report on a Historical and Archaeological Survey." *Bulletin of the British Society for Middle Eastern Studies* 8, no. 1 (1981): 30–32.

Nicolini, Beatrice. "The Makran-Baluch-African Network in Zanzibar and East Africa during the XIXth Century." *African and Asian Studies* 5, no. 3 (2006): 347–70.

Noth, Albrecht. "Isfahan-Nihawand. A Source-Critical Study of Early Islamic Historiography." In Donner, *Expansion of the Early Islamic State*, 241–62.

Ochsenwald, William. "Muslim-European Conflict in the Hijaz: The Slave Trade Controversy, 1840–1895." *Middle Eastern Studies* 16, no. 1 (January 1980): 115–26.

Oleson, John Peter. "The Origins and Design of Nabataean Water-Supply Systems." In *Studies in the History and Archaeology of Jordan V*, edited by Khairieh 'Amr, Fawzi Zayadine, and Muna Zaghloul, 707–19. Amman, JO: Department of Antiquities, 1995.

———. "Water Supply in Jordan through the Ages." In *The Archeology of Jordan*, edited by Burton MacDonald, Russel Adams, and Piotr Bienkowski, 603–14. London: Continuum International Publishing Group, 2001.

Onley, James. *The Arabian Frontier of the British Raj: Merchants, Rulers, and the British in the Nineteenth-Century Gulf*. New York: Oxford University Press, 2007.

Otte, T. G. "'A Course of Unceasing Remonstrance:' British Diplomacy and the Suppression of the Slave Trade in the East, 1852–1898." In Hamilton and Salmon, *Slavery, Diplomacy, and Empire*, 93–124.

Packard, Randall M. *The Making of a Tropical Disease: A Short History of Malaria*. Baltimore: John Hopkins University Press, 2007.

Pankhurst, Richard. "The Ethiopian Slave Trade in the Nineteenth and Early Twentieth Centuries: A Statistical Inquiry." *Journal of Semitic Studies* 9, no. 1 (1964): 220–28.

Parker, Chad H. "Controlling Man-Made Malaria: Corporate Modernisation and the Arabian American Oil Company's Malaria Control Program in Saudi Arabia, 1947–1956." *Cold War History* 12, no. 3 (August 2012): 473–94.

Patterson, Orlando. *Slavery and Social Death: A Comparative Study*. Cambridge, MA: Harvard University Press, 1982.

Peppelenbosch, G. N. "Nomadism on the Arabian Peninsula: A General Appraisal." *Tijdschrift voor Economische en Sociale Geografie* 59 (1968): 335–46.

Peters, F. E. *The Hajj: The Muslim Pilgrimage to Mecca and the Holy Places.* Princeton, NJ: Princeton University Press, 1994.

Pike, Ruthven W. "Land and Peoples of the Hadhramaut, Aden Protectorate." *Geographical Review* 30, no. 4 (October 1940): 627–48.

Pipes, Daniel. "Mawlas: Freed Slaves and Converts in Early Islam." In Willis, *Slaves and Slavery in Muslim Africa*, 1:199–247.

Platt, O. S., Donald J. Brambilla, Wendell F. Rosse, Paul F. Milner, Oswaldo Castro, Martin H. Steinberg, and Panpit P. Klug. "Mortality in Sickle Cell Disease: Life Expectancy and Risk Factors for Early Death." *New England Journal of Medicine* 330 (1994): 1639–43.

Popenoe, Paul. "The Distribution of the Date Palm." *Geographical Review* 16, no. 1 (January 1926): 117–21.

Popovic, Alexandre. *The Revolt of African Slaves in Iraq in the 3rd/9th Century.* Translated by Léon King. Princeton, NJ: Markus Wiener Publishers, 1999.

Potter, Lawrence G., ed. *The Persian Gulf in History.* New York: Palgrave Macmillan, 2009.

Potts, D. T. "Contributions to the Agrarian History of Eastern Arabia I. Implements and Cultivation Techniques." *Arabian Archaeology and Epigraphy* 5 (1994): 158–68.

———. "Date Palms and Date Consumption in Eastern Arabia During the Bronze Age." In *The Date Palm: From Traditional Resource to Green Wealth*, 33–50. Abu Dhabi, UAE: The Emirates Center for Strategic Studies and Research, 2003.

Preston, G. W., A. G. Parker, H. Walkington, M. J. Leng, and M. J. Hodson. "From Nomadic Herder-hunters to Sedentary Farmers: The Relationship between Climate Change and Ancient Subsistence Strategies in South-eastern Arabia." *Journal of Arid Environments* 86 (2012): 122–30.

Reilly, Benjamin. "Arabian Travelers, 1800-1950: An Analytical Bibliography." *British Journal of Middle Eastern Studies*, 2015. doi: 10.1080/13530194.2015.1060155.

———. "*Mutawalladeen* and Malaria: African Slavery in Arabian Wadis." *Journal of Social History* 47, no. 4 (2014): 1–19.

———. "Revisiting Bedouin Desert Adaptations: Lactase Persistence as a Factor in Arabian Peninsula History." *Journal of Arabian Studies* 2, no. 2 (2012): 93–107.

———. "Revisiting Consanguineous Marriage in the Greater Middle East: Milk, Blood, and Bedouins." *American Anthropologist* 115, no. 3 (2013): 374–87.

———. "A Well-Intentioned Failure: British Antislavery Measures and the Arabian Peninsula, 1820-1940." *Journal of Arabian Studies*, forthcoming.

Richards, Martin, Chiara Rengo, Fulvio Cruciani, Fiona Gratrix, James F. Wilson, Rosaria Scozzari, Vincent Macaulay, and Antonio Torroni. "Extensive Female-Mediated Gene Flow from Sub-Saharan Africa into Near Eastern Arab Populations." *American Journal of Human Genetics* 72 (2003): 1058–64.

Ricks, Thomas M. "Slaves and Slave Traders in the Persian Gulf, 18th and 19th Centuries: An Assessment." In Clarence-Smith, *Indian Ocean Slave Trade*, 60–70.

Risso, Patricia. *Oman and Muscat: An Early Modern History*. London: Croom Helm, 1986.

Roberts, Neil. "Water Conservation in Ancient Arabia." *Proceedings of the Seminar of Arabian Studies* 7 (1977): 134–46.

Robinson, Chase F. *Islamic Historiography*. New York: Cambridge University Press, 2003.

Rowley, Gwyn. "Irrigation Systems in the Holy Land: A Comment." *Transactions of the Institute of British Geographers* 11, no. 3 (1986): 356–59.

Rutter, Eldon. "Slavery in Arabia." *Journal of the Royal Central Asian Society* 20, no. 3 (1933): 315–32.

Said, Edward. *Orientalism*. New York: Vintage Books, 1978.

Scarborough, Vernon L. *The Flow of Power: Ancient Water Systems and Landscapes*. Santa Fe, NM: SAR Press, 2003.

Schoff, W. H., trans. and ed. *The Periplus of the Erythraean Sea: Travel and Trade in the Indian Ocean by a Merchant of the First Century*. London: Longman, Green and Company, 1912.

Scoville, Sheila A. "Historiography on the '*Gazetteer* of Arabia': Vol. I." *Proceedings of the Seminar for Arabian Studies* 12 (1982): 73–78.

Segal, Ronald. *Islam's Black Slaves*. New York: Farrar, Straus, and Giroux, 2001.

Sells, Michael A. *Desert Tracings: Six Classic Arabian Odes by 'Alqama, Shánfara, Labíd, 'Antara, Al'A'sha, and Dhu al-Rúmma*. Middletown, CT: Wesleyan University Press, 1989.

Serjeant, R. B. "The Cultivation of Cereals in Mediaeval Yemen." *Arabian Studies* 1 (1974): 25–74.

———. "Société et gouvernement en Arabie du Sud." *Arabica* 14, no. 3 (October 1967): 284–97.

Shahîd, Irfan. *Byzantium and the Arabs in the Sixth Century*. Washington, DC: Dumbarton Oaks, 2010.

Sheriff, Abdul. "The Slave Mode of Production Along the East African Coast, 1810–1873." In Willis, *Slaves and Slavery in Muslim Africa*, 2:161–81.

———. *Slaves, Spices, and Ivory in Zanzibar*. Athens: Ohio University Press, 1987.

———. "The Slave Trade and Its Fallout in the Persian Gulf." In Campbell, *Abolition and Its Aftermath*, 103–19.

Sidebothham, Stephen E. "Aelius Gallus and Arabia." *Latomus* 45, no. 3 (July–September 1986): 590–602.

Sinka, Marianne E., Michael J. Bangs, Sylvie Manguin, Theeraphap Chareonviriyaphap, Anand P Patil, William H. Temperley, Peter W Gething, et al. "The Dominant *Anopheles* Vectors of Human Malaria in the Asia-Pacific

Region: Occurrence Data, Distribution Maps and Bionomic Précis." *Parasites and Vectors* 4 (2011). doi: 10.1186/1756-3305-4-89.

Sikainga, Ahmad Alawad. "Comrades in Arms or Captives in Bondage: Sudanese Slaves in the Turko-Egyptian Army, 1821–1865." In *Slave Elites in the Middle East and Africa*, edited by Toru Miamura and John Edward Philips, 197–224. New York: Kegan Paul International, 2000.

Stack, Lee. "The Slave Trade Between the Sudan and Arabia." *Journal of the Central Asian Society* 8, no. 3 (1921): 163–64.

Stone, Francine, ed. *Studies on the Tihāmah: The Report of the Tihāmah Expedition 1982 and Related Papers.* Harlow, UK: Longman, 1985.

Talhami, Ghada Hashem. "The Zanj Rebellion Reconsidered." *International Journal of African Historical Studies* 10, no. 3 (1977): 443–61.

al-Tawfiq, Jaffar A. "Epidemiology of Travel-related Malaria in a Non-malarious Area in Saudi Arabia." *Saudi Medical Journal* 27, no. 1 (2006): 86–89.

Thompson, Andrew. *Origins of Arabia.* Chicago: Fitzroy Dearborn Publishers, 2000.

Toledano, Ehud R. *Slavery and Abolition in the Ottoman Middle East.* Seattle: University of Washington Press, 1998.

———. *As if Silent and Absent: Bonds of Enslavement in the Islamic Middle East.* New Haven, CT: Yale University Press, 2007.

Trabelsi, Salah. "L'esclavage domanial dans le paysage agraire musulman au Moyen Age." In *Esclavage et dependences serviles*, edited by M. Cottias, A. Stella, and B. Vincent, 305–24. Paris: L'Harmattan, 2006.

Trench, Richard. *Arabian Travelers.* Topsfield, MA: Salem House, 1986.

Urban, B., and A. Buerkert. "Palaeoecological Analysis of a Late Quaternary Sediment Profile in Northern Oman." *Journal of Arid Environments* 73 (2009): 296–305.

Varisco, Daniel Martin. "The Ard in Highland Yemeni Agriculture." *Tools and Tillage* 4, no. 3 (1982): 157–72.

Vassiliev, Alexei. *The History of Saudi Arabia.* New York: New York University Press, 2000.

Vernet, Thomas. "Slave Trade and Slavery on the Swahili Coast, 1500–1750." In Mirzai, Montana, and Lovejoy, *Slavery, Islam, and Diaspora*, 37–76.

Vidal, F. S. *The Oasis of Al-Hasa.* N.p.: Arab-American Oil Company, Local Government Relations, Arabian Research Division, 1955.

Vogel, Horst. "Impoundment-Type Bench Terracing with Underground Conduits in Jibal Haraz, Yemen Arab Republic." *Transactions of the Institute of British Geographers*, n.s., 13, no. 1 (1988): 29–38.

———. "Terrace Farming in Yemen." *Journal of Soil and Water Conservation* 42, no. 1 (1987): 18–21.

Waal, Alex de. *Evil Days: 30 Years of War and Famine in Ethiopia.* New York: Human Rights Watch, 1991.

Ward, Phillip. *Ha'il: Oasis City of Saudi Arabia*. New York: Oleander Press, 1983.

Webb, James L. A., Jr. *Desert Frontier: Ecological and Economic Change along the Western Sahel, 1600–1850*. Madison: University of Wisconsin Press, 1995.

———. *Humanity's Burden: A Global History of Malaria*. Cambridge, UK: Cambridge University Press, 2009.

———. *The Long Struggle Against Malaria in Tropical Africa*. New York: Cambridge University Press, 2014.

White, Sam. *The Climate of Rebellion in the Early Modern Ottoman Empire*. New York: Cambridge University Press, 2011.

———. "The Little Ice Age Crisis of the Ottoman Empire: A Conjuncture in Middle East Environmental History." In Mikhail, *Water on Sand*, 71–90.

Willis, John Ralph, ed. *Slaves and Slavery in Muslim Africa*. 2 vols. New York: Frank Cass, 1985.

Winckler, Onn. "The Surprising Results of the Saudi Arabian 2004 Demographic Census." *International Journal of Middle East Studies* 40, no. 1 (2008): 12–15.

Zahed, Laila. "The Spectrum of β-thalassemia Mutations in the Arab Populations." *Journal of Biomedicine and Biotechnology* 1, no. 3 (2001): 129–32.

Zarins, Juris. "Environmental Disruption and Human Response: An Archaeological-Historical Example from South Arabia." In *Environmental Disaster and the Archeology of Human Response*, edited by Garth Bawden and Richard M. Reycraft, 35–49. Albuquerque: University of New Mexico, Maxwell Museum of Anthropology, 2000.

Index